Urian Pierson James

River Guide

Mississippi Valley

Urian Pierson James

River Guide
Mississippi Valley

ISBN/EAN: 9783742857316

Manufactured in Europe, USA, Canada, Australia, Japa

Cover: Foto ©Andreas Hilbeck / pixelio.de

Manufactured and distributed by brebook publishing software (www.brebook.com)

Urian Pierson James

River Guide

JAMES'
RIVER GUIDE:

CONTAINING

DESCRIPTIONS OF ALL THE CITIES, TOWNS, AND PRINCIPAL OBJECTS OF INTEREST,

ON THE NAVIGABLE WATERS OF THE

MISSISSIPPI VALLEY,

FLOWING WEST FROM THE ALLEGHANY MOUNTAINS, EAST FROM THE ROCKY MOUNTAINS, AND SOUTH FROM NEAR THE NORTHERN LAKES, INCLUDING THE RIVERS OF ALABAMA AND TEXAS, FLOWING INTO THE GULF OF MEXICO; ALSO, AN ACCOUNT OF THE SOURCES OF THE RIVERS;

WITH

FULL TABLES OF DISTANCES,

AND MANY INTERESTING

HISTORICAL SKETCHES OF THE COUNTRY,

STATISTICS OF POPULATION, PRODUCTS, COMMERCE, MANUFACTURES, MINERAL RESOURCES, SCENERY, &C., &C.

ILLUSTRATED WITH FORTY-FOUR MAPS,

AND A NUMBER OF ENGRAVINGS.

REVISED EDITION.

CINCINNATI:
PUBLISHED BY U. P. JAMES.
167 WALNUT STREET.
1871.

ABBREVIATIONS USED IN THIS WORK.

Ala.	stands for	Alabama.	Mo.	stands for	Missouri.
Ark.	"	Arkansas.	Miss.	"	Mississippi.
co.	"	county.	Neb.	"	Nebraska.
Io.	"	Iowa.	O.	"	Ohio.
Ia.	"	Indiana.	Pa.	"	Pennsylvania.
Ill.	"	Illinois.	pop.	"	population.
Kan.	"	Kansas.	R. or Riv.	"	River.
Ky.	"	Kentucky.	Tenn.	"	Tennessee.
La.	"	Louisiana.	Va.	"	Virginia.
Min. or Minn.		Minnesota.	Wis.	"	Wisconsin.

TABLES OF DISTANCES.

The MISSISSIPPI RIVER, from Fort Ripley to the Gulf of Mexico.

PLACES.	From Place to Place. Miles	Whole distance. Miles	PLACES.	From Place to Place. Miles	Whole distance. Miles	PLACES.	From Place to Place. Miles	Whole distance. Miles
Fort Ripley, Min.			Savannah, Ill.	8	422	Portages des Sioux, M.	7	790
Swan River, Min.	18	18	Sabula, Io.	4	426	Randolph, Ill.	4	794
Sauk Rapids, Min.	28	46	Lyons, Io. }	15	441	Alton, Ill.	7	801
Benton, Min.	9	55	Fulton City, Io. }			Missouri River, Mo.	5	806
Itasca, Min.	40	95	Albany, Ill. }	7	448	Chippewa, Ill.	1	807
Rum River, Min.	10	105	Camanche, Io. }			Madison, Ill.	2	809
Manomin, Min.	10	115	Wapsipinecon R., Io.	7	455	Venice, Ill.	8	817
Falls of St. Anthony }	9	124	Cordova, Ill.	4	459	Bremen, Mo.	2	819
Minneapolis, Min. }			Princeton, Io.	1	460	ST. LOUIS, Mo. }	4	823
Fort Snelling, Min. }			Parkhurst, Io.	5	465	Illinoistown, Ill. }		
St. Peter's River, M.	8	132	Port Byron, Ill. }	1	466	Cahokia, Ill.	4	827
Mendota, Min. }			Le Claire, Io. }	1	467	Carondelet, Mo.	1	828
St. Paul, Min.	6	138	Hampton, Ill.	5	472	Jefferson Barracks, M.	5	833
Red Rock, Min.	7	145	Davenport, Io. }			Maramec River, Mo.	9	842
Hastings, Min.	10	155	Rock Island, Ill. }	12	484	Clifton, Mo.	10	852
Vermilion Riv. Min.	3	158	Moline, Ill. }			Harrisonville, Ill.	2	854
Point Douglas, Min }			Rock Island City, Ill.	3	487	Herculaneum, Mo.	2	856
St. Croix River. }	5	163	Rock River, Ill.	2	489	Plattin Rock, Mo.	1	857
Prescott, Wis. }			Buffalo, Io. }	5	494	Selma, Mo.	2	859
Red Wing, Min. }	18	181	Andalusia, Ill. }			Rush Tower, Mo.	4	863
Lake Pepin. }			Iowa, Io.	8	502	Fort Chartres, Ill.	9	872
Kansas, Wis.	25	206	Fairport, Io.	7	509	St. Genevieve, Mo.	11	883
Chippewa River, Wis.	1	207	Muscatine, Io.	6	515	St. Mary's Landing.	10	893
Wabashaw, Min.	10	217	Port Louisa, Io.	16	531	Pratt's Landing, Mo.	2	895
Fountain City, Wis.	15	232	New Boston, Ill. }	10	541	Kaskaskia River, Ill.	3	898
Trempaleau R. Wis. }	10	242	Iowa River, Io. }			Chester, Ill.	1	899
Minnesota City, M. }			Keithsburg, Ill.	7	548	Mary's River, Ill.	4	903
Montoville, Wis.	5	247	Huron, Io.	9	557	Port Perry, Mo.	3	906
Black River, Wis.	8	255	Oquawka, Ill.	10	567	Liberty, Ill.	4	910
Rising Sun. Min.	4	259	Burlington, Io.	15	582	Wittemberg, Mo.	17	927
Brooklyn, Min.	2	261	Skunk River, Io.	8	590	Devil's Bake Oven.	5	932
La Crosse, Wis.	2	263	Pontoosuc, Ill.	7	597	Grand Tower.	1	933
Hokah River, Min.	3	266	Appanoose, Ill.	5	602	Breesville, Ill.	2	935
Brownsville, Min.	5	271	Fort Madison, Io.	3	605	Muddy River, Ill.	4	939
Racoon River, Wis.	5	276	Nauvoo, Ill. }	8	613	Birmingham, Mo. }	4	943
Bad Axe River, Wis.	6	282	Montrose, Io. }			Union Point, Ill. }		
Battlefield, Wis.	2	284	Nashville, Io.	4	617	Devil's Tea Table }		
Lansing, Io.	15	299	Montebello, Ill.	6	623	and Cornice Rocks }	3	946
Lynxville, Wis. }	8	307	Keokuk, Io. }	4	627	Bainbridge, Mo. }	6	952
Wexford, Io. }			Hamilton City, Ill. }			Hamburg, Ill. }		
Prairie Du Chien, W.	10	317	Warsaw, Ill.	4	631	Cape Girardeau, Mo.	10	962
Fort Crawford, Wis.	1	318	Des Moines R., Io.			Thebes, Ill.	9	971
Wisconsin Riv., Wis.	3	321	Fox River, Mo.	2	633	New York, Mo. }		
Cincinnati, Wis. }	7	328	Des Moines City, Mo.	6	639	Commerce, Mo.	3	974
Kilroy, Io. }			Tully, Mo.	12	651	New Philadelphia, M.	7	981
Clayton, Io.	2	330	Lagrange, Mo.	6	657	Ohio City, Mo. }		
Mendota, Wis.	7	337	Quincy, Ill.	12	669	Cairo, Ill. }	21	1002
Guttenburg, Io.	5	342	Fabia's River, Mo. }			MOUTH OF OHIO }		
Cassville, Wis. }			Marion City, Mo. }	7	676	RIVER. }		
Turkey River, Io. }	6	348	Aston, Ill.	3	679	Island No. 1. }	6	1008
Frankfort, Io. }			Booneville, Ill.			Norfolk, Mo. }		
Buena Vista, Io.	5	353	Hannibal, Mo. }	7	686	Beckwith's, Mo.	7	1015
Potosi, Wis.	12	365	Dayton, Ill. }			Baldwinsville, Mo.	5	1020
Peru, Io.	7	372	Saverton, Mo.	8	694	Columbus, Ky.	4	1024
Sinepee, Wis.	2	374	Salt River, Mo.	18	712	Hickman, Ky.	20	1044
Jamestown, Wis.	1	375	Louisiana, Mo.	2	714	New Madrid, Mo.	44	1088
Dubuque, Io. }	5	380	Clarksville, Mo.	12	726	Point Pleasant, Mo.	7	1095
Dunleith, Ill. }			Hamburg, Ill.	15	741	Riddle's Point, Mo.	3	1098
Fevre River, Ill.	15	395	Gilead, Ill.	9	750	Walker's Bend.	18	1116
Moselle, Ill. }	6	401	Riviere au Cuivre, Mo.	15	765	Little Prairie, Mo.	7	1123
Bellevue, Io. }			Deer Plain, Mo.	12	777	Needham's Out-off }		
Makoqueta River, Io.	8	409	Illinois River, Ill. }	6	783	Obion River, Tenn. }	24	1147
Portsmouth, Ill.	5	414	Crafton, Ill. }			Hale's Point. }		

[Continued on next page.]

TABLES OF DISTANCES.—Continued.

PLACES.	From Place to Place. Miles	Whole distance. Miles	PLACES.	From Place to Place. Miles	Whole distance. Miles	PLACES.	From Place to Place. Miles	Whole distance. Miles
Miss'i River Cont'd.			*Miss'i River Cont'd.*			*Alabama R. Contin'd.*		
Bearfield Landing, A.	2	1149	Rodney, Miss.	4	1672	Bell's Landing, Ala.	18	197
Forked Deer R., Ten.	4	1153	Natchez, Miss. }	41	1713	Claiborne, Ala.	22	219
Ashport, Tenn.	2	1155	Vidalia, La. }			Gosport, Ala.	7	226
Osceola, Ark. }	12	1167	Ellis' Cliff, Miss.	18	1731	Gainestown, Ala.	9	235
Plum Point. }			Union Point, La.	3	1734	French's Land'g, Ala.	8	243
1st Chickasaw Bluff, T	6	1173	Homochitto R. Miss.	23	1757	James' Landing, Ala.	6	249
Fulton, Tenn.	4	1177	Port Adams, Miss.	10	1767	Tombigbee Riv. Ala.	40	289
Hatchee Riv., Ten. }	10	1187	Red River, La. }	11	1778	Fort St. Philip, Ala.	22	311
Randolph, Tenn. }			Red River Island and Cut-off. }			MOBILE, Ala.	22	333
Pecan Point, Ark.	10	1197				Gulf of Mexico.	30	363
2d Chickasaw Bluff, T	10	1207	Red R. Landing, La.	6	1784			
Greenock, Ark.	27	1234	Roccourci Bend and Cut-off.	4	1788	**ST. PETERS RIVER.**		
Mound City, Ark.	12	1246				*From South Bend City to the Mississippi.*		
Wolf River, Tenn. }	8	1254	Tunica Bend.	6	1794			
Memphis, Tenn. }			Bayou Sara, La. }	24	1818	South Bend City, M..		
Pickering, Tenn.	2	1256	St. Francisville, La }			Mankato, Min.	3	3
Grayson, Ark.	6	1262	Point Coupee, La. }			St. Peters, Min.	8	11
Norfolk, Miss.	2	1264	Waterloo, La.	5	1823	Traverse Des Sioux }	3	14
Blue's Point, Ark.	18	1282	Thompson's Cr'k, La.	5	1828	Min. }		
Commerce, Miss.	2	1284	Port Hudson, La.	1	1829	Le Sueur, Min.	8	22
Austin, Miss.	6	1290	Thomas' Point.	13	1842	Henderson, Min.	6	28
St. Francis River. }	20	1310	Baton Rouge, La. }	12	1854	Chasca, Min.	34	62
Sterling, Ark. }			W. Baton Rouge, L }			Carver, Min.	2	64
Helena, Ark.	10	1320	Manchac, La.	15	1869	Hennepin, Min.	10	74
Yazoo Pass, Miss. }	8	1328	Manchac Bayou. }			Mouth of St. Peters.	25	99
Delta, Miss. }			Bayou Plaquemine, }	8	1877			
Prier's Point, Miss. }			Plaquemine, La. }					
Horseshoe Bend & Cut-off. }	6	1334	Iberville, La.	10	1887	**ST. CROIX RIVER,**		
			Bayou Goule, La.	10	1897	*From St. Croix Falls to the Mississippi River.*		
Old Town, Ark.	3	1337	Bayou La Fourche, }	14	1911			
Barney's, Ark.	10	1347	Donaldsonville, La. }					
Concordia, Miss.	30	1377	Jefferson College, La.	16	1927	St. Croix Falls, Wis.		
Montgomery'sPoint }	10	1387	Bonnet Carre, La.	24	1951	Osceola, Wis.	9	9
Victoria, Miss. }			Red Church, La.	16	1967	Marine Mills, Min.	9	18
White River, Ark.	4	1391	Carrollton, La.	19	1986	Stillwater, Min.	15	33
Arkansas River. }	16	1407	Lafayette City, La.	5	1991	Hudson, Wis. }	5	38
Napoleon, Ark. }			**NEW ORLEANS.**	2	1993	Lake St. Croix. }		
Bolivia, Miss.	13	1420	Battle Ground, La.	6	1999	Mouth of St. Croix.	16	54
Gaines' Landing, Ark	35	1455	Ducro's Landing, La.	6	2005			
Columbia, Ark.	18	1473	Fort St. Leon, La.	5	2010	**WISCONSIN RIVER,**		
Point Chicot, Ark.	4	1477	English Turn, La. }			*From Wausau to the Mississippi River.*		
Greenville, Miss.	4	1481	Forts St. Philip & Jackson, La. }	55	2065			
Worthington Land- ing, Miss. }	22	1503	Mouths of the Mississippi. }	30	2095	Wausau; or Big } Bull Falls, Wis. }		
Grand Lake Land- ing, Ark. }	6	1509				Little Bull Falls, W.	18	18
Princeton, Miss.	4	1513	**ALABAMA RIVER,**			Stephen's Point, Wis.	26	46
Bunche's Bend and Cut-off. }	10	1523	*From Montgomery to the Gulf of Mexico.*			Plover, Wis.	3	49
Providence, La.	19	1542				Portage City, Wis.	115	164
Tallulah, Miss.	5	1547	Montgomery, Ala.			Prairie du Sac, Wis.	40	204
Tompkinsville, La.	10	1557	Washington, Ala.	13	13	Richland, Wis.	45	249
Brunswick Land- ing, Miss. }	14	1571	Lowndesport, Ala.	10	23	Brooklyn, Wis.	65	314
			Vernon, Ala.	8	31	Mouth of Wisconsin	7	321
Campbellsville, La.	10	1581	Miller's Ferry, Ala.	9	40			
Millikinsville, La.	2	1583	Benton, Ala.	15	55	**ROCK RIVER,**		
Young's Point, La. }	6	1589	Selma, Ala.	26	81	*From Watertown to the Mississippi River.*		
Yazoo River, Miss. }			Cahawba, Ala.	16	97			
Walnut Hills, Miss.	10	1599	Elm Bluff, Ala.	5	102			
Vicksburgh, Miss.	2	1601	Portland, Ala.	19	121	Watertown, Wis.		
Warrentown, Miss.	10	1611	Bridgeport, Ala.	16	137	Jefferson, Wis.	16	16
Palmyra Set, Miss. }	15	1626	Canton, Ala.	5	142	Fort Atkinson, Wis.	8	24
New Carthage, La. }			Prairie Bluff, Ala.	10	152	Janesville, Wis.	34	58
Point Pleasant, La.	10	1636	Upper Peach Tree Landing, Ala. }	11	163	Beloit, Wis.	18	76
Big Black Riv. Miss.	14	1650				Roscoe, Ill.	8	84
Grand Gulf, Miss.	2	1652	Black Bluff Land- ing, Ala. }	13	176	Rockford, Ill.	12	95
Bayou Pierre, Miss. }	10	1662				Byron, Ill.	12	108
Bruinsburgh, Miss. }			Lower Peach Tree Landing, Ala. }	5	181	Oregon, Ill.	10	118
St. Joseph, La.	6	1668				Dixon, Ill.	20	138

[Continued on next page.]

TABLES OF DISTANCES.—Continued.

PLACES.	From Place to Place.	Whole distance.
Rock River Contin'd.		
Sterling, Ill.............	12	150
Lyndon, Ill.............	16	166
Prophetstown, Ill.....	2	168
Erie, Ill.................	10	178
Camden, Ill............	35	213
Mouth of Rock River	1	214
IOWA RIVER,		
From Iowa City to the Mississippi River.		
Iowa City, Io..........		
Port Allen, Io.........	35	35
Concord, Io............	10	45
Wapello, Io............	12	57
Mouth of Iowa.....	23	80
DES MOINES RIVER,		
From Ft. Des Moines to the Mississippi.		
Fort Des Moines, Io.		
Dudley, Io..............	14	14
Lafayette, Io...........	5	19
Bennington, Io........	10	29
Red Rock, Io..........	16	45
Amsterdam, Io........	12	57
Bellefontaine, Io.....	12	69
Auburn, Io..............	12	81
Des Moines City, I...	8	89
Eddyville, Io...........	2	91
Chillicothe, Io.........	8	99
Ottumwa, Io...........	12	111
Iowaville, Io...........} New Market............}	20	131
Portland, Io............	6	137
Philadelphia, Io.......	8	145
Pittsburgh, Io..........	7	152
Keosauqua, Io........} Pleasant Hill, Io.....}	5	157
Bentonsport, Io.......} Vernon, Io..............}	8	165
Bonaparte, Io..........	5	170
Farmington, Io........	8	178
Black Hawk, Mo.....	3	181
Croton, Io...............	3	184
Athens, Mo.............	5	189
Belfast, Io...............	6	195
Niagara, Mo............	5	200
St. Francisville, Mo.	5	205
Churchville, Mo.......	14	219
Mouth of the Des Moines..............}	1	220
ILLINOIS RIVER,		
From Dresden to the Mississippi River.		
Dresden, Ill.............		
Morris, Ill...............	10	10
Clarkson, Ill............	4	14
Marseilles, Ill..........	17	31
Ottawa, Ill..............	9	40
Utica, Ill.................	10	50
La Salle, Ill.............	5	55
Peru, Ill..................	2	57
Hennepin, Ill..........} West Hennepin......}	17	74
Henry, Ill................	13	87

PLACES.	From Place to Place.	Whole distance.
Illinois River Cont'd.		
Lacon, Ill................	6	93
Chillicothe, Ill........} Peoria Lake............}	13	106
Rome, Ill................	4	110
Spring Bay, Ill........	4	114
Detroit, Ill..............	7	121
Little Detroit, Ill.....	2	123
Peoria, Ill...............	5	128
Wesley City, Ill......	4	132
Pekin, Ill................	7	139
Liverpool, Ill..........	28	167
Havana, Ill.............	9	176
Bath, Ill.................	12	188
Sangamon River......	18	206
Fredericksville, Ill...	3	209
Beardstown, Ill.......	4	213
La Grange, Ill.........	8	221
Meredosia, Ill.........	9	230
Naples, Ill..............	7	237
Florence, Ill............	10	247
Montezuma, Ill........	6	253
Bridgeport, Ill.........	6	259
Newport, Ill............	8	267
Hardin, Ill..............	14	281
Guilford, Ill............	4	285
Monterey, Ill..........	4	289
Mouth of the Illinois	13	302
MISSOURI RIVER,		
From the Head Waters to the Mississippi River.		
"Gates of the Rocky Mountains"........}	441	441
Great Falls..............	110	551
Mouth of Yellow Stone River..........}	675	1226
Sioux City, Io.........	1075	2301
Tekama, Neb..........	60	2361
De Soto, Neb..........	30	2391
Fort Calhoun, Neb...	15	2406
Florence, Neb.........	10	2416
Council Bluff's City, Io..................}	10	2426
Omaha City, Neb....		
Council Point, Io.....	5	2431
Trader's Point, Io....	3	2434
Bellevue, Neb.........	2	2436
St. Mary's, Io.........	5	2441
California City, Io..} Platte River............}	2	2443
Plattsville, Io..........	2	2445
Plattsmouth, Neb....	1	2446
Bethlehem, Io.........	1	2447
Kenosha, Neb.........	10	2457
Nebraska City, Neb.	10	2467
Brownsville, Neb....	30	2497
Iowa Point, Mo.......	40	2537
Nodeway City, Mo..	30	2567
St. Joseph, Mo........	25	2592
Leechman, Mo........	25	2617
Duniphan, Kan.......	8	2625
Atchinson, Kan.......	9	2634
Kickapoo City, Kan.	12	2646
Weston, Mo............	10	2656
Ft. Leavenworth, K.	4	2660
Little Platte Riv. Io.	20	2680
Parkville, Mo..........	2	2682

PLACES.	From Place to Place.	Whole distance.
Missouri Riv. Cont'd.		
Wyandotte City, K...} Kansas River...........} Kansas, Mo..............}	12	2694
Randolph, Mo.........	5	2699
Wayne City, Mo.....	7	2706
Liberty Landing, Mo	5	2711
Livingston, Mo.......	5	2716
Owen's Landing, Mo.	1	2717
Richfield, Mo.........	10	2727
Sibley, Mo..............	10	2737
Napoleon, Mo.........	6	2743
Camden, Mo...........	6	2749
Wellington, Mo.......	7	2756
Lexington, Mo.......	8	2764
Crooked River, Mo..	6	2770
Waleonda, Mo........	15	2785
Waverly, Mo..........	3	2788
Hill's Landing, Mo..	10	2798
Miami, Mo..............	20	2818
De Witt, Mo...........	6	2824
Grand River, Mo.....	5	2829
Brunswick, Mo.......	2	2831
Old Jefferson, Mo....	25	2856
Cambridge, Mo.......	2	2858
Chariton River, Mo.	5	2863
Glasgow, Mo...........	3	2866
Bluffport, Mo..........	5	2871
Arrow Rock, Mo.....	10	2881
La Mine River, Mo.	10	2892
Booneville, Mo.......		
Old Franklin, Mo...}	6	2897
Rocheport, Mo........	12	2909
Mt. Vernon, Mo......	8	2917
Providence, Mo.......	6	2923
Nashville, Mo.........	2	2925
Maniteau, Mo.........	3	2928
Marion, Mo.............	6	2934
Stonesport, Mo.......	10	2944
Jefferson City, Mo..}	6	2950
Hibroia, Mo............		
Formosa, Mo..........		
Osage River..........}	9	2959
Cote Sans Dessein, Mo.......................}	5	2964
Smith's Landing, Mo.......................}	9	2973
Portland, Mo..........	16	2989
Gasconade River, Mo.......................}	10	2999
Hermann, Mo..........	6	3004
Bridgeport, Mo.......	1	3005
Pinckney, Mo.........} Griswold, Mo..........}	12	3017
Washington, Mo.....	16	3033
Bascora, Mo............	1	3034
South Point, Mo......	2	3036
Portununa, Mo........	6	3042
Mt. Pleasant, Mo.....	1	3043
St. Albans, Mo........	8	3051
Missouriton, Mo......	1	3052
Johnson's Ferry, M} Port Royal, Mo......}	2	3054
Pittman's Ferry, Mo.	5	3059
St. Charles, Mo.......	18	3077
Jamestown, Mo.......	16	3093
Bellefontaine, Mo...	2	3095
Columbus, Mo........		
Mouth of the Missouri..................}	4	3099

[Continued on next page.]

TABLES OF DISTANCES.—Continued.

PLACES.	From Place to Place	Whole distance	PLACES.	From Place to Place	Whole distance	PLACES.	From Place to Place	Whole distance
KASKASKIA RIVER,			**RED RIVER,**			*Ohio River Contin'd.*		
From Shelbyville to the Mississippi Riv.			*From Lanesport to the Mississippi River.*			Coalport, O..........	1	257
						Middleport, O........	1	258
Shelbyville, Ill........			Lanesport, Ark.......			Sheffield, O..........		
Vandalia, Ill.........	50	50	Fulton, Ark........	100	100	West Columbia, Va...	1	259
Keysport, Ill.........	27	77	Conway, Ark........	100	200	Cheshire, O..........	3	262
Carlyle, Ill..........	12	89	Shreveport, La......	90	290	Addison, O..........	3	265
Covington, Ill.......	14	103	Nachitoches, La.....	100	390	Point Pleasant, Va..	4	269
Fayetteville, Ill.....	26	129	Alexandria, La......	80	470	Great Kanawha R		
Athens, Ill..........	9	138	Mouth of Red River.	150	620	Gallipolis, O........	4	273
Lively, Ill..........	2	140				Big Racoon Creek, O.	5	278
Tamaraxa, Ill.......	3	143				Blandenburg, O.....	6	284
Evansville, Ill.......	20	163	**OHIO RIVER.**			Millersport, O.......	14	298
Kaskaskia, Ill.......	8	171	*From Pittsburgh to the Mississippi R.*			Haskellville, O......	3	301
Mouth of the Kaskaskia..	7	178				Guyandotte, Va...		
			Pittsburgh, Pa.......			Guyandotte R., V.	10	311
WHITE RIVER,			Manchester, Pa......	2	2	Proctorsville, O.....		
From Worth to the Mississippi River.			Middleton, Pa.......	9	11	Burlington, O........	8	319
			Sewickleyville, Pa...	2	13	Big Sandy River...		
			Economy, Pa........	6	19	Catlettsburg, Ky...	4	323
Worth, Ark..........			Baden, Pa...........	4	23	Coal Grove, O.......	4	327
Johnson, Ark........	55	55	Freedom, Pa.........	2	25	Ironton, O...........	5	332
Liberty, Ark.........	28	83	Rochester, Pa.......	4	29	Hanging Rock, O....	4	336
Athens, Ark.........	25	108	Beaver, Pa..........			Greenupsburgh, Ky..	6	342
Mt. Olive, Ark.......	6	114	Jacobsburg, Pa......	1	30	Wheelersburg, O....	8	350
Fylamore, Ark.......	6	120	Georgetown, Pa......			Sciotoville, O........	3	353
Batesville, Ark......	45	165	Glasgow, Pa.........	14	44	Portsmouth, O......		
Jacksonport, Ark....	35	200	Liverpool, O.........	4	48	Scioto River, O......	9	362
Elizabeth, Ark.......	10	210	Wellsville, O........	4	52	Springville, Ky.....		
Augusta, Ark........	65	275	Elliottsville, O......	8	60	Alexandria, O.......	3	365
Des Arc, Ark........	35	310	Newburg, O.........	2	62	Bradford, O.........	3	369
Clarendon, Ark......	38	348	Steubenville, O......	9	71	Rockville, O.........	11	380
Crockett's Bluff, Ark.	33	381	Wellsburg, Va.......	7	78	Vanceburg, Ky......	2	382
Unas Coe, Ark.......	8	389	Warrenton, O........	7	85	Rome, O.............	7	389
Mouth of White Riv.	50	439	Tiltonville, O........	3	88	Concord, Ky........	7	396
			Burlington, O........	4	92	Manchester, O.......	7	403
			Martinsville, O......	1	93	Maysville, Ky......	12	415
ARKANSAS RIVER,			Wheeling, O.........			Aberdeen, O........		
From Fort Gibson to the Mississippi R.			Bridgeport, O........	1	94	Charleston, Ky......	7	422
			Bellaire, O..........	4	98	Ripley, O...........	2	424
Ft. Gibson, Ind. Ter.			Mannyville, Va......	8	106	Lavana, O...........		
Fort Coffee, Ind. Ter.	100	100	Elizabethtown, Va...			Dover, Ky..........	2	426
Fort Smith, Ark.....	20	120	Moundsville..........	1	107	Higginsport, O.......	4	430
Van Buren, Ark.....	10	130	Big Grave Creek.....			Augusta, Ky........	4	434
Ozark, Ark..........	60	190	Steinerville, O.......	8	115	Rockspring, Ky.....	4	438
Roseville, Ark.......	12	202	Clarington, O........	7	122	Mechanicsburg, O...	4	442
Patterson's Bluff, Ark	20	222	New Martinsville, Va	8	130	Neville, O...........		
Spadra Bluff, Ark....	15	237	Sistersville, Va......	9	139	Fosterville, Ky.....	3	445
Pittsburgh, Ark......	5	242	Newport, O.........	12	151	Moscow, O..........	2	447
St. Martin's, Ark....	10	252	Marietta, O.........			Point Pleasant O...		
Scotia, Ark..........	2	254	Muskingum River.	19	170	Belmont, Ky........	3	450
Norristown, Ark.....			Harmer, O..........			New Richmond, O...	5	455
Dardenelle, Ark.....	20	274	Vienna, Va..........	6	176	Palestine, O.........	4	459
Lewisburg, Ark......	40	314	Parkersburg, Va.....			California, O........		
Greene Grove, Ark..	18	332	Little Kanawha R.	7	183	Little Miami River	11	470
Little Rock, Ark.....	40	372	Belpre, O...........			Columbia, O........	2	472
Straw Hat, Ark......	70	442	Blannerhassett's I.	2	185	Dayton, Ky........	1	473
Pine Bluff, Ark......	20	462	Centre, O...........					
Rob Roy, Ark.......	12	474	Troy, O.............			**CINCINNATI, O...**		
New Gascony, Ark..	10	484	Hockhocking Riv....	12	197	Newport, Ky.......	3	476
Richland, Ark.......	8	492	Belleville, Va.......	4	201	Licking River......		
Swan Lake, Ark.....	5	497	Murraysville, Va....	5	207	Covington, Ky.....		
Niccatico, Ark.......	10	507	Shade River, O.....	1	208	Industry, O.........	10	486
South Bend, Ark.....	30	537	Ravenswood, Va....	11	219	Claysville, O........		
Arkansas Post, Ark..	25	562	Letartsville, O.......	23	242	Home City, O.......	2	488
Red Fork, Ark.......	10	572	Graham's Station, O.	6	248	North Bend, O......	4	492
Wellington, Ark.....	20	592	Racine, O...........	1	249	Great Miami River.	4	496
Mouth of the Arkansas..	30	622	Minersville, O.......	6	255	Lawrenceburg, Ia...	2	498
			Pomeroy, O.........	1	256	Petersburg, Ky.....	2	500

* Ashland, Ky.

[*Concluded on next page.*]

TABLES OF DISTANCES.—Continued.

PLACES.	From Place to Place. Miles.	Whole distance. Miles.	PLACES.	From Place to Place. Miles.	Whole distance. Miles.	PLACES.	From Place to Place. Miles.	Whole distance. Miles.
Rock River Contin'd.			**Illinois River Cont'd.**			**Missouri Riv. Cont'd.**		
Sterling, Ill.	12	150	Lacon, Ill.	6	93	Wyandotte City, K.		
Lyndon, Ill.	16	166	Chillicothe, Ill. }	13	106	Kansas River, }	12	2694
Prophetstown, Ill.	2	168	Peoria Lake }			Kansas, Mo. }		
Erie, Ill.	10	178	Rome, Ill.	4	110	Randolph, Mo.	5	2699
Camden, Ill.	35	213	Spring Bay, Ill.	4	114	Wayne City, Mo.	7	2706
Mouth of Rock River	1	214	Detroit, Ill.	7	121	Liberty Landing, Mo	5	2711
			Little Detroit, Ill.	2	123	Livingston, Mo.	5	2716
IOWA RIVER,			Peoria, Ill.	5	128	Owen's Landing, Mo.	1	2717
From Iowa City to the Mississippi River.			Wesley City, Ill.	4	132	Richfield, Mo.	10	2727
			Pekin, Ill.	7	139	Sibley, Mo.	10	2737
Iowa City, Io.			Liverpool, Ill.	28	167	Napoleon, Mo.	6	2743
Port Allen, Io.	35	35	Havana, Ill.	9	176	Camden, Mo.	6	2749
Concord, Io.	10	45	Bath, Ill.	12	188	Wellington, Mo.	7	2756
Wapello, Io.	12	57	Sangamon River	18	206	Lexington, Mo.	8	2764
Mouth of Iowa	23	80	Frederiksville, Ill.	3	209	Crooked River, Mo.	6	2770
			Beardstown, Ill.	4	213	Waleouda, Mo.	15	2785
DES MOINES RIVER,			La Grange, Ill.	8	221	Waverly, Mo.	3	2788
From Ft. Des Moines to the Mississippi.			Meredosia, Ill.	9	230	Hill's Landing, Mo.	10	2798
			Naples, Ill.	7	237	Miami, Mo.	20	2818
			Florence, Ill.	10	247	De Witt, Mo.	6	2824
Fort Des Moines, Io.			Montezuma, Ill.	6	253	Grand River, Mo.	5	2829
Dudley, Io.	14	14	Bridgeport, Ill.	6	259	Brunswick, Mo.	2	2831
Lafayette, Io.	5	19	Newport, Ill.	8	267	Old Jefferson, Mo.	25	2856
Bennington, Io.	10	29	Hardin, Ill.	14	281	Cambridge, Mo.	2	2858
Red Rock, Io.	16	45	Guilford, Ill.	4	285	Chariton River, Mo.	5	2863
Amsterdam, Io.	12	57	Monterey, Ill.	4	289	Glasgow, Mo.	3	2866
Bellefontaine, Io	12	69	Mouth of the Illinois	13	302	Bluffport, Mo.	5	2871
Auburn, Io.	12	81				Arrow Rock, Mo.	10	2881
Des Moines City, Io.	8	89	**MISSOURI RIVER,**			La Mine River, Mo.	10	2892
Eddyville, Io.	2	91	*From the Head Waters to the Mississippi River.*			Booneville, Mo. }	6	2895"
Chillicothe, Io.	8	99				Old Franklin, Mo. }		
Ottumwa, Io.	12	111				Rocheport, Mo.	12	2909
Iowaville, Io. }	20	131	"Gates of the Rocky } Mountains" }	441	441	Mt. Vernon, Mo.	8	2917
New Market }						Providence, Mo.	6	2923
Portland, Io.	6	137	Great Falls	110	551	Nashville, Mo.	2	2925
Philadelphia, Io.	8	145	Mouth of Yellow } Stone River }	675	1226	Moniteau, Mo.	3	2928
Pittsburgh, Io.	7	152				Marion, Mo.	6	2934
Keosauqua, Io. }	5	157	Sioux City, Io.	1075	2301	Stonesport, Mo.	10	2944
Pleasant Hill, Io. }			Tekama, Neb.	60	2361	Jefferson City, Mo. }	6	2950
Bentonsport, Io. }	8	165	De Soto, Neb.	30	2391	Hibreria, Mo. }		
Vernon, Io. }			Fort Calhoun, Neb.	15	2406	Osage River	9	2959
Bonaparte, Io.	5	170	Florence, Neb.	10	2416	Cote Sans Dessein, } Mo. }	5	2964
Farmington, Io.	8	178	Council Bluff's City, Io.	10	2426	Smith's Landing, } Mo. }	8	2972
Black Hawk, Mo.	3	181						
Croton, Io.	3	184	Omaha City, Neb.					
Athens, Mo.	5	189	Council Point, Io.	5	2431	Portland, Mo.	16	2988
Belfast, Io.	6	195	Trader's Point, Io.	3	2434	Gasconade River, } Mo. }	10	2998
Niagara, Mo.	5	200	Bellevue, Neb	2	2436			
St. Francisville, Mo.	5	205	St. Mary's, Io.	5	2441	Hermann, Mo.	6	3004
Churchville, Mo.	14	219	California City, Io. }	2	2443	Bridgeport, Mo.	1	3005
Mouth of the Des } Moines }	1	220	Platte River }			Pinckney, Mo. }	12	3017
			Plattsbills, Io.	2	2445	Griswold, Mo. }		
			Plattsmouth, Neb.	1	2446	Washington, Mo.	16	3033
ILLINOIS RIVER,			Bethlehem, Io	1	2447	Bascom, Mo.	1	3034
From Dresden to the Mississippi River.			Kenosha, Neb	10	2457	South Point, Mo.	2	3036
			Nebraska City, Neb.	10	2467	Portmuna, Mo.	6	3012
Dresden, Ill.			Brownsville, Neb.	30	2497	Mt. Pleasant, Mo.	1	3043
Morris, Ill.	10	10	Iowa Point, Mo.	40	2537	St. Albans, Mo.	8	3051
Clarkson, Ill.	4	14	Nodoway City, Mo.	30	2567	Missouriton, Mo.	1	3052
Marseilles, Ill.	17	31	St. Joseph, Mo.	25	2592	Johnson's Ferry, M }	2	3054
Ottowa, Ill.	9	40	Leachman, Mo.	25	2617	Por' Royal, Mo. }		
Utica, Ill.	10	50	Duniphan, Kan.	8	2625	Pittman's Ferry, Mo.	5	3059
La Salle, Ill.	5	55	Atchinson, Kan.	9	2634	St. Charles, Mo.	18	3077
Peru, Ill.	2	57	Kickapoo City, Kan.	12	2646	Jamestown, Mo.	16	3093
Hennepin, Ill. }	17	74	Weston, Mo.	10	2656	Bellefontaine, Mo.	2	3095
West Hennepin. }			Ft. Leavenworth, K.	4	2660	Columbus, Mo. }		
Henry, Ill.	13	87	Little Platte Riv. Io.	20	2680	Mouth of the Missouri }	4	3099
			Parkville, Mo.	2	2682			

[Continued on next page.]

TABLES OF DISTANCES.—Continued.

PLACES.	From Place to Place	Whole Distance	PLACES.	From Place to Place	Whole Distance	PLACES.	From Place to Place	Whole Distance
KASKASKIA RIVER,			**RED RIVER,**			*Ohio River Contin'd.*		
From Shelbyville to the Mississippi Riv.			*From Lanesport to the Mississippi River.*			Coalport, O........	1	257
						Middleport, O...... }	1	258
						Sheffield, O......... }		
Shelbyville, Ill......			Lanesport, Ark......			West Columbia, Va...	1	259
Vandalia, Ill.........	50	50	Fulton, Ark..........	100	100	Cheshire, O..........	3	262
Keysport, Ill.........	27	77	Conway, Ark.........	100	200	Addison, O...........	3	265
Carlyle, Ill...........	12	89	Shreveport, La.......	90	290	Point Pleasant, Va. }	4	269
Covington, Ill	14	103	Nachitoches, La......	100	390	Great Kanawha R }		
Fayetteville, Ill......	26	129	Alexandria, La.......	80	470	Gallipolis, O.........	4	273
Athens, Ill...........	9	138	**Mouth of Red River.**	150	620	Big Racoon Creek, O.	5	278
Lively, Ill............	2	140				Blandenburg, O......	6	284
Tamaroora, Ill.......	3	143				Millersport, O.......	14	298
Evansville, Ill.......	20	163	**OHIO RIVER.**			Haskellville, O......	3	301
Kaskaskis, Ill.......	8	171	*From Pittsburgh to the Mississippi R.*			Guyandotte, Va... }	10	311
Mouth of the Kaskaskia }	7	178				Guyandotte R., V. }		
						Proctorsville, O.... }		
WHITE RIVER,			Pittsburgh, Pa.......			Burlington, O........	8	319
From Worth to the Mississippi River.			Manchester, Pa.......	2	2	Big Sandy River... }	4	323
			Middleton, Pa	9	11	Catlettsburg, Ky. }		
			Sewickleyville, Pa...	2	13	Coal Grove, O........	4	327
Worth, Ark...........			Economy, Pa.........	6	19	Ironton, O............	5	332
Johnson, Ark.........	55	55	Baden, Pa............	4	23	Hanging Rock, O.....	4	336
Liberty, Ark..........	28	83	Freedom, Pa..........	2	25	Greenupsburgh, Ky...	6	342
Athens, Ark..........	25	108	Rochester, Pa........	4	29	Wheelersburg, O.....	8	350
Mt. Olive, Ark.......	6	114	Beaver, Pa........... }	1	30	Sciotoville, O........	3	353
Fylamore, Ark.......	6	120	Jacobsburg, Pa...... }			**Portsmouth, O....** }	9	362
Batesville, Ark.......	45	165	Georgetown, Pa...... }	14	44	Scioto River, O..... }		
Jacksonport, Ark.....	35	200	Glasgow, Pa.......... }			Springville, Ky......	4	48
Elizabeth, Ark........	10	210	Liverpool, O..........	4	48	Alexandria, O........	3	365
Augusta, Ark.........	65	275	Wellsville, O.........	4	52	Bradford, O..........	3	369
Des Arc, Ark.........	35	310	Elliottsville, O.......	8	60	Rockville, O..........	11	380
Clarendon, Ark.......	38	348	Newburg, O..........	2	62	Vanceburg, Ky.......	2	382
Crockett's Bluff, Ark.	33	381	Steubenville, O......	9	71	Rome, O..............	7	389
Unas Coe, Ark.......	8	389	Wellsburg, Va.......	7	78	Concord, Ky.........	7	396
Mouth of White Riv.	50	439	Warrenton, O........	7	85	Manchester, O.......	7	403
			Tiltonsville, O.......	3	88	**Maysville, Ky....** }	12	415
			Burlington, O........	4	92	Aberdeen, O........ }		
ARKANSAS RIVER,			Martinsville, O.......	1	93	Charleston, Ky......	7	422
From Fort Gibson to the Mississippi R.			Wheeling, Va........ }	1	94	Ripley, O............	2	424
			Bridgeport, O....... }			Lavana, O............	2	426
Ft. Gibson, Ind. Ter.			Bellaire, O...........	4	98	Dover, Ky...........		
Fort Coffee, Ind. Ter.	100	100	Mannyville, Va......	8	106	Higginsport, O.......	4	430
Fort Smith, Ark......	20	120	Elizabethtown, Va... }	1	107	Augusta, Ky.........	4	434
Van Buren, Ark......	10	130	Moundsville......... }			Rockspring, Ky......	4	438
Ozark, Ark...........	60	190	Big Grave Creek.... }			Mechanicsburg, O...	4	442
Roseville, Ark	12	202	Steinerville, O.......	8	115	Neville, O............		
Patterson's Bluff, Ark	20	222	Clarington, O........	7	122	Fosterville, Ky...... }	3	445
Spadra Bluff, Ark....	15	237	New Martinsville, Va	8	130	Moscow, O...........	2	447
Pittsburgh, Ark......	5	242	Sistersville, Va......	9	139	Point Pleasant O... }	3	450
St. Martin's, Ark.....	10	252	Newport, O..........	12	151	Belmont, Ky......... }		
Scotia, Ark...........	2	254	Marietta, O.......... }	19	170	New Richmond, O...	5	455
Norristown, Ark..... }	20	274	Muskingum River. }			Harmer, O...........	4	459
Dardenelle, Ark...... }			Vienna, Va..........	6	176	Palestine, O.........		
Lewisburg, Ark......	40	314	Parkersburg, Va.... }	7	183	California, O........ }	11	470
Greene Grove, Ark...	18	332	Little Kanawha R. }			Little Miami River }	2	472
Little Rock, Ark....	40	372	Belpre, O.............			Columbia, O.........		
Straw Hat, Ark......	70	442	Blannerhassett's I. }	2	185	**Dayton, Ky........** }	1	473
Pine Bluff, Ark......	20	462	Centre, O............ }					
Rob Roy, Ark........	12	474	Troy, O..............	12	197	**CINCINNATI, O...** }	3	476
New Gascony, Ark...	10	484	Hockhocking Riv... }			Newport, Ky........ }		
Richland, Ark........	8	492	Belleville, O.........	4	201	Licking River....... }		
Swan Lake, Ark.....	5	497	Murraysville, Va....	5	207	Covington, Ky...... }		
Niceattoo, Ark.......	10	507	Shade River, O.....	1	208	Industry, O.......... }	10	486
South Bend, Ark....	30	537	Ravenswood, Va....	11	219	Claysville, Ky....... }		
Arkansas Post, Ark..	25	562	Letartsville, O.......	23	242	Home City, O........	2	488
Red Fork, Ark	10	572	Graham's Station, O.	6	248	North Bend, O.......	4	492
Wellington, Ark......	20	592	Racine, O............	1	249	Great Miami River..	4	496
Mouth of the Arkansas }	30	622	Minersville, O.......	6	255	Lawrenceburg, Ia...	2	498
			Pomeroy, O..........	1	256	Petersburg, Ky......	2	500

* Ashland, Ky.   [*Concluded on next page.*]

TABLES OF DISTANCES.—Continued.

PLACES.	From Place to Place.	Whole Distance
Ohio River Contin'd.		
Aurora, Ia.	2	502
Belleview, Ky.	6	508
Rising Sun, Ia.	3	511
Millersburg, Ia.	3	514
Big Bone Lick Cr'k } Hamilton, Ky. }	9	523
Patriot, Ia.	2	525
Warsaw, Ky.	11	536
New York, Ia.	1	537
Vevay, Ia. } Ghent, Ky. }	10	547
Carrollton, Ky. } Kentucky River. }	10	557
Preston, Ky. } Madison, Ia. } Milton, Ky. }	10	567
Hanover Landing, Ia.	6	573
New London, Ia.	6	579
Bethlehem, Ia.	6	585
Westport, Ky.	6	591
Charleston L'd'g, Ia.	12	603
Utica, In.	5	608
Jeffersonville, Ia.	9	617
Louisville, Ky.	1	618
Shippingsport, Ky.	2	620
Portland, Ky. } New Albany, Ia. }	1	621
Bridgeport, Ia.	9	630
Blakesville, Ia.	6	636
Salt River, Ky. } West Point, Ky. }	4	640
Brandenburg, Ky.	18	658
Mauckport, Ia.	3	661
Northampton, Ia.	7	668
Amsterdam, Ia.	3	671
Blue River, Ia.	6	678
Leavenworth, Ia.	2	680
Fredonia, Ia.	5	685
Alton, Ia.	13	698
Concordia, Ky.	10	708
Rome, In.		
Stephensport, Ky.	12	720
Sinking Creek, Ky. } Cloverport, Ky. } Tobinsport, In. }	10	730
Hawesville, Ky. } Cannelton, Ia. }	14	744
Troy, Ia. } Anderson River. }	6	750
Maxville, Ia.	1	751
Batesville, Ia.	2	753
Lewisport, Ky.	3	756
Rockport, Ia.	13	769
Owensburg, Ky.	9	778
Ben Harbor, Ky.	3	781
Enterprise, Ia.	3	784
Point Isabel, Ia.	1	785
Newburg, Ia.	13	795
Green River, Ky.	6	804
Evansville, Ia.	9	813
Verona, Ia.	7	820
Henderson, Ky.	5	825
West Franklin, Ia.	14	839
Mount Vernon, Ia.	12	851
Uniontown, Ky.	10	861
Wabash River.	5	866
Raleigh, Ky.	6	872
Shawneetown, Ill.	5	877
Caseyville, Ky.	10	887

PLACES.	From Place to Place.	Whole Distance
Ohio River Contin'd		
Battery Rock, Ill.	2	889
Cave-in-rock, Ill.	12	901
Elizabethtown, Ill.	6	907
Golconda, Ill.	23	930
Cumberland River } Smithland, Ky. }	15	945
Tennessee River. } Paducah, Ky. }	12	957
Belgrade, Ill.	8	965
Fort Massac, Ill.	2	967
Metropolis, Ill.	1	968
Hillaman, Ill.	8	976
Wilkinsonville, Ill.	7	983
Caledonia, Ill.	10	993
America, Ill.	3	996
Emporium, Ill.	8	999
Cairo, Ill. } Mouth of Ohio. }	6	1005
MUSKINGUM RIVER,		
From Coshocton to the Ohio River.		
Coshocton, O.		
Dresden, O.	17	17
Zanesville, O.	16	33
Duncan's Falls, O. } Taylorsville, O. }	9	42
Engleport, O.	11	53
McConnelsville, O } Malta, O. }	10	63
Newcastle, O.	3	66
Windsor, O.	7	73
Big Rock, O.	8	81
Beverly, O. } Waterford, O. }	10	91
Lowell, O.	10	101
Mth. of Muskingum	12	113
SCIOTO RIVER,		
From Columbus to the Ohio River.		
Columbus, O.		
Circleville, O.	26	26
Chillicothe, O.	19	45
Piketon, O.	20	65
Jasper, O.	2	67
Lucasville, O.	10	77
Mouth of Scioto	13	90
KENTUCKY RIVER,		
From Boonesboro' to the Ohio River.		
Boonesboro', Ky.		
Cogar's Landing, Ky		
Monday's Land'g. K.	4	4
Cumming's L'dg, Ky.	4	8
Oregon, Ky.	10	18
McCowan's L'dg. Ky.	3	21
Wilson's Land'g, Ky.	4	25
Sherlock's L'd'g, Ky.	4	29
Woodford L'd'g, Ky.	4	33
Frankfort, Ky.	12	45
Flat Creek L'd'g, Ky	15	60
Monterey, Ky.	3	63
Owenton's Land'g, K	5	68
Lockport, Ky.	6	74
Gratz, Ky.	3	77

PLACES.	From Place to Place.	Whole Distance
Kentucky Riv. Cont'd.		
Drennon's Springs, K	8	85
Springport, Ky.	1	86
Marion, Ky.	4	90
Law's Landing, Ky.	3	93
Worthsville, Ky.	4	97
Mouth of Kentucky.	8	105
WABASH RIVER,		
From Lafayette to the Ohio River.		
Lafayette, Ia.		
Wheaton, Ia.	9	9
La Grange, Ia.	3	12
Maysville, Ia.	5	17
Independence, Ia.	1	18
Atica, Ia.	8	26
Williamsport, Ia.	2	28
Portland, Ia.	8	36
Baltimore, Ia.	6	42
Covington, Ia.	4	46
Perryville, Ia.	9	55
Vermilion River.	10	65
Lodiville, In.	2	67
Newport, Ia.	7	74
Montezuma, Ia.	6	80
Armiesburg, Ia.	2	82
Clinton, Ia.	10	92
Numa, Ia.	2	94
Harrison, Ia.	14	108
Terre Haute, Ia.	4	112
Darwin, Ia.	25	137
Yorke, Ill.	16	153
Hudsonville, Ill.	9	162
Merom, In.	8	170
Russellville, Ill.	25	195
Vincennes, Ia.	18	213
Mt. Carmel, Ill.	36	249
Graysville, Ill.	45	294
New Baltimore, Ia.	9	303
New Harmony, Ia.	6	309
Chainville, Io.	20	329
Mouth of Wabash	40	369
CUMBERLAND RIV.		
From Nashville to the Ohio River.		
Nashville, Tenn.		
Clarksville, Tenn.	55	55
Palmyra, Tenn.	15	70
Dover, Tenn.	30	100
Tobaccoport, Tenn.	15	115
Canton, Ky.	16	131
Rockcastle, Ky.	5	136
Eddyville, Ky.	17	153
Mth. of Cumberland	50	203
TENNESSEE RIVER,		
From Muscle Shoals to the Ohio River.		
Muscle Shoals. } Florence, Ala. } Tuscumbia, Ala. }		
Waterloo, Ala.	30	30
Savannah, Tenn	35	65
Carrollville, Tenn.	35	100
Perryville, Tenn.	20	120
Reynoldsburg, Tenn.	50	170
Mouth of Tennessee.	110	284

INDEX TO RIVERS.

	PAGE		PAGE		PAGE
Alabama River	60	Gasconade River	78	Racoon River, Io.	70
Alleghany River	86	Grand River, Ind. Ter.	80	Racoon River, Wis.	14
Amite River	46	Grand River, Mo.	77	Red Cedar River	68
Anderson River	118	Great Kanawha River	102	Red River	81
Aransas River	65	Great Miami River	112	Rio Grande	65
Arkansas River	80	Green River	120	Rock River	68
		Guadulupe River	65	Rum River	12
Bad Axe River	14	Guyandotte River	102	
Bark River	69			Sabine River	62
Bayou Goule	48	Hatchee River	34	Salt River, Ky	116
Bayou La Fourche	48	Hockhocking River	100	Salt River, Mo.	20
Bayou Pierre	40	Hokah River	13	San Antonio River	65
Bayou Plaquemine	46	Holston River	128	Sangamon River	72
Bayou Sara	44	Homochitto River	42	San Jacinto River	64
Beaver River	92			Scioto River	124
Big Barren River	120			Shade River	100
Big Black River	40	Illinois River, Ill.	71	Sinking Creek	118
Big Bone Lick Creek	112	Illinois River, Ind. Ter.	80	Skunk River	17
Big Grave Creek	96	Iowa River	69	Spoon River	72
Big Racoon Creek	102			St. Croix River	67
Big Sandy River	102	Kankakee River	71	St. Francis River	36
Big Stone River	74	Kansas River	76	St. Peters River	67
Black River, Ark	80	Kaskaskia River	79	Sunflower River	81
Black River, Wis	13	Kentucky River	125	Swan River	11
Blue River, Ark	81				
Blue River, Ia	118	La Mine River	77	Talapoosa River	60
Brazos River	64	Lavacca River	65	Tallahatchee River	81
		Licking River	110	Tennessee River	128
Cahaba River	60	Little Blue River	118	Thompson's Creek	46
Canadian River	80	Little Kanawha River	93	Tombigbee River	60
Cash River	122	Little Miami River	106	Trempaleau River	13
Chagres River	66	Little Platte River	76	Trinity River	62
Chariton River	77			Turkey River	14
Cheat River	84	Makoqueta River	15	Tuscarawas River	124
Chippewa River	68	Manchac Bayou	46		
Clearwater River	68	Maramec River	26	Upper Iowa River	14
Clinch River	127	Mary's River	28		
Colorado River	64	Mission River	65	Vermilion River, Ia.	126
Cocsa River	60	Mississippi River	9	Vermilion River, Min.	13
Copper River	20	Missouri River	73		
Crawfish River	69	Monongahela River	84	Wabash River	125
Crooked River	77	Muddy River	28	Walhounding River	124
Cumberland River	127	Muskingum River	124	Wapsipinecon River	16
				White River, Ark	70
Des Moines River	70	Neasho River	80	White River, Ia	126
Des Plaines River	71	Neches River	62	Willow River	67
		Nueces River	65	Wisconsin River	68
Fabin's River	20			Wolf River	34
False River	46	Obion River	32		
False Washita River	81	Ohio River	83	Yallabusha River	81
Fevre River	15	Osage River	78	Yazoo Pass, or Bayou	36
Forked Deer River	34			Yazoo River	81
Fox River, Ill	71	Platte River	75	Yellow Stone River	74
Fox River, Io	18	Plover River	68	Youghioghoney River	84
Fox River, Wis	68				

8

JAMES'

RIVER GUIDE.

THE MISSISSIPPI RIVER.

The Mississippi is the largest and most magnificent river in North America, and with its main branch, the Missouri, the longest in the world. It takes its rise near the dividing ridge of the Red River of the north, and in a small lake called Itasca. This beautiful lake, which is some 5 or 7 miles in length, reposes amidst hills of marine sand, of the drift epoch, and consists of pure springs of water, gushing out in copious rills, within a visible basin. Its distance from the Gulf of Mexico, is estimated at 3160 miles. The entire altitude of the lake, as determined by Mr. Nicollet, in 1836, is 1575 feet, which is 105 feet below the summit of its environing hills; and its latitude, at Schoolcraft's Island, the only island in it, is 47° 13' 35" N. Lat., and it flows into the Gulf of Mexico in 29° N. Lat.

The face of the country about its head, presents a very similar appearance to that at its estuary. It is formed of many small branches; but soon becomes a broad stream, moving a wide expanse of waters, with a current scarcely perceptible—sometimes along a marshy bed—through interminable swamps; at others, over a white sand bottom, with its waters transparent, and at others, "it is compressed to a narrow and rapid current, between ancient and hoary limestone bluffs. A great number of streams, rising in the same plateau, and interlocking with the waters of Red River, and other streams of Lake Winnipeg, unite to form the St. Peters and Mississippi." The following are among the most considerable of its tributaries: Rapid, St. Croix, Cannon River, Buffalo Bluff, Black, Root, Upper Iowa, Yellow, Bad Axe, Wisconsin, Turkey River, La Mine, Fevre River, Tete de Mort, Wipisipiuscon, Little Loutour, Rock River, Iawa, Des Moines, Waconda, Fabian, Justioni, Oahaka, or Salt River, Bœuf of Cuivre, Dardenne, Illinois, Missouri, Maramec, Kaskaskia, Big Muddy, Ohio, Wolf, St. Francis, White River, Arkansas, Yazoo, Red River, and Bayou Sara.* 1100 miles below its source, and 771 above St. Louis, are the Falls of St. Anthony. Here the river is about 600 yards wide, and is precipitated over a ledge of limestone, 17 feet high. The scenery around the falls is grand and imposing. Below this point, the river is bounded by limestone bluffs, from 100 to 400 feet high, and first begins to exhibit islands. Its current is broke by the Rapids, at the mouth of the Rock river and Des Moines, which partially obstruct navigation, for a portion of the summer.

The scenery along the Upper, or Rock River Rapids, is very fine. On the western side, the land rises in gentle slopes, which are terminated in the distance

* Flint's Geography.

by a beautiful chain of hills. On the opposite side, a broad, flat plain, of more than a mile in width, and several miles in length, presents itself. The celebrated Black Hawk War originated in the determination of the Sacs and Fox Indians to maintain possession of this splendid tract of country.

"Below the rapids, the river assumes its medial width and character from that point to the entrance of the Missouri. It is a still more beautiful river than the Ohio; somewhat gentler in its current—a third wider, with broad, clean sand-bars, except in time of high waters, when they are all covered. At every little distance, there are islands, sometimes a number of them parallel, and broadening the stream to a great width. These islands, are, many of them, large, and have, in the summer season, an aspect of beauty, as they swell gently from the clear stream, a vigor and grandeur of vegetation, which contribute much to the magnificence of the river." "Where it receives the Missouri, it is a mile and a half wide. The Missouri, itself, enters with a mouth not more than half a mile wide. The united streams below have thence, to the mouth of the Ohio, a medial width of little more than half a mile. This mighty affluent seems rather to diminish than increase its width; but it perceptibly alters its depth, its mass of waters, and, what is to be regretted, wholly changes its character. It is no longer the gentle, placid stream, with smooth shores, and clean sand-bars; but has a furious and boiling current, a turbid and dangerous mass of sweeping waters, jagged and dilapidated shores, and, wherever its waters have receded, deposits of mud. It remains a sublime object of contemplation; but its character of calm magnificence, that so delighted the eye above, is seen no more."* The surface of the river is covered with huge boils or swells, which render it a matter of considerable difficulty, in some places, to navigate a boat. "In its course, accidental circumstances shift the impetus of its current, and propel it upon the point of an island, bend, or sand-bar. In these instances, it tears up the island, removes the sand-bars, and sweeps away the tender, alluvial soil of the bends, with all their trees, and deposits the spoils in another place. At the season of high waters, nothing is more familiar to the ears of the people on the river, than the deep crash of a landslip, in which larger or smaller masses of the soil on the banks, with all the trees, are plunged into the stream. Such is its character, from the Missouri to the Balize—a wild, furious, whirling river, never navigated safely.

"No person who descends this river for the first time, receives clear and adequate ideas of its grandeur, and the amount of water which it carries. If it be in the spring, when the river below the mouth of the Ohio is generally over its banks, although the sheet of water that is making its way to the gulf, is, perhaps, 30 miles wide, yet, finding its way through deep forests and swamps, that conceal all from the eye, no expanse of water is seen, but the width, that is curved out between the outline of woods on either bank; and it seldom exceeds, and oftener falls short of a mile. But when he sees, in descending from the Falls of St. Anthony, that it swallows up one river after another, with mouths as wide as itself, without affecting its width at all—when he sees it receiving in succession the mighty Missouri, the broad Ohio, St. Francis, White, Arkansas, and Red Rivers, all of them of great depth, length, and volume of water—when he sees this mighty river absorbing them all, and retaining a volume, apparently unchanged, he begins to estimate rightly the increasing depth of current, that must roll on in its deep channel to the sea. Carried out of the Balize, and sailing with a good breeze for hours, he sees nothing on any side but the turbid waters of the Mississippi, long after he is out of sight of land.

"Between the mouth of the Ohio and St. Louis, on the west side of the river, the bluffs are generally near it, seldom diverging from it more than 2 miles.

---

* Flint's Geography.

They are for the most part, perpendicular masses of limestone; sometimes shooting up into towers and pinnacles, presenting, as Mr. Jefferson well observed, at a distance, the aspect of the battlements and towers of an ancient city. Sometimes the river sweeps the base of these perpendicular bluffs, as happens at the Cornice rocks, and at the cliffs above St. Genevieve. They rise here between 200 and 300 feet above the level of the river. There are many imposing spectacles of this sort near the western bank of the Mississippi, in this distance. We may mention among them, that gigantic mass of rocks, forming a singular island in the river, called the 'Grand Tower,' and the shot tower at Herculaneum.

"From the sources of the river to the mouth of the Missouri, the annual flood ordinarily commences in March, and does not subside until the last of May, and its medial height is 15 feet. At the lowest stages, 4 feet of water may be found from the rapids of Des Moines to the mouth of the Missouri. Between that point and the mouth of the Ohio, there are 6 feet in the channel of the shallowest places at low water; and the annual inundation may be estimated at 25 feet. Between the mouth of the Ohio and the St. Francis, there are various shoal places, where pilots are often perplexed to find a sufficient depth of water, when the river is low. Below that point, there is no difficulty for vessels of any draught, except to find the right channel. Below the mouth of the Ohio, the medial flood is 50 feet; the highest, 60. Above Natchez, the flood begins to decline. At Baton Rouge, it seldom exceeds 30 feet; and at New Orleans, 12. Some have supposed this gradual diminution of the flood to result from the draining of the numerous affluxes of the river, that convey away such considerable portions of its waters, by separate channels to the sea. To this should be added, no doubt, the check, which the river, at this distance, begins to feel from the reaction of the sea, where this mighty mass of descending waters finds its level." *

The banks of the river, from Cairo down, are clothed, in many instances, with a rich verdure of trees, down to the water's edge, interspersed here and there with towns and fine plantations. About 500 miles below, commences the great cotton growing region, and, below the mouth of Red River, the sugar plantations. From thence to New Orleans, the banks of the river are lined with a succession of fine plantations and dwellings, delightfully surrounded with shrubbery. From Columbia, Arkansas, the forest of cotton and other trees presents a most singular appearance, being, in many places, covered with a peculiar kind of moss, which depends from the branches, in long, thick masses, and gives an almost funereal aspect to them. It is the moss commonly used, when manufactured, for mattresses, &c.

A traveler, in some well written sketches, very truthfully remarks, that, "No person can pass down the Mississippi, and view the immense bodies of uncultivated lands, lying contiguous to its banks, without reflecting on the great changes which time will produce. In a century, or two at the most, the banks of the river will present continuous lines of cultivated plantations, similar to those on the coast. The lands are as rich as nature can make them, being all of alluvial formation; and the soil of such a depth that there is no danger of its ever being exhausted. When we read of the myriads of people, who formerly existed in the valley of the Nile, and compare the capabilities of the Mississippi valley with it, we can comprehend the great destiny, awaiting only the development of time, in store for this *already* far-famed region."

Fort Ripley, formerly Fort Gaines, is 6 miles south of Crow Wing river, at the mouth of the Nokay, in Cass co., Minnesota, and 122 miles north of St. Paul.

Swan River, Benton co., Minn., 18 miles south of Fort Ripley. Near the mouth of this river, on the east side of the Mississippi, is a small settlement.

---

*Flint's Geography.

Sauk Rapids, county seat of Benton co., Minn., 28 miles below. The village is situated on the east side of the Mississippi, in the center of a very fine farming country. Population about 300.

Benton, 9 miles below, in the same county.

St. Cloud, 4 miles below, in Stearns co., Minn. Pop. 3,000.

Itasca, about 36 miles below, in Benton co., is a small village.

Rum River, 10 miles below, rises to the north of the Mississippi, in Mille Lacs, and after a course of about 80 miles, falls into the Mississippi at this point.

Manomin, 10 miles below, in Ramsey co., Minn.

Falls of St. Anthony, 9 miles below. These falls are about 18 feet perpendicular, and about 30 rods in width, divided by a conical island, leaving nearly two-thirds on the west side. The entire fall of the river in a distance of a few miles, is about 100 feet, affording almost unlimited water-power.

St. Anthony's Falls, Ramsey co., Minn. The town of St. Anthony is beautifully situated on the side and summit of a hill, rising up from a precipice, from which a fine view of the falls and surrounding country can be obtained. It is the seat of the University of Minnesota, endowed by a liberal donation of lands by the General Government. There are a number of stores, 2 printing offices, 2 hotels, a number of saw and grist-mills, and manufacturing establishments. Population about 4500. The land in the vicinity of the falls, consists of prairie, interspersed with openings of various extent, and is generally admirably adapted to agricultural purposes. It is also well watered by numerous small lakes and streams, whose never-failing springs add much to the strength and fertility of the soil. These lakes and streams are well stocked with fish.

The falls of St. Anthony were named by Father Hennepin, a companion of the enterprising M. De la Salle, who, in 1680, ascended the Mississippi river as far as the falls, and reported that he had discovered its source. The Mississippi river was discovered by Marquette, seven years before.

Minneapolis, county seat of Hennepin co., Minn., is a thriving town opposite St. Anthony's Falls. Population about 13,000.

Fort Snelling, 8 miles below, in the same county. This fort is situated on the west side of the Mississippi, and at the mouth of

St. Peter's River, (See page 67.)

Mendota, the capital of Dakota co., Minn., is just below the mouth of St. Peter's river, which must, at no distant day, bear upon its waters the valuable products of a fertile and luxuriant soil. Mendota contains a number of stores, and a population of about 1,000.

St. Paul, 6 miles below, is the capital of Minnesota, and county seat of Ramsey co.. This is the head of steamboat navigation. St. Paul is pleasantly situated on a high bluff, from which a fine view of the river may be had. It contains a fine State House, 6 or 8 churches, a number of hotels, 3 printing offices, several mills, and flourishing schools, a large number of stores, and mechanic's shops of various kinds. It is rapidly increasing in wealth, and commands the trade of a large extent of growing country, with a soil of exceeding fertility. Population 20,031.

Red Rock, Ramsey co., Minn., 7 miles below. Its name is derived from a large rock, which the Indians painted red, and styled *Wakon*, or Spirit-rock.

Red Rock was first settled by the Methodist missionaries, in 1837, under the superintendence of the Rev. Alfred Brunson. An Indian school was established, at an expenditure of $30,000; but, after a few years, the mission failed. The soil in this region is well adapted to the growth of corn.

Hastings, 10 miles below, in Minnesota.

Vermilion, or Rapid River, enters the Mississippi 3 miles below; it rises in Minnesota, and flows north-east on a line nearly parallel with the St. Peters river.

Point Douglas, Washington co., Minn., 5 miles below. This village is situated on a point of land formed by the junction of the St. Croix with the Mississippi river. It has an excellent steamboat landing.

St. Croix River, (See page 67.)

Prescott, the county seat of Pierce co., Wis., is just below the junction of the St. Croix with the Mississippi.

Red Wing, 18 miles below, is the county seat of Goodhue co., Minn., and at the upper part of Lake Pepin.

Lake Pepin, is formed by an expansion of the Mississippi. It is about 25 miles long, and 4 wide; the water is clear and the current very gentle. On the eastern side of the lake, is the celebrated *Maiden's Rock*, which rises perpendicularly 500 feet. Near the head of the lake, on the east side, is the mouth of Rush river, which empties into the lake; and, on the opposite side is the Cannon river. The shores of this lake abound with *carnelian* and other valuable stones.

Kansas, 25 miles below Red Wing, at the lower extremity of Lake Pepin, in Dunn co., Wis.

Chippewa River, empties into the Mississippi 1 mile below, from Wisconsin. (See page 68.)

Wabashaw, in Wabashaw co., Minn., about 10 miles below the mouth of the Chippewa.

Fountain City, 15 miles below, in Buffalo co., Wis.

Winona, Winona co., Minn., 7 miles below. Pop. 7,000.

Trempeleau, 3 miles below, in Jackson co., Wis., at the mouth of Trempeleau River. Population 800.

Minnesota City, opposite, in Winona co., Minn.

Montoville, 5 miles below, in Trempaleau co., Wis.

Mountain Island, is a high rocky island, and one of the most remarkable places on the upper Mississippi. Its altitude has been variously estimated at from 300 to 500 feet, and, from a distance, has the appearance of rising from the middle of the river. It is a conspicuous and noted landmark.

Black River, 8 miles below Montoville, rises near the center of Wisconsin. It is navigable for small boats about 50 miles. Before entering the Mississippi, it separates into two branches, forming a delta of some extent.

Rising Sun, 4 miles below, in Winona co., Minn.

Brooklyn, 2 miles below.

La Crosse, capital of La Crosse co., Wis., 2 miles below, is located upon a beautiful prairie of the same name, at the mouth of La Crosse river, and contains a court-house, 2 churches, a land office, a number of stores and mills, and commands a considerable portion of the lumber trade of La Crosse river. Population about 6000.

Hokah, or Root River, enters the Mississippi from Minnesota 3 miles below the mouth of the La Crosse.

Brownsville, 5 miles below, in Minnesota.

Racoon River, a small stream, flows into the Mississippi from Wisconsin, 5 miles below.

Bad Axe River, rises in Wisconsin and joins the Mississippi 6 miles below the mouth of Racoon river.

Battle Field, 2 miles below the mouth of Bad Axe river, in Bad Axe co., Wis.

Upper Iowa River, rises in Minnesota and flows southerly, then northeast, through the north-eastern part of Iowa, and enters the Mississippi a short distance below the mouth of Bad Axe river, near the boundary line between Iowa and Minnesota.

Lansing, 15 miles below, in Alamake co., Iowa. Population 2.500.

Lynxville, 8 miles below, in Crawford co., Wis.

Wexford, Alamake co., Iowa, is nearly opposite Lynxville.

Prairie du Chien, capitol of Crawford co., Wis., is about 100 miles west of Madison. It is situated on the borders of an extensive prairie, and occupies the site of an old Indian village, from whose chief, called by the French, Chien, it derives its name. The town contains a court-house, a fine academy, and several churches. There are excellent hunting-grounds in the vicinity of this place. The water courses and marshes are covered with wild rice, which the Indians gather for food. Numerous mounds are scattered over the land—the remains of a people whose history is unknown to us, and whose existence might have been doubted, had they not, like the builders of the pyramids, left these unmistakable evidences of their having "lived, and moved, and had a being." The terminus of the Milwaukee & Mississippi Railroad is here. Population about 4500. Prairie du Chien is 10 miles below Wexford.

Fort Crawford, 1 mile below Prairie du Chien, in the same county. Fort Atkinson, Iowa, near the head waters of Turkey river, is nearly due west from this station.

Wisconsin River, enters the Mississippi, from Wisconsin, 3 miles below. (See page 68.)

Cincinnati, Grant co., Wis., 7 miles below the mouth of the Wisconsin river.

Kilroy, opposite Cincin., in Clayton co., Iowa.

Clayton, 2 miles below, in the county of same name, Iowa. Lead mines are worked near this place.

Mendota, Grant co., Wis., 7 miles below.

Guttenburg, formerly *Prairie du Port*, 5 miles below, in Clayton co., Io., is a thriving village. It is situated on a high bluff. Rich lead mines are worked in this neighborhood.

Cassville, Grant co., Wis., 6 miles below. A large quantity of lead is shipped at this point, from mines in the vicinity. Population about 300.

Turkey River rises in Iowa, and after a course of 150 miles, passing diagonally through Clayton co., enters the Mississippi, opposite Cassville. It is not navigable for steamboats.

Frankford, Clayton co., Io., is a small village at the mouth of Turkey river.

Buena Vista, Clayton Co., Io., 5 miles below.

Potosi, 12 miles below, in Grant co., Wis., on Grant river, near its mouth,

Lead abounds in this region. Potosi is an important and flourishing town, having a large trade. Population about 3000.

Peru, Dubuque co., Io., 7 miles below, near the mouth of Little Makoquette river.

Sinapee, Grant co., Wis., 2 miles below.

Jamestown, 1 mile below, in the same county.

Dubuque, capitol of Dubuque co., Io., 5 miles below. It is situated on a gently sloping prairie, in one of the richest lead districts in the world. It contains a land office, 6 or 8 churches, 4 printing offices, 2 banks, several large hotels, a court-house, a number of stores, and workshops of all descriptions. The branch of the Illinois Central Railway, passing through Galena, terminates here. It is the terminus, also, of the Dubuque & Keokuk Railroad. The town was settled by the French and Canadians, about 1784. Population 18 500.

Dunleith, opposite Dubuque, in Jo Daviess co., Ill.

Fevre River, a small, sluggish stream, empties into the Mississippi, from Ill., 15 miles below. It is navigable for steamboats to Galena, during most of the year. On account of the narrowness of this stream, large boats have difficulty in getting up and down.

Galena, Jo Daviess co., Ill., is situated on Fevre river, seven miles from its mouth. It is located near the center of a rich lead district, extending, on both sides of the Mississippi, from the Wisconsin to the vicinity of Rock river. It derives its name from *galena*, a kind of lead ore found in the vicinity. In 1822, the process of smelting was first commenced; since that time there has been as high as 10,000,000 of pounds smelted in one year. The ore lies in horizontal *strata*, varying in thickness from a few inches to several feet, and yields 75 per cent of pure lead. Galena was first settled in 1826, and was then an outpost in the wilderness. An immense amount of business is now transacted here, as it is a place of import and export for the products of a very extensive and fertile region. There are several churches, 3 printing offices, a number of extensive manufactories, including mills, (flouring and saw mills,) sheet lead manufactories, &c., &c. Population about 9000. The Chicago & Galena Rail road has a terminus here, and a branch of the Illinois Central Railroad passes through.

Moselle, in same county, 6 miles below the mouth of Fevre river.

Bellevue, nearly opposite Moselle, is the county seat of Jackson co., Io. It is a thriving place, beautifully situated on a high bluff. It has a fine landing, and a splendid farming region in the interior.

Makoqueta River, enters the Mississippi from Iowa, 8 miles below. It furnishes a large amount of water-power. Its whole length is about 100 miles.

Portsmouth, Carroll co., Ill., 5 miles below.

Savannah, Carroll co., Ill., 8 miles below, a short distance above the mouth of Plum creek. It contains a court-house, jail and a number of stores. Population about 1000.

Sabula, Clinton co., Io., 4 miles below, is a small village.

Lyons, Clinton co., Io., is a place of considerable business, 15 miles below.

Fulton City, Whiteside co., Ill., is a flourishing village nearly opposite Lyons. Population 3.000

Albany, Whiteside co., Ill., 7 miles below, has an active trade. Population about 800.

Camanche, Clinton co., Io., nearly opposite Albany, is a lively business place. Population about 1.300.

Wapsipinecon River, rises in the north-eastern part of Iowa, and after a winding course of about 200 miles, enters the Mississippi 7 miles below Camancha. It affords excellent water-power for mills.

Cordova, Rock Island co., Ill., 4 miles below.

Princeton, Scott co., Io., 1 mile below.

Parkhurst, 5 miles below, in the same county.

Port Byron, Rock Island co., Ill., a small town, 1 mile below, is near the head of the upper rapids. Population 1.500.

Le Claire, Scott co., Io., 1 mile below, is a thriving village.

Hampton, Rock Island co., Ill., 5 miles below. It has considerable trade in earthenware. Population about 300.

Davenport, county seat of Scott co., Io., 12 miles below, is one of the most flourishing cities on the upper Mississippi. It is situated at the foot of the upper rapids in the midst of a fertile region of country. Stone coal is found in the vicinity. Davenport was settled in 1837. It now contains a number of flouring and saw mills, over 100 stores, many important manufacturing establishments, 8 or 10 churches and 3 or 4 printing offices. Population 20.042. A splendid rail-road bridge crosses the Mississippi at this point. The terminus of the Davenport and Missouri Railroad is here. The scenery in the vicinity of Davenport is very beautiful. The town stands on an elevated plain with a range of hills in the background.

Rock Island, is the name given a large island in the Mississippi just below Davenport. Fort Armstrong, an old U. S. Blockhouse in the time of Black Hawk's wars is on the southern extremity of the Island, it stands upon a rock, near twenty feet above the surface of the river. There is a recess in this rock called *Black Hawk's Cave*, where, it is said, he often concealed himself. It was here that Col. Davenport was murdered, July, 1845, by a party of lawless wretches. The Mississippi at this point is very rapid; it falls 21 feet 10 inches in the distance of 15 miles. Ledges of rock extend across the river, and, at low water, greatly obstruct the navigation.

The country around Rock Island is exceedingly rich. It consists mostly of prairie land, rising in a succession of little knolls, which at a distance, appear like the swells of the ocean, as it rolls about the verdant islands of the East. After leaving the river, the land rises gradually into a chain of rounded hills, thinly covered with trees. The Indians regard this as *their promised land*.

Moline, Rock Island co., Ill., is a thriving manufacturing village opposite the head of Rock Island, and has considerable water-power from the rapids of the river. Population 4.000.

Rock Island City, 3 miles below, opposite the foot of Rock Island, is the capital of Rock Island co., Ill. A number of extensive manufactories are carried on here, having the advantages of excellent water-power. It is the terminus of the Chicago & Rock Island Railroad. Population about 10.000. A fine railroad bridge crosses the river at this point.

Rock River, enters the Mississippi 2 miles below. (See page 68.)

Buffalo, Scott co., Io., 5 miles below the mouth of Rock river.

Andalusia, Rock Island co., Ill., nearly opposite Buffalo.

Iowa, Muscatine co., Io., 8 miles below.

Fairport, 7 miles below in the same county.

Muscatine, 6 miles below, county seat of Muscatine co., Io., is one of the most flourishing towns in the State. Iowa city is 32 miles north-west. Muscatine was laid out in 1836, being previously an Indian trading post. It is the shipping point for a large and fertile region of country. It contains a fine court-house, 9 or 10 churches, 3 printing offices, 7 hotels, a large number of stores and warehouses, 2 steam flouring and 2 steam saw mills. Population about 7500.

Port Louisa, Louisa co., Io., 16 miles below.

New Boston, 10 miles below, in Mercer co., Ill., is a thriving village with an active trade, it has a good landing, and is surrounded by a fertile country. Population about 800.

Iowa River, enters the Mississippi from Iowa, just below New Boston. (See page 69.)

Keithsburg, county seat of Mercer county, Ill., 7 miles below the mouth of Iowa river, is a flourishing village. Large amounts of produce are shipped from here. It is a good landing place. Population about 600.

Huron, Des Moines co., Io., 9 miles below.

Oquawka, capitol of Henderson co., Ill., 10 miles below, is a place of active business. It contains 2 or 3 printing offices, a court-house, a number of stores, and a population of about 3000.

Burlington, 15 miles below, is the county seat of Des Moines co., Io., and before 1839 was the capitol of the State. The river here is a broad and beautiful stream. The town is very pleasantly situated, partly on high ground, overlooking delightful scenery. Burlington contains a number of fine churches, schools, academies, &c., 4 printing offices, and a large number of business houses, mills, foundries, manufactories of different kinds, extensive pork packing houses, &c. Population about 12,000. The terminus of the Burlington & Peoria Railroad is here; also, the Burlington & Missouri Railroad.

Skunk River, empties into the Mississippi 8 miles below Burlington, from Iowa. It rises near the center of the State, and furnishes extensive water-power through a rich region of country.

Pontoosuc, 7 miles below, in Hancock co., Ill., is a flourishing village, surrounded by a fertile country. Population about 600.

Appanoose, 5 miles below in same county.

Fort Madison, county seat of Lee co., Io., 3 miles below. It became a town in 1835; since that time it has increased rapidly. The town occupies the site of an old fortification, built in 1808, as a defense against the Indians, who, in 1813, obliged the garrison to abandon and burn the fort. It contains a handsome court-house, a number of elegant churches, the Iowa Penitentiary, several spacious hotels, and is largely engaged in various branches of manufacturing and trade. There are 2 or 3 printing offices here, and it is a shipping point for large quantities of produce, and an extensive lumber depot. Population about 4500.

Nauvoo, 8 miles below, in Hancock co., Ill., the sacred city of the Mormons, is the most remarkable city in the Union. It is situated on a high slope, elevated several feet above the surface of the river. The location is one of the best in the West. The land was purchased by the Mormons, and the city laid out in 1840, under the direction of Joe Smith. It was 12 miles in circumference—streets regular, crossing each other at right-angles. The dwellings were mostly plain, with the exception of the Great Temple, which was one of the finest buildings in the West; it was 130 feet long, 88 feet wide, 65 feet to the top of the cornice, and 163 to the top of the cupola, and cost over half a million of dollars. It was designed to accommodate a congregation of 3,000 persons. The basement of the temple contained the *baptistry*, or brazen sea, in which new converts were baptized. This pool was supported by twelve gilded, colossal oxen, and was designed to imitate the brazen sea of Solomon. In the erection of this magnificent structure, most of the male population were engaged. Each one considered it his duty to contribute as far as he was able, believing he was erecting a temple which would stand till the end of time. The Mormons, supposing themselves the true *Latter Day Saints*, into whose hands the earth would soon pass, did not, at all times, pay a due regard to the rights and privileges of others. This constantly brought them into difficulty; and though often in fault, yet they were persecuted beyond measure. Smith and others of his sect were arrested and thrown into prison, where, in June, 1844, they were murdered by a lawless mob, without even the *form* of a trial. In October, 1848, the temple was fired, and soon reduced to a heap of ruins. The city is now in the hands of a band of French Socialists. Only a small number of the dwellings are occupied—the Mormon population, which at one time exceeded 15000, removed to Utah, and built the " *Great Salt Lake City.*" The present population of Nauvoo is about 4000.

The Mormons first appeared in the United States about 1830. Joseph Smith, their prophet, pretended to have found an addition to the Bible, engraved on twelve golden plates. After being submitted to Professor Anthon, and others, who pronounced the inscriptions a mess of jargon, he, by Divine assistance, was enabled to get a correct translation, which he published under the title of the *Book of Mormon.*

Montrose, nearly opposite Nauvoo, in Lee co., Io., is situated on an elevated prairie which commands a view of the river and country for 20 miles around. Numerous Indian mounds, the depositories of the ancient dead, are found in the vicinity. This town stands at the head of the Lower Rapids, and is the place of reshipping in time of low water. Population about 1000.

Nashville, Lee co., Io., is a small village 4 miles below.

Montebello, Hancock co., Ill., 6 miles below.

Keokuk, 4 miles below, in Lee co., Io., situated at the foot of the Des Moines, or Lower rapids, is a place of large business. In low water large boats from below can not pass the rapids; their freight is discharged at Keokuk, conveyed to Montrose, and reshipped on smaller boats. The fall of the rapids is 24 feet in 12 miles. Keokuk stands upon a limestone rock formation, which affords an excellent building material. The place contains 8 or 9 churches, several academies and schools, 2 printing offices, flouring mills and foundries, and a large number of stores, &c. Population nearly 12,000.

Hamilton City, Hancock co., Ill., nearly opposite Keokuk.

Warsaw, 4 miles below, in Hancock co., Ill., stands on a high bluff at the foot of the rapids, near the site of old Fort Edwards. The situation is very favorable for trade, and a large business is done in receiving and shipping merchandise and produce. Warsaw contains several mills, a large number of business houses, and manufactories. Population about 4000.

Des Moines River, enters the Mississippi from Iowa, nearly opposite Warsaw. (See page 70.)

Alexandria, Clark co., Mo., on Fox river near its entrance into the Mississippi.

Fox River, a small stream, rises in Daviss co., Io., and enters the Mississippi from Mo., about 2 miles below the mouth of the Des Moines river.

Des Moines City, 6 miles below, in Clark co., Mo.

Tully, Lewis co., Mo., 12 miles below, is a flourishing place. Large quantities of produce are shipped from here. It is pleasantly situated, and contains

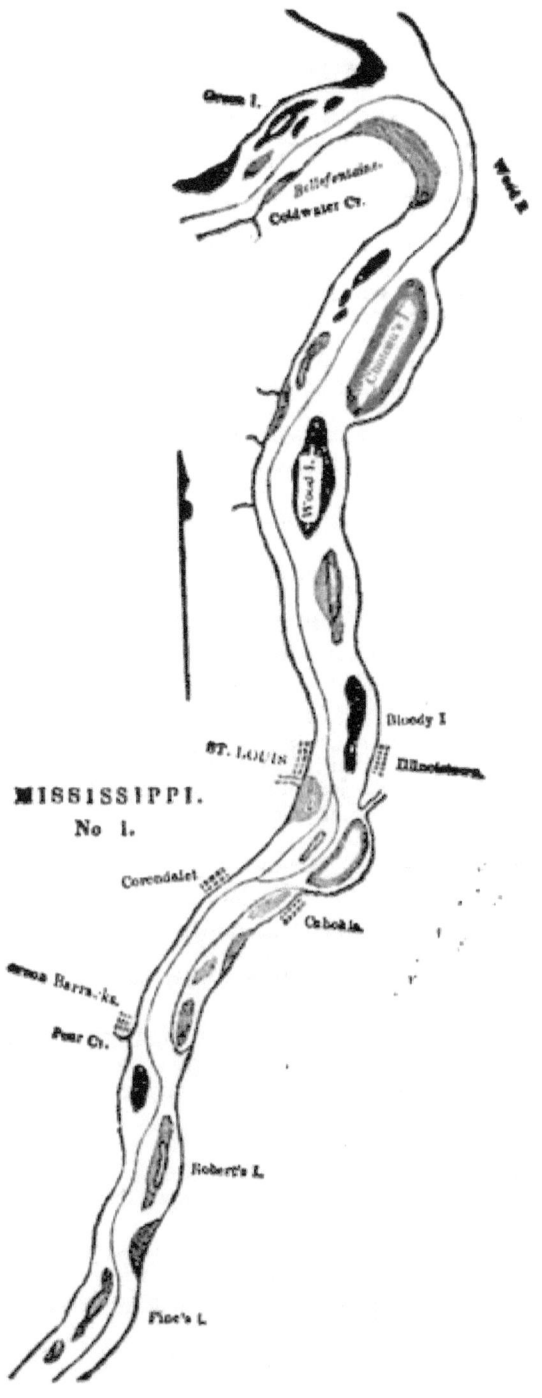

2 or 3 churches, 2 steam mills, and a number of stores. Population about 800. Laid out in 1833.

Lagrange, 6 miles below, in same county, near the mouth of Wyaconda river, is a place of considerable business. It contains several churches, a college, a flouring mill, &c. Population about 2.500.

Quincy, 12 miles below, is the county seat of Adams co., Ill. It is situated on a beautiful elevation 125 feet above the Mississippi, and commands a fine view of the river for 5 or 6 miles in each direction. It contains a large public square, a good court-house, a land office, 8 or 10 printing offices, about 20 churches; 3 banks, a number of extensive mills and manufactories, and a large number of stores and commission houses, also foundries, machine shops, distilleries, pork houses, &c. The country in its vicinity is a beautifully rolling and rich prairie, and one of the finest agricultural regions in the State. Large quantities of produce are annually shipped from here, by steamboats and other craft, which can navigate the river, from this place down, at any season of the year. Population about 25000. Quincy is the terminus of the Northern Cross Railroad.

Fabin's River, enters the Mississippi opposite Quincy. Near its mouth this river branches—north Fabin's and south Fabin's—the sources of each branch being about 150 miles from the point where they unite. Neither branch is navigable for steamboats.

Marion City, 7 miles below, in Marion co., Mo., is a thriving village and the shipping port for the interior. The soil of this county is very rich, and abounds in fine timber, bituminous coal, salt springs, and lead.

Aston, opposite Marion city, in Adams co., Ill.

Booneville, 3 miles below, in same county.

Hannibal, Marion co., Mo., 7 miles below, is a shipping port for large quantities of pork, hemp, tobacco and other produce raised in the vicinity. Stone coal and an excellent limestone for building purposes are abundant near the place. Hannibal is the terminus of the Hannibal and St. Joseph Railroad. It contains a large number of stores and warehouses, 2 or 3 printing offices and a population of about 9000.

Dayton, opposite Hannibal, in Adams co., Ill.

Saverton, 8 miles below, in Ralls co., Mo.

Salt River, empties into the Mississippi 18 miles below. Three branches of this river—the north, middle, and south forks—unite at Florida, Monroe co., Mo., about 85 miles from its mouth, and form the main stream, to which point it is navigable for small steamers.

Cincinnati, Ralls co., Mo., is on Salt river, about 20 miles below Florida.

Louisiana, Pike co., Mo., 2 miles below the mouth of Salt river, contains a number of stores and warehouses, and 2 printing offices. Population about 3.500.

Clarksville, 12 miles below, in same county.

Hamburgh, 15 miles below, in Calhoun co., Ill., is a flourishing town. It has a good landing, and employs considerable capital in mercantile and manufacturing pursuits. Population 800.

Gilead, Calhoun co., Ill., 9 miles below, is situated a short distance from the river. It was formerly the county seat. Population about 800.

Riviere au Cuivre, a small stream, enters the Mississippi, from Mo., 15 miles below Gilead.

Deer Plain, 12 miles below, in Calhoun co. Mo.

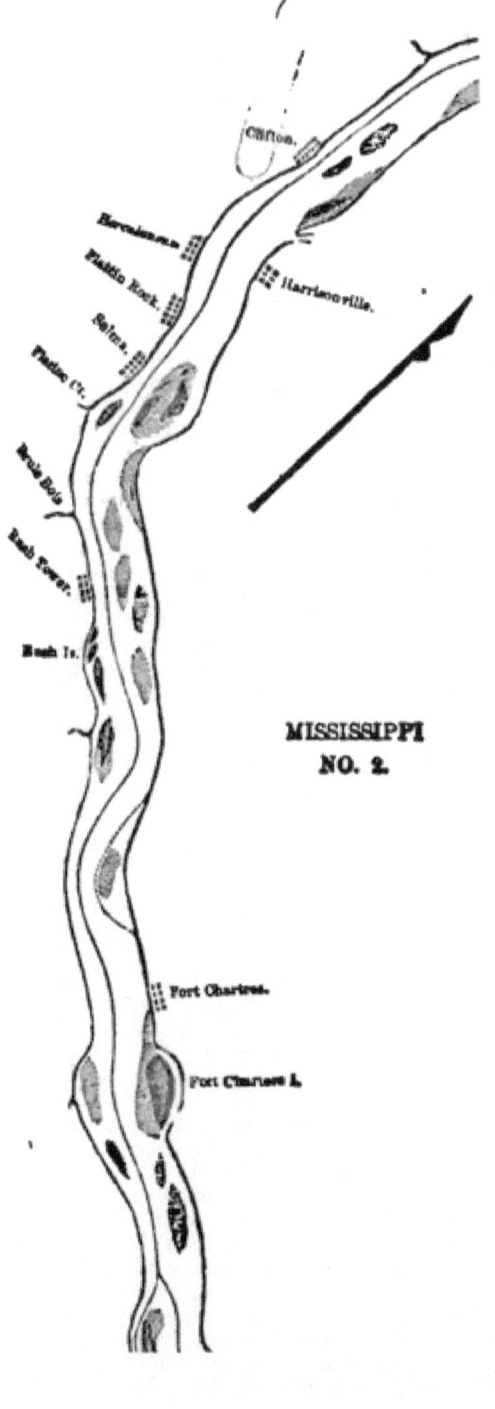

Illinois River, enters the Mississippi 6 miles below Deer Plain. (See page 71.)

Grafton, Jersey co., Ill., just below the mouth of the Illinois river, is a small village. Population about 350.

Portage des Sioux, St. Charles co., Mo., 7 miles below.

Randolph, 4 miles below, in Jersey co., Ill.

Alton, 7 miles below, in Madison co., Ill., was laid out in 1818. Up to the year 1832, it contained only a few houses and a steam mill. In that year, the Penitentiary of the State was erected here. After which it improved rapidly, and many fine buildings were put up. It is handsomely laid out in wide, beautiful streets, and contains 6 or 8 churches, a lyceum and theological seminary, and a large number of stores, commission houses, pork houses and manufactories. It is favorably situated for trade, and has an excellent landing. Alton is the terminus of the Chicago and Mississippi Railroad, also of the Terre Haute & Alton Railroad. Population about 12.000. This city is surrounded, for several miles in extent, with one of the finest bodies of timber in the State. Bituminous coal exists in great abundance only a short distance from the town. Inexhaustible beds of limestone, for building purposes, and easily quarried, are within its precincts. A species of freestone, easily dressed, and used for monuments and architectural purposes, and that peculiar species of lime, used for water-cement, are found in great abundance, in the vicinity. The corporate bounds extend 2 mile along the river, and half-a-mile back. The city plat was laid out, by the proprietors, upon a liberal scale. There are 5 squares reserved for public purposes, and a large reservation was made on the river for a public landing and promenade.

Missouri River, enters the Mississippi 5 miles below Alton. (See page 73.)

Chippewa, 1 mile below the mouth of the Missouri river, in Madison co., Ill.

Madison, 2 miles below, in same co.

Venice, in same co., 8 miles below.

Bremen, 2 miles below, in St. Louis co., Mo.

St. Louis, 4 miles below, was selected by Mr. Laclede (the manager for a company of merchants, who had obtained the monopoly of the Indian fur trade, on the Mississippi and Missouri rivers), as a depot for their merchandise. Mr. Laclede, after examining numerous points on the Mississippi,

ST. LOUIS FROM BLOODY ISLAND.

foresaw and predicted the future importance of the town, to which he gave the name of St. Louis, in honor of Louis XV of France, and in Dec., 1763, he had a portion of the ground, on which it stands, cleared, and returned to Fort Chartres, to make preparation for the establishment of his new colony. He was accompanied in his visit by two young creoles of New Orleans, Augustus and Pierre Chouteau, whom he despatched, in the February following, with men and materials to complete the settlement. During the summer of 1764, many of the French from the vicinity of Fort Chartres, removed to St. Louis. This emigration was soon checked by the cession of that territory to the King of Spain. It was not, however, until 1770 that Spain obtained possession of St. Louis. In 1771, it contained 120 houses, mostly of stone, and a population of about 800, exclusive of 150 negroes; the whites being mostly French.

In 1780, the garrison consisting of only 50 or 60 men, was attacked by a large body of Indians, numbering from 900 to 1500. "The women and

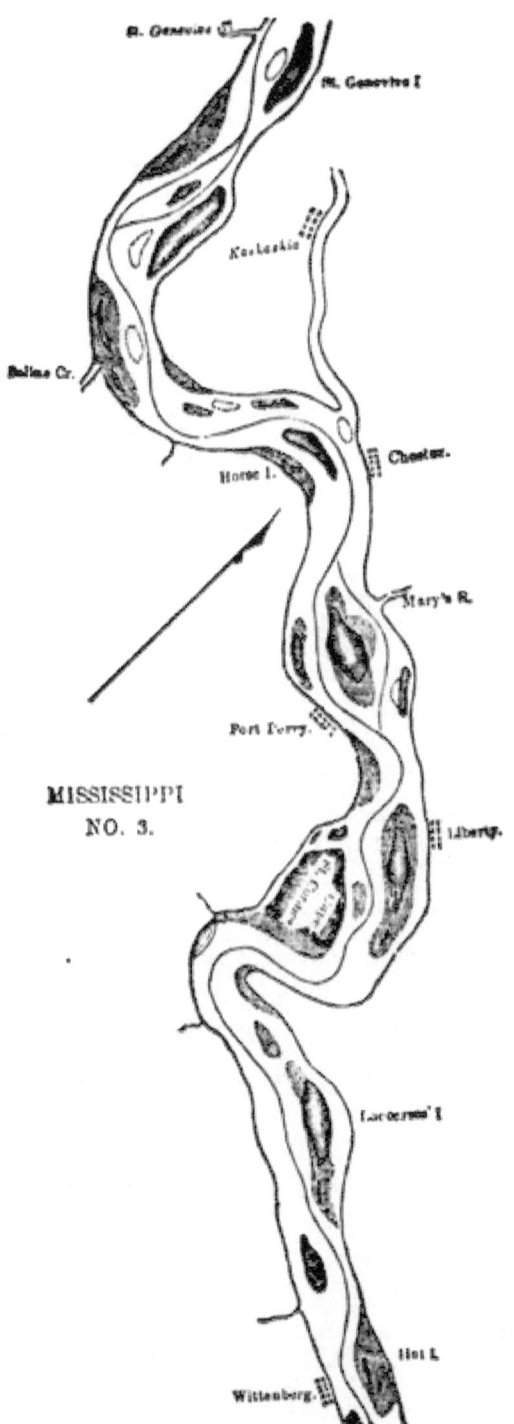

children who could not take part in the defense, took shelter in the house of Auguste Chouteau, whilst all those, both men and women, who were within the palisades, commenced so vigorous a resistance, that the enemy was forced to retreat. But, with their characteristic ferocity, threw themselves upon those of the inhabitants, who engaged in the cultivation of their fields, had not time to reach the palisades, and it is said that 60 were killed and 13 made prisoners. The year this attack took place is called by the French, "*l'Anee du Grand Coup*—the year of the great blow."

After this, the inhabitants finding their garrison insufficient to protect them, sent Mr. A. Chouteau to New Orleans for assistance. Cruzat was made commander of St. Louis, and a wooden fort erected on the most elevated spot within the city, upon which several heavy pieces of ordnance were mounted, and still later, 4 stone turrets were added, from which cross fires could be kept up. No traces of this fortification are now to be seen.

St. Louis is the capitol of St. Louis co., Mo., and the largest town in the State, situated in Lat. 38° 37' north. It rests on a bed of limestone rising from 20 to 60 feet above the floods of the Mississippi. At this elevation an extensive plain opens to view. The city extends along the river many miles. Some of the prominent buildings of St. Louis are, a splendid court-house, erected at a cost of over half a million of dollars, the Planter's House, United States Hotel, Virginia Hotel, Missouri Hotel, City Hospital, Marine Hospital, Home for the Friendless, Church of the Messiah (Unitarian), Catholic Cathedral, St. George's, Church (Episcopal), and the U. S. Arsenal. St. Louis contains about 85 churches, of different denominations, the University of St. Louis, the Missouri University, a Mercantile Library Association, in a very flourishing condition, with a large and increasing library and fine reading room. The public schools receive the special attention of the citizens; a large number of pupils are in daily attendance, and the seminaries and private schools are, also, well patronized. There are some 25 or 30 printing offices in St. Louis, a number of them issuing daily, tri-weekly, and weekly newspapers, with a large circulation. The city is supplied with water, from reservoirs, forced up from the river by stationary engines, and distributed through iron pipes.

The location of St. Louis, for commerce, is second to none in the West. It is the center of an immense and fertile region, watered by the largest rivers in the world. There are a vast number of steamboats in its trade, many of them of the largest class, navigating the rivers from near the Alleghany to the Rocky Mountains, and from the northern lakes to the Gulf of Mexico. The flouring, the pork packing, and the sugar refining business, are carried on here very extensively, and a great number of important manufacturing establishments on a large scale. The terminus of the St. Louis and Pacific Railroad, is here; and the Ohio & Mississippi Railroad, and others, have their terminus in Illinois, opposite.

The population of the city has increased rapidly: in 1810, it was less than 2000; in 1830, it was 7000; in, 1840, it was 16000; in 1845, 35,000; in 1850, 70,000; in 1860, about 150,000; and in 1870, 314,000.

Illinoistown, St. Clair co., Ill., on the east side of the Mississippi, opposite St. Louis, is the western terminus of the Ohio & Mississippi Railroad. Population about 600.

Cahokia, 4 miles below, in St. Clair co., Ill., is one of the oldest settlements in the State. It was occupied by the Cuoquias, a tribe of Illinois Indians, long before the discovery of the Mississippi. The French settled on it shortly after La Salle descended the Mississippi, probably about the year 1683. In 1766, it contained 40 families, and now about 50. The majority of the houses are built of pickets, one story high, having piazzas on each side, and, being white-washed,

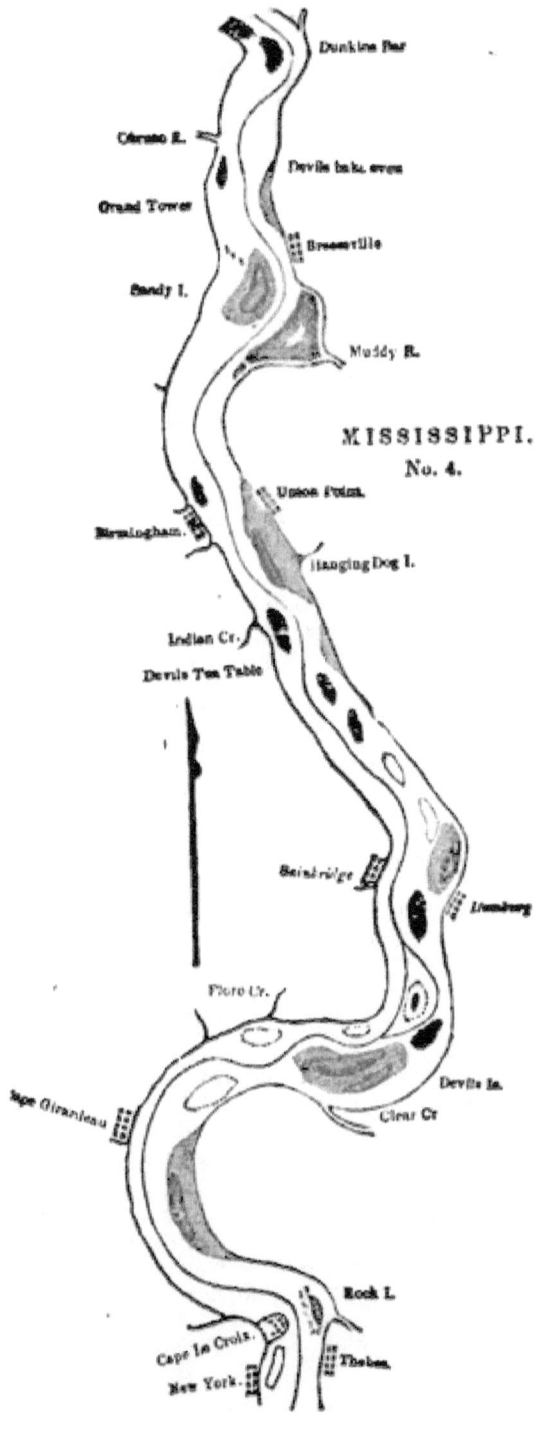

present a pleasant appearance. The inhabitants are principally French. By an act of Congress, passed in 1788, a grant of 400 acres of land, adjoining the village, was made to each family. The situation is somewhat elevated, but unhealthy, and Americans seldom pass a season in it without suffering from the miasma of the surrounding ponds. Stone coal is found in the vicinity.

Carondalet, St. Louis co., Mo., formerly called Vide Poche (empty pocket), 1 mile below, is a small village principally occupied by the French, who supply vegetables for the St. Louis market. It was settled in 1767.

Jefferson Barracks, St. Louis co., 5 miles below, is one of the most extensive U. S. military establishments in the West, and has a large cavalry school attached, from which the mounted troops upon the frontiers are supplied.

Maramec River, rises in Crawford and Washington counties, Mo., and flows north-east, then south-east, and enters the Mississippi 9 miles below Jefferson Barracks. It is navigable some 60 miles.

Clifton, 10 miles below, in Jefferson co., Mo.

Harrisonville, 2 miles below, in Monroe co., Ill.

Herculaneum, Jefferson co., Mo., 2 miles below, is a flourishing town. There are a number of shot towers here, and in the vicinity, and being a principal port of the lead district, a large amount of lead and shot are annually exported — Population 700.

Plattin Rock, 1 mile below, in same co.

Selma, 2 miles below, in same co., has a good landing, and carries on considerable trade in lead. Shot are also made here in large quantities. Population about 400.

Rush Tower, 4 miles below, in same co., is a small village.

Fort Chartres, 9 miles below, in Randolph co., Ill., was an old French fort, built in 1720, as a defence against the Spaniards. It was taken possession of by the English in 1765 by virtue of the treaty of Fontainbleau. It is now a heap of ruins. The walls are fast crumbling away, and vines and trees are springing up around these venerable remains. This fort was designed to be the strongest on the continent: Its walls were built of solid masonry, in quadrangular form, 490 feet in circumference. It was the head quarters of the commandant in upper Louisiana, and the center of fashion in the West.

St. Genevieve, capitol of St. Genevieve co., Mo., 11 miles below, is pleasantly situated, and a place of considerable business. It exports large quantities of lead, iron, copper, limestone and a white silicious sand, a very fine article used at Pittsburgh and other places for making glass. St. Genevieve was settled by the French about 1750. It contains the usual county buildings, and 2 printing offices. Population about 2000. Directly back of this town, a few miles, is Potosi. It is located in the finest mineral district in the United States. The Iron Mountain, the greatest natural curiosity in the West, is in the vicinity. This mountain is said to be an almost solid mass of ore.

St. Mary's Landing, 10 miles below, in same county, is a small village.

Pratt's Landing, Perry co., Mo., 2 miles below, is a small place.

Kaskaskia River, enters the Mississippi from Illinois, 3 miles below. (See page 79.) This is the southern terminus of the great American Bottom, which extends northerly, on the river, for 80 miles.

Chester, Randolph co., Ill., 1 mile below the mouth of the Kaskaskia river. The town is built on an elevated bottom, and is the commercial depository of a fine country. It is a flourishing place. Population about 1860.

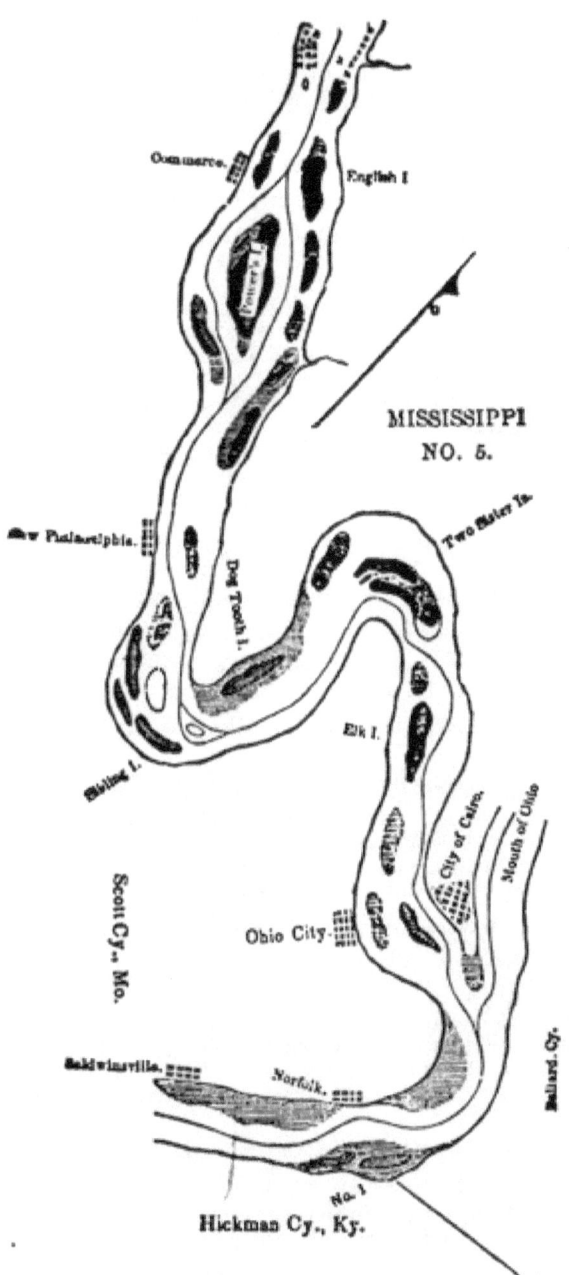

Mary's River, 4 miles below, rises in Illinois and flows south-west into the Mississippi. It is a small stream, and not navigable.

Port Perry, Perry co., Mo., 3 miles below, is a small village.

Liberty, Randolph co., Ill., 4 miles below.

Wittemberg, 17 miles below, in Perry co., Mo.

Devil's Bake-oven and Grand Tower, 5 and 6 miles below. These are names given to a portion of a gigantic range of rocks, rising to a considerable height on both sides of the river, nearly midway between St. Louis and the mouth of the Ohio. The summits of this range are covered with vegetation, which looks smilingly down upon the water as it dashes against its base. The current here is very swift; and by its force and constant wearing away of the cliffs, it has separated a large portion, which stands, like a gigantic column in the midst of the waves. Such is "Grand Tower," which rises nearly 50 feet above the surface of the river.

Those hardy boatmen, who navigated our western waters before the introduction of steam, dreaded this place more than any other on the river. The only way they could ascend the river, was to pull their boats along the Illinois shore by means of ropes. The Indians, who were always on the lookout for plunder, would conceal themselves in the bushes, and, when a favorable opportunity offered, fall upon them. Thus many valuable lives and cargoes were lost, in attempting that which steam now performs in perfect safety.

Breeseville, Jackson co., Ill., 2 miles below, is a small village.

Muddy River, 4 miles below, rises in Illinois and flows south-west into the Mississippi. It is navigable only for a short distance.

Birmingham, 4 miles below, in Cape Girardeau co., Mo., near the mouth of Apple creek, is a small village.

Union Point, opposite Birmingham, in Union co., Ill.

Devil's Tea-table and Cornice Rocks, 3 miles below, are great natural curiosities. The water has worn the rocks into regular shapes, representing continuous rows of cornice work and other architectural devices of the greatest beauty, which hang majestically over the river.

Bainbridge, 6 miles below, in Cape Girardeau co., Mo.

Hamburg, Union co., Ill., opposite Bainbridge.

Cape Girardeau, in the county of the same name, 10 miles below. It has a number of good stores and mills, 2 academies, 3 schools, and 1 convent. It is the seat of St. Mary's college, founded in 1830; which now has a president, 5 professors, and a library of 2500 volumes. Population 3000. The country around it is very fertile, and thickly inhabited, for forty or fifty miles back, to the New Madrid settlements.

Thebes, 9 miles below, capital of Alexander co., Ill.

New York, nearly opposite Thebes, in Scott co., Mo.

Commerce, 3 miles below, in same co., contains a number of stores. It has considerable trade, and a fine region of country back. Population about 400.

New Philadelphia, 7 miles below, in same co.

Ohio City, Mississippi co., Mo., 21 miles below, is a flourishing place, nearly opposite Cairo and the mouth of the Ohio river.

Ohio River, and Cairo—(See pages 88 and 122.)

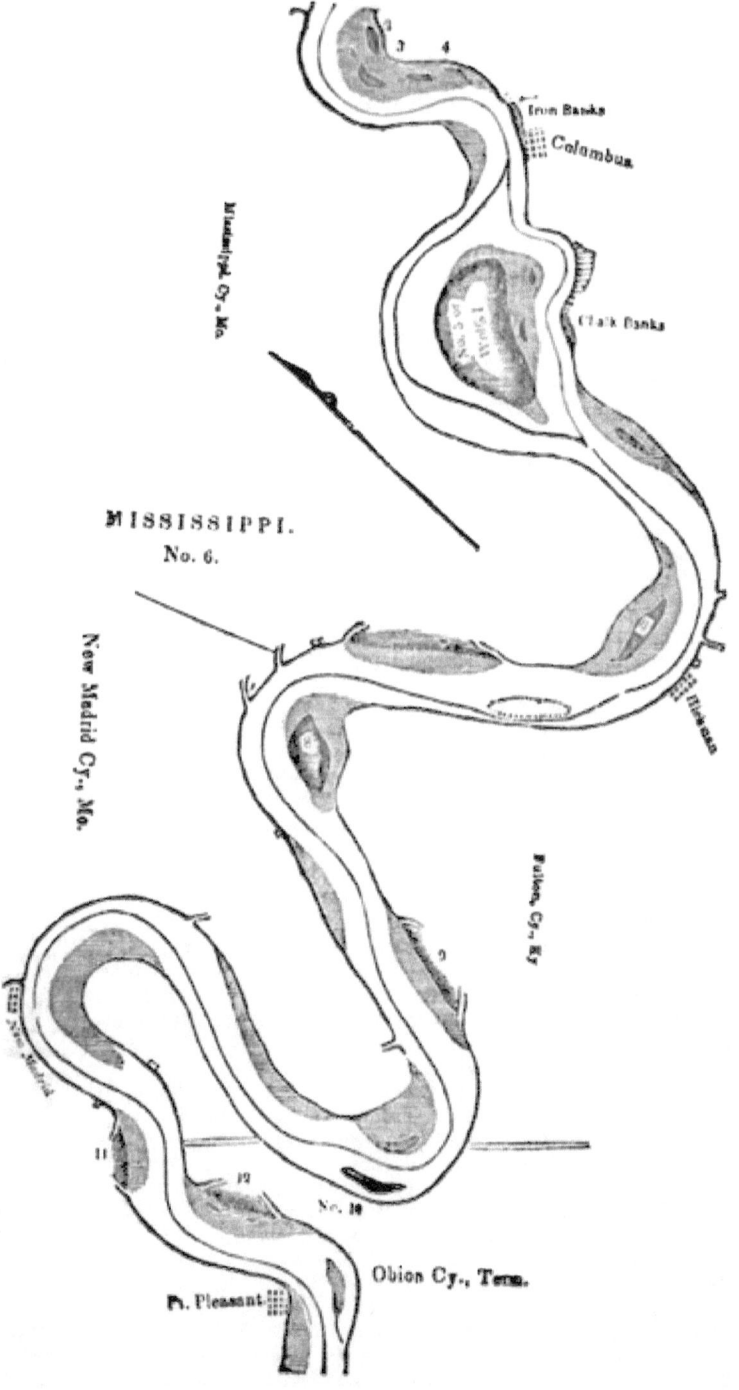

Island No. 1, 6 miles below the mouth of the Ohio, opposite which, in Kentucky, a short distance from the river, are the remains of Fort Jefferson, erected by Gen. George Rogers Clark, in the spring of 1780. This fort was built by order of Gov. Jefferson, of Virginia, in order to protect the navigation of the Mississippi, and secure it to that State, in which this territory was then included.

Norfolk, Mississippi co., Mo., opposite Island No. 1.

Bickwith's, 7 miles below, in same co., is a small village.

Baldwinsville, 5 miles below, in same co., is a small place Population about 200.

Columbus, 4 miles below, capitol of Ballard co., Ky It contains several extensive warehouses, and a population of about 600. Just above it are the Iron banks, extending along the river, on the same side, for about 2 miles. They derive the name from the color of the banks resembling iron rust.

Hickman, formerly Mills Point, county seat of Fulton co., Ky., 20 miles below, is a flourishing town. It contains 10 or 12 stores, and commission and forwarding houses, 2 or 3 churches, a printing office, a large tobacco stemery, and a bank. Large quantities of tobacco, corn, cotton, cattle, poultry, &c., are annually shipped from here, it being the depot for the products of a large and fertile section of country. It is the starting point for the stage route to Nashville. Population about 2,000.

Island No. 10, 32 miles below Hickman.

New Madrid, 12 miles below, is the county seat of New Madrid co., Mo. It carries on a large trade in shipping produce, cattle, lumber, &c. It has a printing office and a population of about 500. This point was the scene of a violent earthquake in 1811. The following account of it is from the pen of Dr. Hildreth of Marietta, O., and published in Perkins' Annals of the West.

"The center of its violence was thought to be near the Little Prairie, 25 or 30 miles below New Madrid—the vibrations from which were felt all over the valley of the Ohio, as high up as Pittsburgh. * * * * New Madrid, having suffered more than any other town on the Mississippi from its effects, was considered as situated near the focus, from whence the undulations proceeded. From an eye-witness, who was then about 40 miles below that town, in a flat-boat, on his way to New Orleans, with a load of produce, and who narrated the scene to me, the agitation which convulsed the earth and the waters of the mighty Mississippi, filled every living creature with horror. The first shock took place in the night (Dec. 16, 1811), while the boat was lying at the shore, in company with several others. At this period, there was danger apprehended from the Southern Indians, it being soon after the battle of Tippecanoe, and for safety several boats kept in company, for mutual defense, in case of an attack. In the middle of the night, there was a terrible shock and jarring of the boats, so that the crews were all awakened, and hurried on deck, with their weapons of defense in their hands, thinking the Indians were rushing on board. The ducks, geese, swans, and various other aquatic birds, whose numberless flocks were quietly resting in the eddies of the river, were thrown into the greatest tumult, and, with loud screams, expressed their alarms in accents of terror. The noise and commotion soon became hushed, and nothing could be discovered to excite apprehension; so that the boatmen concluded that the shock was occasioned by the falling in of a large mass of the bank of the river near them. As soon as it was light enough to distinguish objects, the crews were all up, making ready to depart. Directly a loud roaring and hissing was heard, like the escape of steam from a boiler, accompanied by the most violent agitation of the shores, and tremendous boiling up of the waters of the Mississippi, in huge swells rolling the waters below, back on the descending stream, and tossing the boats about so violently that the men, with difficulty,

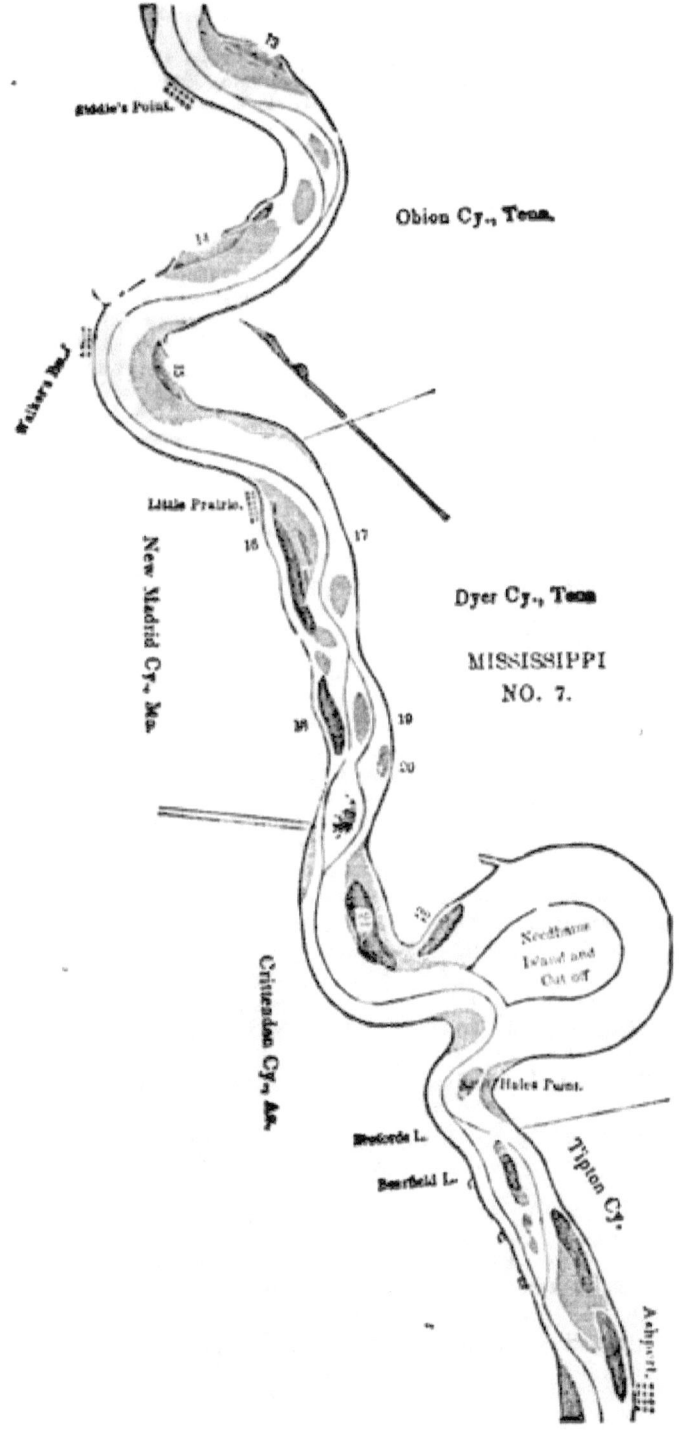

could keep their feet. The sand-bars and points of the islands gave way, swallowed up in the tumultuous bosom of the river, carrying down with them the cotton-wood trees, cracking and crashing, tossing their arms to and fro, as if sensible of their danger, while they disappeared beneath the flood. The water of the river, which, the day before, was tolerably clear, being rather low, changed to a reddish hue, and became thick with mud, thrown up from its bottom; while the surface, lashed violently by the agitation of the earth beneath, was covered with foam, which, gathering into masses the size of a barrel, floated along on the trembling surface. The earth on the shores opened in wide fissures, and, closing again, threw the water, sand, and mud, in huge jets, higher than the tops of the trees. The atmosphere was filled with a thick vapor, or gas, to which the light imparted a purple tinge, altogether different, in appearance, from the autumnal haze of Indian summer, or that of smoke. From the temporary check to the current, by the heaving up of the bottom, the sinking of the banks and sand-bars into the bed of the stream, the river rose, in a few minutes 5 or 6 feet; and, impatient of the restraint, again rushed forward with redoubled impetuosity, hurrying along the boats, now set loose by the horror-struck boatmen, as in less danger on the water than at the shore, where the banks threatened every moment to destroy them by the falling earth, or carry them down in the vortices of the sinking masses. Many boats were overwhelmed in this manner, and their crews perished with them. It required the utmost exertions of the men, to keep the boat, of which my informant was the owner, in the middle of the river, as far from the shores, sand-bars, and islands, as they could. Numerous boats were wrecked on the snags and old trees thrown up from the bottom of the Mississippi, where they had quietly rested for ages; while others were sunk or stranded on the sand-bars and islands. At New Madrid, several boats were carried, by the reflux of the current, into a small stream that puts into the river just above the town, and left on the ground by the returning waters, a considerable distance from the Mississippi. * * * The sulphurated gasses that were discharged during the shocks, tainted the air with their noxious effluvia, and so strongly impregnated the water of the river, to the distance of 150 miles below, that it could hardly be used for any purpose for several days. New Madrid, which stood on a bluff, 15 or 20 feet above the summer floods, sunk so low, that the next rise covered it to the depth of 5 feet. The bottoms of several fine lakes in the vicinity were elevated, so as to become dry land, and have since been planted with corn." Slight oscillations and shocks continued to be felt for years, along this region.

Point Pleasant, 7 miles below, in the same county, is a thriving village. Large quantities of corn are shipped from this place.

Riddle's Point, 3 miles below, in the same co., is a landing place for goods destined for the interior, and for the receipt of produce. The whole country, for miles, along the river, is extremely rich, yielding immense quantities of corn.

Walker's Bend, 18 miles below. This is simply a large bend of the river, so named by the boatmen.

Little Prairie, 7 miles below, in New Madrid co., Mo. Population 500. This is the point where, it is thought, was the center of the vibrations of the great earthquake.

Needham's Cut-off, 24 miles below. These cut-offs are channels formed by the current, in the circular bends of the river. The floods are constantly washing away the banks, thus opening new channels for the current. These frequent changes, in the channel, render the navigation of the river quite intricate.

Obion River, rises in West Tennessee and flows south-west into the Mis-

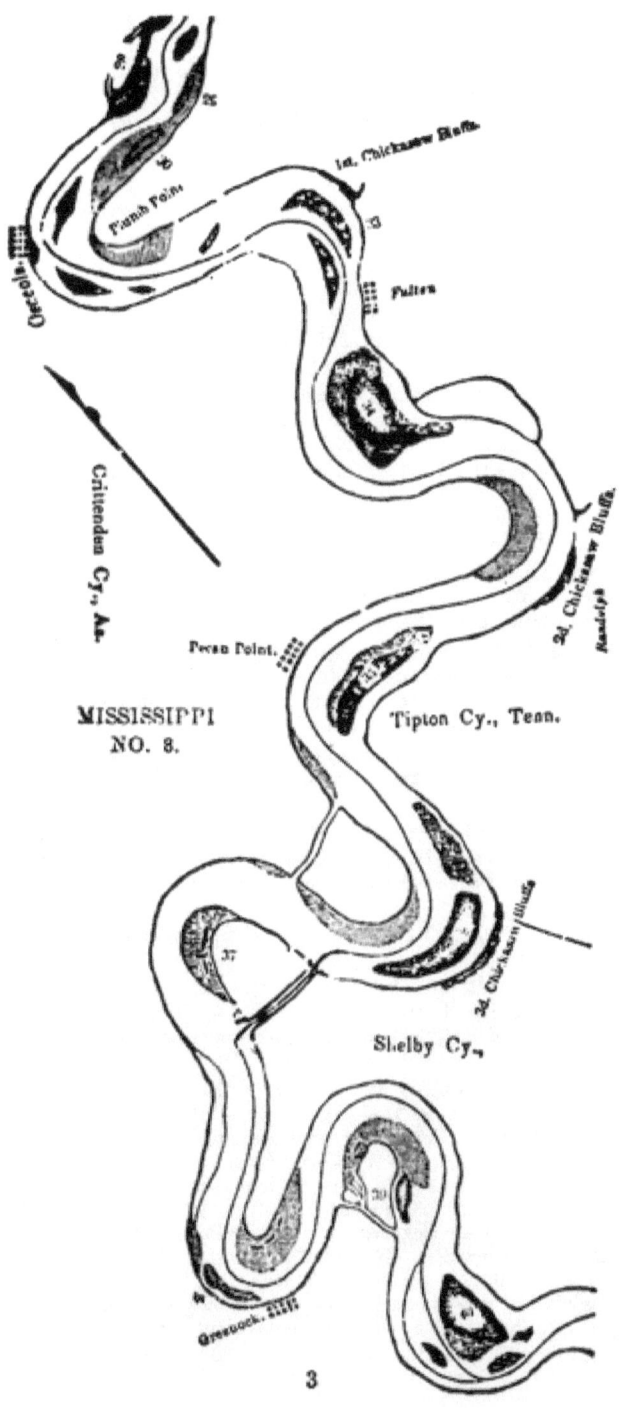

sissippi, just above Needham's Cut-off—its whole length is estimated at 150 miles. It is navigable for 60 miles.

Hale's Point, at the lower side of Needham's Cut-off.

Bearfield Landing, 2 miles below, in Mississippi co., Ark.

Forked Deer River flows from West Tennessee, and enters the Mississippi 4 miles below Bearfield. It is navigable for keel boats, some 150 miles, to Jackson.

Ashport, Lauderdale co., Tenn., 2 miles below, near the lower end of the Canadian Reach. It has several warehouses and a steam saw-mill   Population 200

Osceola, 12 miles below, county seat of Mississippi co., Ark., is a small village, just at the head of *Plum Point Bars*.

Plum Point.— This is one of the most difficult places to pass on the Mississippi. From the frequent changes in the channel, bars have been thrown up, in which a large amount of drift has become imbedded, rendering navigation very difficult. Quite a number of boats have been lost here.

1st Chickasaw Bluff, 6 miles below. These bluffs, which are 4 in number, are merely ordinary banks, extending for a few miles along the river. The highest is elevated about 30 feet above high water mark. After passing these banks, the country bordering on the river is very low.

Fulton, Lauderdale co., Tenn., 4 miles below, on the lower extremity of the 1st Chickasaw Bluff. It contains several warehouses, and a number of dwellings and has some trade in cotton. It is supported by a rich country. Population 400.

Hatchee River enters the Mississippi 10 miles below Fulton. It rises in Mississippi, and flows through Hardeman and Haywood counties, Tenn., and is the boundary line between Lauderdale and Tipton counties, Tenn. It is navigable to Bolivar, the county seat of Hardeman co., about 75 miles.

Randolph, Tipton co., Tenn., at the mouth of the Hatchee river, near the head of the 2d Chickasaw bluff. Large quantities of cotton are shipped from this place.

Pecan Point, 10 miles below, in Mississippi co., Ark.

3rd Chickasaw Bluff, 10 miles below. This bluff is separated from the main channel of the river by a slough, which is only navigable in high stages of water.

Greenock, Crittenden co., Ark., 27 miles below is a small village. Population about 200.

Mound City, 12 miles below, in same co.

Wolf River rises in the northern part of the State of Mississippi, and flows in a westerly direction till it joins the Mississippi just above Memphis. It is not navigable.

Memphis, 8 miles below Mound city, in Shelby co., Tenn., is beautifully situated on the 4TH CHICKASAW BLUFF, just below the mouth of Wolf river. This spot was formerly the site of Fort Assumption, used for the purpose of protecting the country against the Chickasaws, to chastise whom a French army of nearly 4000, white, red, and black, were gathered here. They remained in a state of inactivity, from the summer of 1739 to the spring of 1740, during which time, hundreds of them sickened and died, when in March of the last named year, peace was concluded. The bluff, on which Memphis stands, is 30 feet above the highest floods, and its base is washed by the river, for a distance of 3 miles, while a bed of sand-stone, the only known stratum of rocks below the Ohio, juts into the stream and forms a convenient landing. From the Ohio to Vicksburgh, a distance of 600 miles, it is the only site for a commercial mart, on

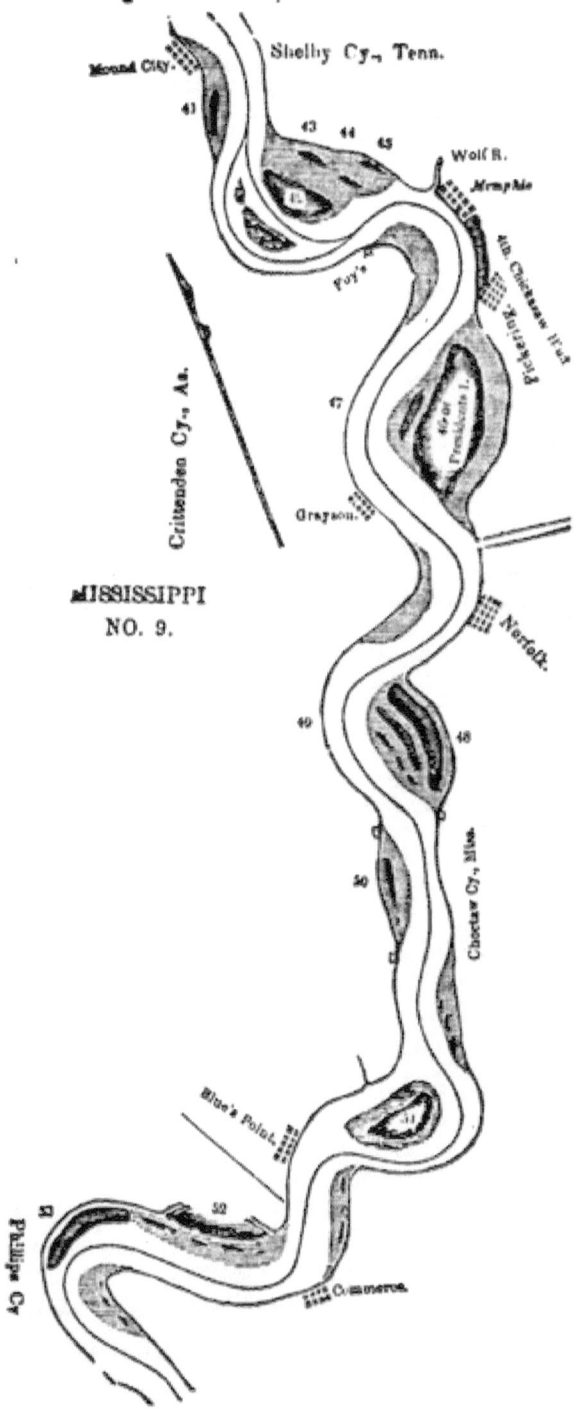

either side of the Mississippi. The beautiful situation of Memphis, and its connection with a fine country, together with the great distance from any other point on the river, where a large city can be built, give it superior advantages. Immense quantities of cotton are grown in the interior country, and this is the principal mart and shipping point for it. 120,000 bales are annually shipped from this place. It contains sixteen churches, 2 medical schools, a number of private schools, a large number of stores and extensive warehouses, 6 or 8 printing offices, and a population of about 41,000. Memphis is the western terminus of the Memphis & Charleston Railroad.

Pickering, 2 miles below, in same co., contains several large commission houses. It has an excellent landing.

Grayson, Crittenden co., Ark., 6 miles below.

Norfolk, 2 miles below, in De Soto co., Miss., is a small village.

Blue's Point, 18 miles below, in Crittenden co., Ark.

Commerce, De Soto co., Miss., 2 miles below, is a small village.

Austin, county seat of Tunica co., Miss., 6 miles below, is a flourishing town. Population about 300.

St. Francis River enters the Mississippi from Arkansas, 20 miles below Austin. It rises in Missouri, and flows almost parallel with the Mississippi for a great distance, and drains the lakes and cypress swamps along its course. Its whole length is about 450 miles, and for 150 miles it is navigable at some seasons of the year.

Sterling, Phillips co., Arkansas, is a small trading post, at the mouth of the St. Francis river.

Helena, county seat of Phillips co., Ark., 10 miles below, is a flourishing town. It contains a court-house, a jail, a U. S. land office, and several printing offices. In the summer of 1852, Helena was nearly destroyed by fire. Population about 500. There is a very handsome range of hills immediately back of it—the only ones seen along the river for some distance. Considerable cotton, brought down the St. Francis river, and from the interior country, is shipped from this place.

Yazoo Pass or Bayou, 8 miles below, in Koahoma co., connects the Mississippi river with the Yazoo river at this point, enabling flat-boats to pass through an immense section of fertile country, on the latter river, a distance of nearly 300 miles. Extensive cotton plantations are all along the course of the Yazoo.

Delta, capital of Koahoma co., Miss., on the lower side of the bayou, is a small village.

Prier's Point, 6 miles below, in same county.

Horse-Shoe Bend and Cut-off, just below. This is a large bend of the river, so called from its resemblance to a horse-shoe. A cut-off has been made across it.

Old Town, Phillips co., Ark., 3 miles below.

Barney's, 10 miles below, in same co.

Concordia, Bolivar co., Miss., 30 miles below, is a small village.

Montgomery's Point, 10 miles below, in Desha co., Ark., is the landing place for goods destined to the White river country.

Victoria, opposite, in Bolivar co., Miss., is also a landing point for the interior country.

It was near this point that the great De Soto first beheld the Mississippi, some-

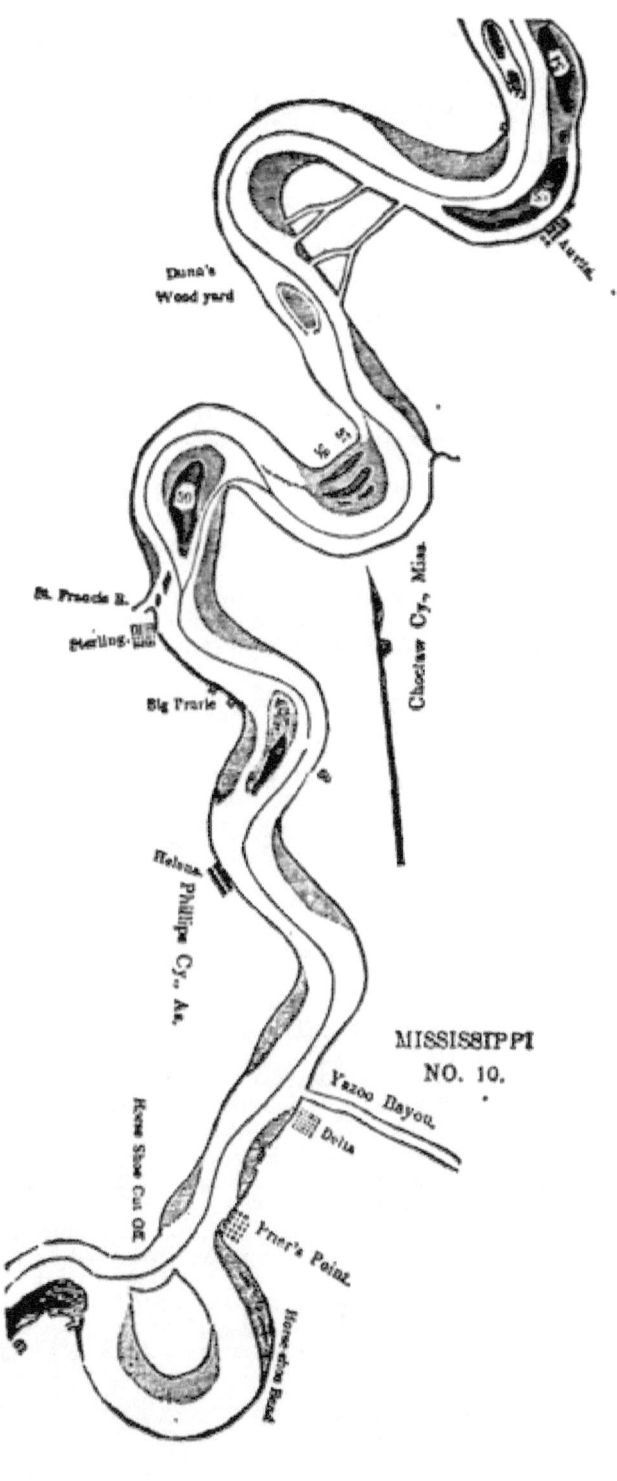

where between Helena and the mouth of White river. This expedition, ever memorable in the history of our country, sailed from Havana on the 12th of May, 1539. After a voyage of two weeks, the fleet landed in a small bay on the coast of Florida. Fired by a thirst for gold, and ambitious to be the first discoverers of the country, they eagerly plunged into the wilds of Florida and began their search for gold. The natives opposed them at every step. In order to make himself as secure as possible, De Soto always contrived to get possession of the chief of the country through which he was passing, whom he held a prisoner, as security for the good conduct of his people. After wandering about for more than 2 years, through a populous and hostile country, he at length reached the Mississippi. He crossed the river and wandered about Arkansas, in the neighborhood of White river. Provisions failing, and suffering from the coldness of the winter, he again directed his course toward the Mississippi, which he reached about 20 miles below the mouth of the Arkansas river. The fatigues and disappointments of the expedition began to weigh so heavily on his mind, that they brought on a fever, which soon terminated his existence. He died at the age of 42, a stranger in a strange land.

White River enters the Mississippi from Arkansas, 4 miles below Victoria. (See page 79.)

Arkansas River empties into the Mississippi 16 miles below the mouth of White river. (See page 80.)

Napoleon, just below the mouth of Arkansas river, in Desha co., Ark., is the depot and landing place for goods destined for, and produce brought down, that river. The U. S. Government has established a marine hospital here. Population about 1100.

Bolivia, capital of Bolivar co., Miss., 13 miles below the mouth of Arkansas river, is a small place.

Gaines' Landing, Chicot co., Ark., 35 miles below.

Columbia, 18 miles below, is the county seat of Chicot co., Ark. It is a very pleasant place, containing a number of stores, a court-house, and a population of about 400. Here commences the great cotton growing region, and the banks of the river are almost one succession of plantations. Just below this commences the growth of the Spanish moss.

Point Chicot, 4 miles below, in Ark., was formerly the county seat of Chicot co.

Greenville, 4 miles below, county seat of Washington co., Miss., is a small village. Population about 300.

Worthington Landing, 22 miles below in Washington co., Miss.

Grand Lake Landing, 6 miles below, in Chicot co., Ark. Grand Lake is a short distance back of the landing.

Princeton, county seat of Washington co., Miss., 4 miles below, is a landing point for the plantations in the neighborhood of Lake Washington, 5 miles in the interior. It is a small village. Population about 300.

Bunche's Bend and Cut-off is 10 miles below Princeton. This cut-off runs through a swamp, and is but a few miles across; while the main channel flows round a circular bend of nearly 18 miles.

Providence, 19 miles below, capital of Carroll parish, La., is a very handsome village, and has considerable trade in shipping cotton and supplying the planters in the interior. Population about 350. Just back of the town is the lake, from which it derives its name, on the banks of which there are a number of fine cotton plantations. On the opposite side of the river, is a very large, fine plantation, with a number of houses and negro quarters, giving it the appearance of a town.

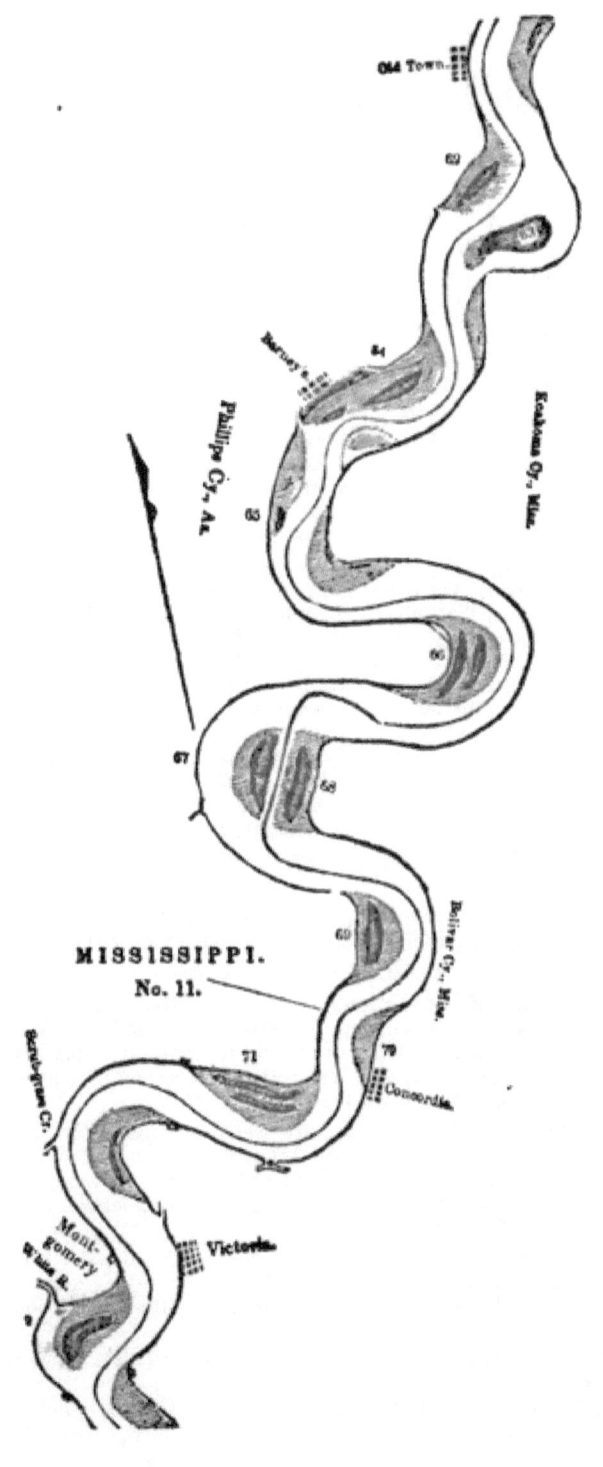

40   THE MISSISSIPPI RIVER.

Tallalula, capital of Issaquena co., Miss., 5 miles below, is a small place. Population about 250.

Tompkinsville, 10 miles below, in Carroll parish, La., is a neat little place, extending for some distance along the river, and containing the residences of a number of wealthy planters.

Brunswick Landing, 14 miles below, in Issaquena co., Miss.

Campbellsville, 10 miles below, in Carroll parish, La.

Millikinsville, La., 2 miles below, is a large settlement of planters, with many fine residences.

Young's Point, 6 miles below, in Madison parish, La.

Yazoo River enters the Mississippi, from the State of that name, nearly opposite Young's Point. (See page 81.)

Walnut Hills, 10 miles below the mouth of Yazoo river, in Warren co., Miss., extend along the river for about 2 miles. They rise to the height of near 500 feet, and display the finest scenery on the lower Mississippi. They are under a state of high cultivation, which renders them very attractive in their appearance.

Vicksburgh, 2 miles below, capital of Warren co., Miss., is built on a hill, the highest point of which is nearly 300 feet above the river. It was settled in 1824 by Neivitt Vick, Esq., and became a city in 1836. This City is the depot of all the Yazoo country. The soil is exceedingly fertile, producing abundant crops of grain, cotton and tobacco. About 100,000 bales of cotton are annually shipped from Vicksburgh to New Orleans. It contains a court-house, 5 or 6 churches, 3 academies, a theater, and several public and private schools, and 3 printing offices. Population about 4000.

The city presents a fine view from the river; the location being high, and the houses built in terraces on the side of the hill, give the whole a beautiful appearance. A railroad extends to Jackson, the capital of the State, 46 miles in the interior. The Mississippi river is some 300 feet deep at this point.

Warrentown, 10 miles below, in Warren co., Miss., is a pleasant town. Population about 300.

Palmyra Settlement, 15 miles below in same county.

New Carthage, Madison parish, La., nearly opposite, is a small village.

Point Pleasant, 10 miles below in Tensas parish, La.

Big Black River, rises in Choctaw co., Miss., and after a course of about 200 miles, enters the Mississippi 14 miles below Point Pleasant. It flows, mostly through a level and fertile region, chiefly occupied by cotton plantations. It is navigable for some 60 miles. The point at which this river joins the Mississippi is called Grand Gulf, and the town of

Grand Gulf, is situated 2 miles below, in Claiborne co., Miss. It is very pleasantly situated, on an elevated bank, and has considerable trade in cotton, and also in supplies for the neighboring plantations. It contains 2 or 3 churches, a town hall, a hospital, a theater, a cotton press, a steam saw and grist mill, and a population of about 1000.

Bayou Pierre empties into the Mississippi 10 miles below. Keel-boats can ascend it as far as Port Gibson, which is a flourishing town, 28 miles from its mouth. It is the county seat of Claiborne co., Miss., and contains a population of about 1200.

Bruinsburgh, Claiborne co., Miss., is a small place at the mouth of Bayou Pierre.

St Joseph, capital of Tensas parish, La., 6 miles below, is a small village. It contains a court-house and a number of stores. Population 200.

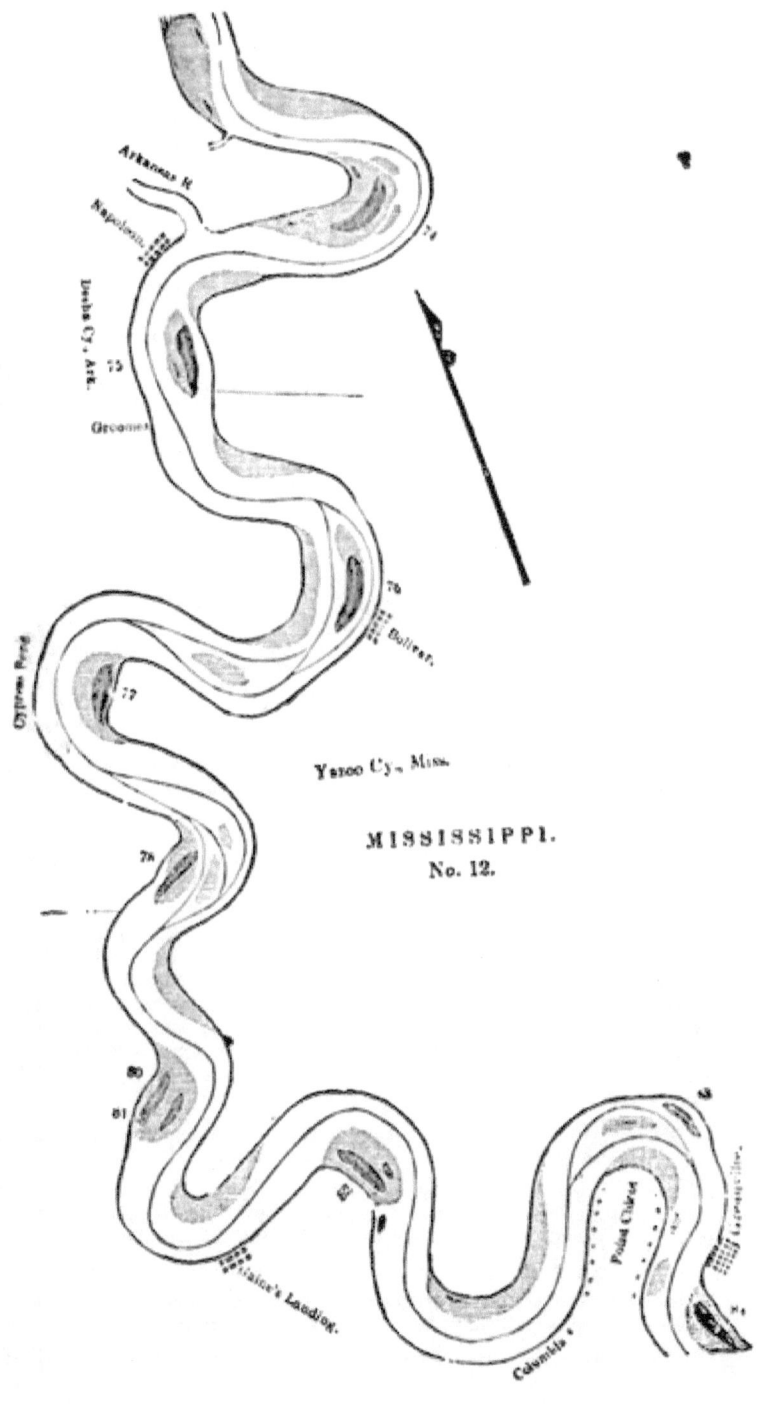

Rodney, Jefferson co., Miss., 4 miles below, is a pleasant town, containing a printing office, a number of stores and warehouses. Population about 500.

Natchez, 41 miles below, capital of Adams co., Miss., is built mostly on a high bluff, near 200 feet above the river, and is the largest town in the State. It was founded by D'Iberville in 1700. That portion of the city on the margin of the river is termed "NATCHEZ, UNDER THE HILL." Most of the heavy mercantile business is done in this part of the town. The upper town stands on the bluff. From this point a fine view of the surrounding country can be obtained. As far as the eye can reach, along the margin of the river, it beholds rich and well-cultivated plantations; while, beyond this, mingling with the blue mists that float along the edge of the horizon, nothing can be seen but a boundless waste of deep and impenetrable swamps. The streets are generally regular and broad. In 1840, a severe tornado swept over this city and destroyed a large amount of property. This city is one of the principal cotton ports on the Mississippi; the streets are often rendered impassible by the piles of cotton bales waiting to be shipped. The city contains a large number of stores, 5 or 6 churches, 4 banks, a hospital, an orphan asylum, several seminaries and public schools, a Masonic hall, a number of steam mills, and 4 or 5 printing offices.

Natchez carries on an extensive inland and foreign trade: many large vessels come up to the town, receive their freight, and sail to foreign ports. There are several large founderies here, which are extensively engaged in making engines, cotton presses, and sugar mills. Population, about 7000.

D'Iberville, whose name occupies a large space in the early history of our country, and especially in those events which transpired on the lower Mississippi, was no ordinary man. No where did he display himself to more advantage, than in the discovery of the mouth of the Mississippi, the last great act in his eventful life. He set sail for the Mississippi on the 17th of October, 1698, with 2 frigates, 2 small vessels, and about 200 settlers. On the 2d of March they succeeded in entering this mighty river in two small barges; they probably proceeded as far as the mouth of Red river, and then returned, by way of the bayou which bears his name, and Lakes Pontchartrain and Maurepas, to St. Louis bay. After building a fort, and leaving his two brothers in command, he sailed for France.

In December, 1699, D'Iberville returned from Europe, with new plans of colonization. In company with his brother, he ascended this great river for the purpose of selecting a site for a town. When he arrived in the country of the Natchez, the Great Sun, their principal chief, came out to welcome them. A high bluff, on which Natchez now stands, was selected, and called Rosalie, in honor of the Countess Pontchartrain. The fort, however, was not built till 1716, 16 years after the selection of the site. Up to this time, no permanent settlement had been made at Natchez. The few traders and hunters who had taken up their abode among the Indians, did not attempt to form a settlement. But after the completion of the fort, the tide of emigration poured in so rapidly, that it soon became the most important place in Louisiana.

Vidalia, Concordia parish, La., is a small place, opposite Natchez. It is the county seat, and contains a court-house and printing office.

Ellis' Cliffs is a high ridge on the east side of the Mississippi, 18 miles below. They extend for several miles along the river, and tend to relieve the eye of the low and monotonous scenery of the lower Mississippi.

Union Point, Concordia parish, La., 3 miles below, is a small town.

Homochitto River rises in the State of Mississippi, and flows west into the Mississippi river, 23 miles below. It is a small stream, and not navigable.

Port Adams, 10 miles below, in Wilkinson co., Miss., is a small village,

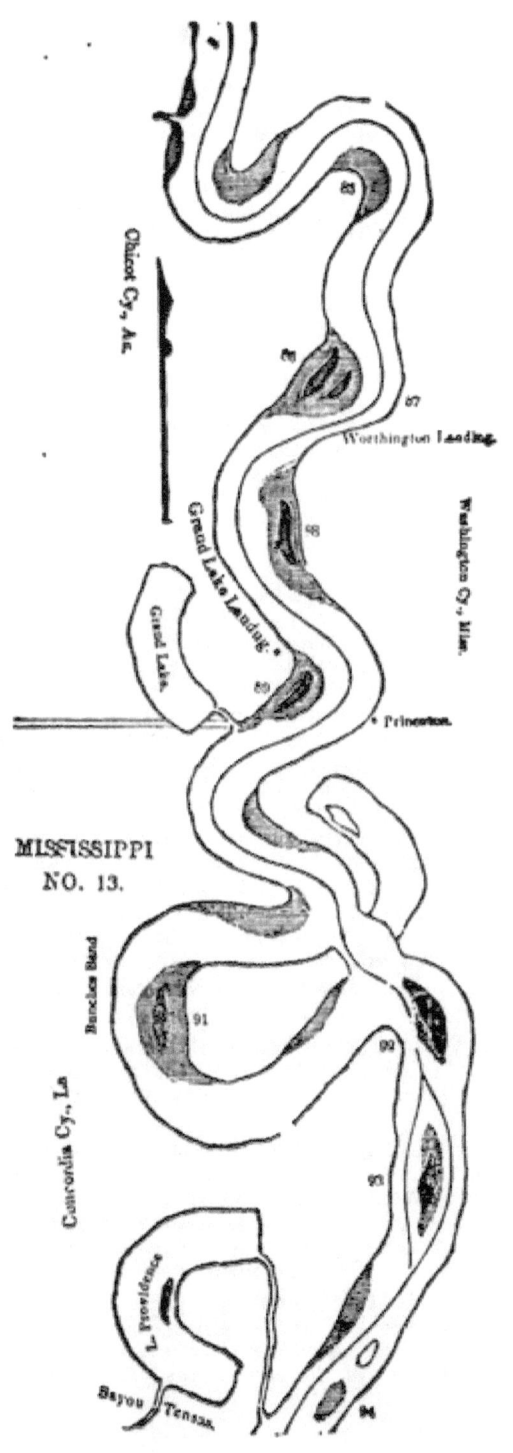

and is considered the port of Woodville, a thriving town, a short distance in the interior.

Red River, upper mouth, enters the Mississippi 11 miles below Port Adams. (See page 81.)

Red River Island and Cut-off.—At the mouth of Red river, the main channel of the Mississippi makes quite a long bend, leaving a very narrow strip of land between. Captain Shreve, of the United States' Engineers, cut a channel across this bend, which, upon admitting the waters, soon became sufficiently wide and deep to allow the largest boats to pass with ease.

From this point, the waters of the Mississippi no longer flow in one regular channel; but, separating into a number of branches or bayous, they wend their way through lakes and swamps to the Gulf, in lines nearly parallel with the parent stream, thus dividing the southern part of the State into a number of islands. The largest of these bayous is ATCHAFALAYA, which leaves the river 3 miles below Red river, and pursues a southern course till it falls into Atchafalaya bay on the Gulf coast. At Plaquemine, 128 miles below, there is another bayou, which also connects with the Gulf. At Donaldsonville, 81 miles above New Orleans, the justly celebrated Bayou La Fourche commences. It can be compared to nothing but a beautiful ship canal. The plantations along this bayou are so numerous that they resemble one continuous town stretching from one extremity to the other. On the east, the principal outlet is the Iberville, which communicates with the Gulf, through Lakes Maurepas, Pontchartrain, and Borgne. The land included between these bayous is called the *delta* of the Mississippi. This land is frequently inundated, and amounts to several thousand square miles. To prevent these overflows as much as possible, embankments have been thrown up along the river, called the *levee*. On the east side, the levee commences about 60 miles above New Orleans, and extends for near 130; on the west side it begins at Point Coupee, 172 miles above New Orleans. From this point down to New Orleans, the river is lined with beautiful plantations, upon which are many fine and costly residences. The whole has the appearance of a town, extending along the margin of the river.

Red River Landing, Point Coupee parish, La., 6 miles below, is a small place, where those going up Red river usually stop.

Raccourci Bend and Cut-off, 4 miles below. The cut-off here, was made in 1848, by order of the State. The distance by the main channel is about 25 miles—by the cut-off it is only about half a mile. The width of the channel is 400 yards, and sufficiently deep to admit the largest boats.

Tunica Bend is a large bend 6 miles below. Island number 122 is in the the lower part of this bend.

Bayou Sara, West Feliciana parish, La., 24 miles below, is a flourishing town, and a shipping point of large quantities of cotton. The country through which the bayou, of same name, passes, is rich, thickly settled, and under a high state of cultivation.

St. Francisville, capital of West Feliciana parish, La., just below bayou Sara, is a pleasant place, being built mostly on a hill, about 1 mile from the river. It is connected with Woodville, a distance of 26 miles, by a Railroad. The portion of the town on the hill is well built, and contains several fine houses. Along the margin of the river, there are a number of extensive warehouses, from which a large amount of cotton is annually shipped. Population 500.

Point Coupee, capital of Point Coupee parish, La., is opposite St. Francisville. It is a settlement of wealthy planters, mostly French, and extends several miles along the river. At this place, the *Grand Levee* or embankment commences. The tendency of the lower Mississippi to seek new channels to

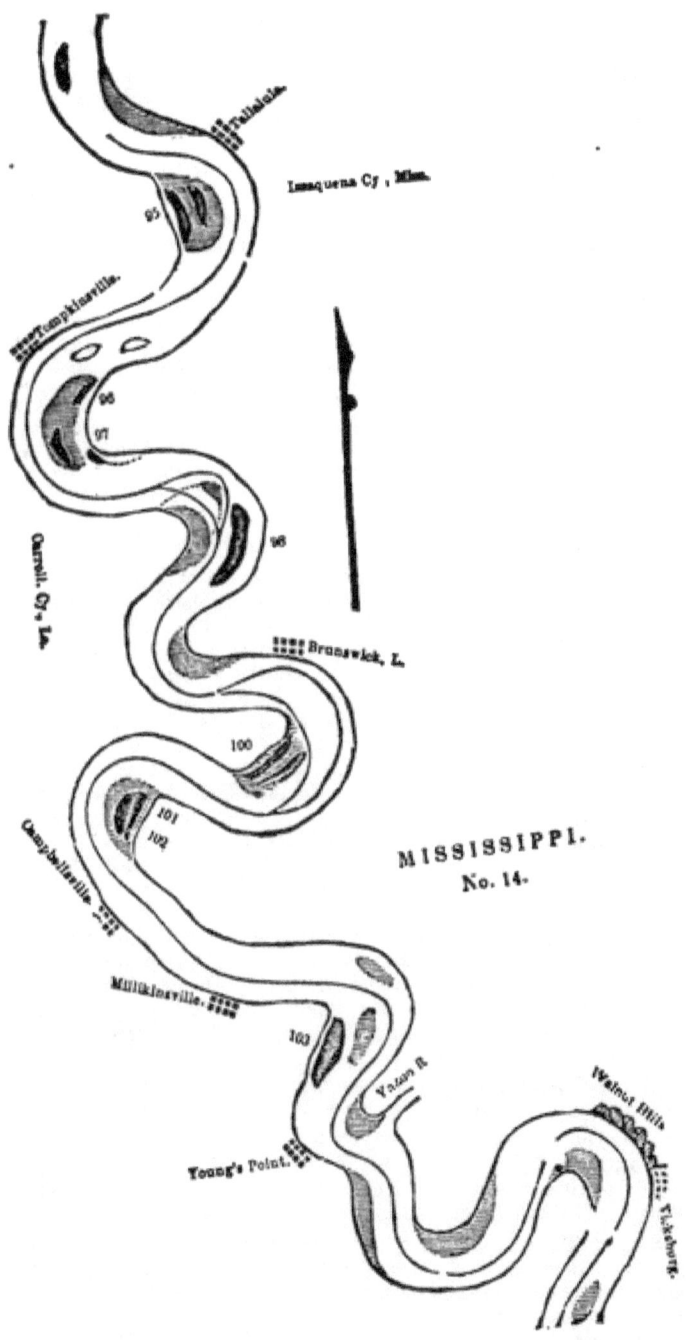

the Gulf, has been apparent for a long time. The cut-offs that have been made above, though they have shortened the distance several miles, have, by giving the water a more direct course, greatly increased its rapidity, volume, and pressure against its banks. This is no doubt the cause of the *crevasse*, which has often been the means of destroying entire plantations, and burying villages in water. The land on the river from this point to the Gulf, is, with few exceptions, below the surface of the water, even at its ordinary stage.

Waterloo, Point Coupee parish, La., 5 miles below, at the outlet of False river. It is a handsome settlement, surrounded by rich and beautiful plantations. Population about 300.

Thompson's Creek, enters the Mississippi from the east a short distance above Port Hudson. Jackson, East Feliciana parish, La., is situated on the east side of Thompson's creek, about 12 miles from St. Francisville. It is the seat of Louisiana College, founded in 1825, which has an able faculty, and about 2000 volumes in its libraries.

Port Hudson, 6 miles below Waterloo, in East Feliciana parish, La., on White Cliffs, is a place of considerable business, large amounts of cotton and sugar are annually shipped from here. It is at the terminus of the Clinton and Port Hudson Railroad. Population about 300.

Thomas' Point, is situated in an acute bend of the river, 13 miles below.

Baton Rouge, 12 miles below, is the capital of Louisiana, and seat of justice of Baton Rouge parish. It is pleasantly situated on the last bluff that is seen, in descending the river. The site is 30 or 40 feet above the highest overflow of the river. The bluff rises by a gentle and gradual swell, and the town, as seen from the river, in the months when the greatest verdure prevails, rising so regularly and beautifully from the banks, with its singularly shaped French and Spanish houses, and its green squares, looks like a finely painted landscape. It is one of the most beautiful and pleasantly situated places on the lower Mississippi.

From Baton Rouge to New Orleans, the "coast," as it is called, is lined with as fine plantations as there are in the South. Every spot, susceptible of cultivation, is transformed into a beautiful garden, containing specimens of all those choice fruits and flowers which flourish only in tropical climes. From the esplanade, the prospect is delightful, commanding a great extent of the coast, with its handsome houses and rich cultivation, and an extensive view of the back country at the east.

Baton Rouge contains a fine State-house, a court-house, penitentiary, Baton Rouge College, 4 or 5 churches, an extensive U. S. arsenal and barracks, 2 or 3 printing offices, 2 academies and a number of schools. Population about 5000. The penitentiary is a fine brick building, 320 feet long, three stories high, and contains 240 cells for convicts. Baton Rouge College has 4 professors, and a library of 10,000 volumes.

West Baton Rouge, is a small place on the opposite side of the river.

Manchac, 15 miles below, in East Baton Rouge parish, La., is a small place at the mouth of Bayou Manchac.

Manchac Bayou leaves the Mississippi at this point. About 20 miles from the river it is connected with the Amite river, and by means of Lakes Maurepas, Pontchartrain and Borgne, opens a communication with the Gulf.

Bayou Plaquemine, 8 miles below, affords the best communication to the rich settlements of Attakapas and Opelousas. It is navigable for small vessels for some miles in the interior, and its banks are lined with splendid sugar and cotton plantations.

Plaquemine, just below, is a pleasant town. Considerable trade with the surrounding plantations is carried on here. It contains a population of about 600.

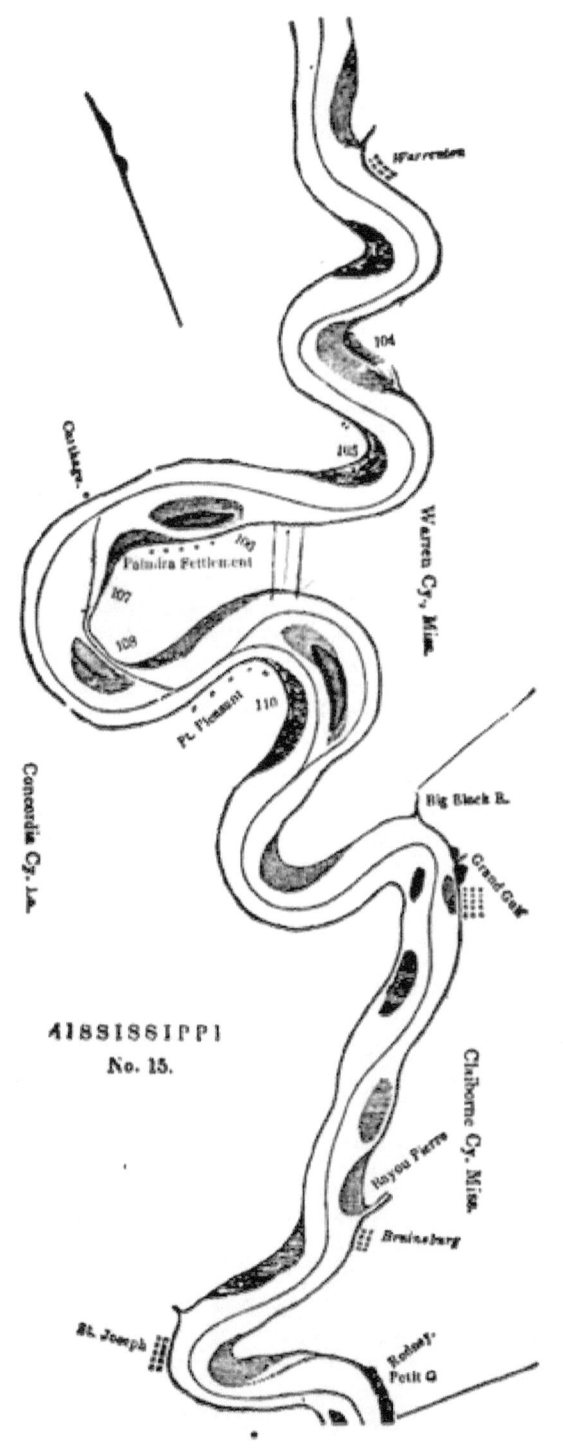

Iberville, 10 miles below, capital of Iberville parish.

Bayou Goule, in same parish, 10 miles below, is a small place.

Bayou La Fourche, 14 miles below, leaves the Mississippi at Donaldsonville, and flows in a direct line to the Gulf. It is very thickly settled on both sides, by some of the richest planters in the State. It is navigable during most of the year for a distance of 60 miles.

Donaldsonville, capital of Ascension parish, La., is just below Bayou La Fourche. It was formerly the capital of the State. It is pleasantly situated, and is a place of considerable trade and wealth. Population about 1000.

Jefferson College, founded in 1831, is a thriving institution, 16 miles below, in St. James parish.

Bonnet Carre, 24 miles below, is the capital of St. John the Baptist parish, La.

Red Church, 16 miles below, in St. John the Baptist parish, La.

Carrollton, 19 miles below, in Jefferson parish, La., is a flourishing town, 7 miles above New Orleans, with which it is connected by a Railroad that runs to the center of the city. The *Carrollton Gardens* are much admired by all who visit them. They are public, and laid out with great taste. Here, among beautiful flowers, thick shrubbery, and finely laid out walks and arbors, and umbrageous branches of green trees filled with innumerable bright-plumaged and melodious singing birds of the South, one may spend a day, almost oblivious of the near vicinity of that great city, with its thousands of inhabitants, gathered from all countries under the sun. The population of Carrollton is about 1000.

Lafayette City, 5 miles below, is but a continuation of New Orleans. The Railroad leading from New Orleans to Carrollton, passes through it. A steam ferry is constantly running from this to the opposite shore, and another to New Orleans. Most of the flat-boats, bound for New Orleans, land at Lafayette. Population about 5000.

New Orleans, 2 miles below, in Orleans parish, La., is situated on the Mississippi river, near the southern extremity of the Mississippi valley, in 29° 57' north latitude and 90° 7' west longitude. It is the great commercial capital of the South, and is, by the river, about 100 miles from the Gulf. New Orleans is the seat of justice for Orleans parish.

NEW ORLEANS FROM THE MISSISSIPPI.

This city is built on a strip of low marshy land lying between Lake Pontchartrain and the Mississippi river, and on the convex shore of a large bend, which resembles a crescent, or new moon, for which reason it is often called the *Crescent City.* The ground gradually falls back toward the lake, and in no part of the city is it sufficiently elevated to throw the waste water into the river. In time of heavy rains many of the streets are flooded with water. On the opposite side of the river is the town of Algiers. This place is extensively engaged in ship building; it contains several large ship yards, which employ a great number of hands.

New Orleans has, probably, twice as much boat navigation above it, as any other city on the globe. By means of the basin, the canal, and the Bayou St. John, it communicates with Lake Ponchartrain, with the Florida shore, with Mobile, Pensacola, and the whole Gulf shore. It also communicates, by means of the bayous Plaquemine and La Fourche, with the Attakapas country, and has

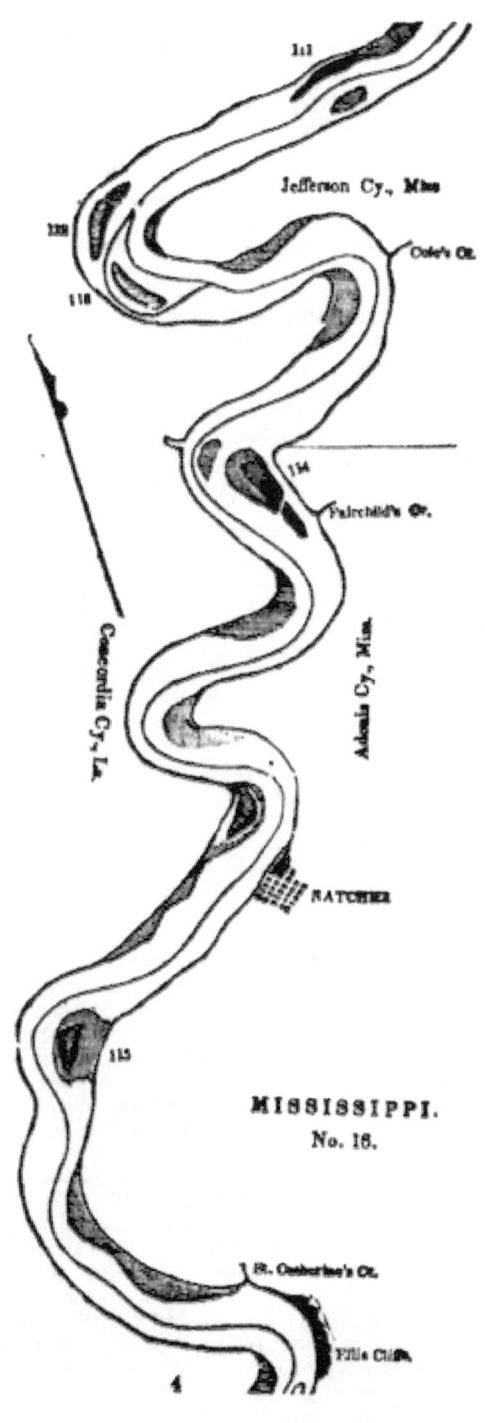

many other communications, by means of the numerous bayous and lakes, with the lower parts of Louisiana. Its wharves may be seen, at all seasons of the year, lined with all kinds of craft, rough flat-boats, which have traveled from the Alleghanies, with lumber, or from further west, with provisions, &c.; steamers, from the hundred navigable rivers, which flow into the Mississippi; ships and other sea vessels from all quarters of the globe, here meet, to land the productions of all climes, and bring together the inhabitants of all countries, colors, and languages. The greater part of the business is transacted between October and June. During the summer, the city is generally unhealthy, and is visited by that scourge, the Yellow Fever. During the winter and spring, the climate is generally reputed healthy, and thousands flock here from all quarters of the world—some for health, others for pleasure, and still more in connection with the immense business of all kinds which is here transacted. The Carondelet, or old canal, runs in a line with Orleans street, the center street of the city, to Bayou St. John. This canal is about 2 miles long, and from 25 to 30 feet in width, and from 4 to 7 feet in depth. The basin is in the center of the city, near the Catholic Cemetery. It is about 5 miles from the canal, down the bayou, to its junction with Lake Pontchartrain, where there is a large dam about ¾ of a mile in extent; at the extremity, there is a light house. There is another canal running through the city to the lake, which does a large amount of business. The New Orleans and La Fourche Canal extends through Algiers to Bayou La Fourche, a distance of 85 miles. This is a very important work, as it brings in communication with New Orleans, some of the richest agricultural portions of the State. There are 4 railroads in this city: the Orleans and Carrollton Railroad, which runs to Carrollton, a distance of 7 miles; the New Orleans Street Railroad, which starts near the river, in the lower part of the city, and extends to Lake Pontchartrain, a distance of 6 miles. The third is the Mexican Gulf Railway, which starts off at right angles from the Pontchartrain road, at the corner of the Elysian Fields and Good Children streets, and runs eastward to Proctorsville, on Lake Borgne, a distance of 27 miles. The 4th is to Jackson, Miss. The Shell Road is the pride of New Orleans. It extends to the lake. This road is made of small, white sea-shells, which soon become broken and cemented together. The cemeteries of New Orleans attract much notice. There are several, which are laid out in a handsome manner, the most celebrated are the "French Cemetery," in the city, and "Cypress Grove Cemetery," about 3 miles out on the Shell Road, leading to Lake Ponchartrain. The taste and elegance displayed in many of the vaults, and the constant attention manifested, to show respect for the memory of departed friends, are truly gratifying to the finer feelings of our nature. On account of the marshy state of the soil, it is impossible to dig graves, as a foot below the surface, they would be filled with water. To obviate this, the tombs are built entirely above ground, and well cemented, with apertures just large enough for a single coffin, and rising up, in many instances, to the height of 3 or 4 tiers. The walks between the vaults are covered with beautiful white shells, from the sea beach; and along the edges may be found almost every variety of shrubbery and flowers, which grow so luxuriantly in the south. These cemeteries are free to all visitors.

PUBLIC BUILDINGS.—The St. Charles' Hotel is one of the finest buildings in the city. It was erected at a cost of nearly $600,000. The Veraudah, at the corner of St. Charles and Common streets, is another fine building. The Municipal Hall is a beautiful marble edifice. The St. Louis Hotel is a beautiful and costly structure. The Custom House is one of the largest buildings of the kind in the Union; it is built of New England granite. The United States Branch Mint is a large edifice of the Ionic order, 282 feet long and 168 feet deep. The Catholic Cathedral is also a large and splendid building. The Odd Fellows' Hall is a fine and extensive building, also the Merchants' Exchange Many of the

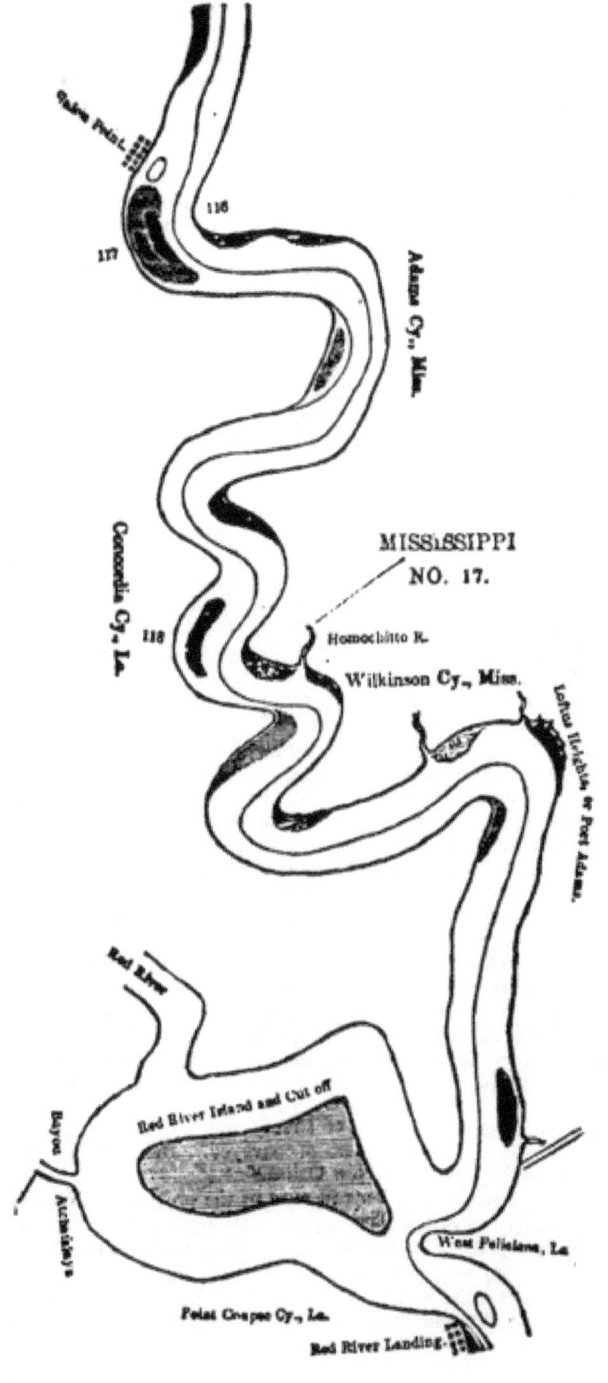

churches are costly and splendid edifices, of which the city contains between 40 and 50 of the various denominations, and several Jewish synagogues. The markets also deserve attention. They are conducted on a different plan from those of most of our Western cities. There are stands erected along the sides of the market-house for the sale of coffee, chocolate, cakes, pies; &c. These are the boarding places of hundreds of people who wander about without any fixed place of residence. The city contains several public squares, which are ornamented with fine trees and shrubbery. There are 4 or 5 theaters here,—the St. Charles, the Orleans, the American, and others. The University of Louisiana was founded in 1835, and has an elegant building at the corner of Common and Philippe streets. There are departments of medicine, law, political economy, and commerce, with able professors in each. New Orleans has a large number of excellent public schools, in which about 16,000 children annually receive instruction.

The benevolent institutions in New Orleans are numerous and extensive; among them may be mentioned the Charity Hospital, the U. S. Naval Hospital, Stone's Hospital, the Franklin Infirmary.

The city contains about 25 printing offices, some of them on an extensive scale, issuing daily and weekly papers with a large circulation, several of them in the French language.

The Commerce of New Orleans is very large, extending to nearly all quarters of the globe. The article of greatest value is cotton, but immense quantities of other produce are annually shipped—flour, sugar, pork, tobacco, hemp, and numerous other articles from all the north-western and south-western States. There are 9 or 10 well managed banks here, with a heavy capital.

The population in 1850 was 126,000; in 1860, 174,000; in 1870, 192,000.

In 1718 (Louisiana then being under the dominion of the French), colonists were sent from Europe, who laid out New Orleans with great ceremony. This colony was under the direction of John Law, the noted financier. The Mississippi company, under Law, received their charter in 1717, and it granted them the exclusive right of trading in the Mississippi country, for 25 years, with the monopoly of the Canada beaver trade. In 1718, the monopoly of trading in tobacco was also granted them. In 1719, the exclusive right of trading in Asia and the East Indies, and, soon after, the farming of the public revenue, together with the extension of all these rights to the year 1770—and, also, the exclusive right of coining for 9 years. They also had the grant, formerly given to Crozat, but resigned by him, of an exclusive monopoly of Louisiana, for 15 years, and the absolute ownership of whatever mines might be opened, for this was, in fact, the great object of all the explorers of the Mississippi country. They relied, not so much on the fertility of the soil, as the immense wealth that would be realized from the rich mines of precious metals, which they hoped to find. In 1717, about 2000 subjects of the Western Duchy, embarked from Europe, under the direction of the company. In 1720, the company failed, and the Germans, thus deserted, dispersed into different portions of the country. Large sums were advanced by the crown to uphold the company, and much expended for military protection against the Indians. But all failed to keep it up. In 1731, the government obtained a judgment against them, of twenty millions of francs, to cancel which, the entire property and privileges were re-conveyed. In 1721, the Council General was removed from Biloxi to New Orleans.

In 1759, Great Britain had over-run most of the province of New France, and obtained possession of Quebec, Ticonderoga, Crown Point and Niagara. During this war, Spain had formed a family compact with France, and taken sides against England. In 1762, hostilities ceased between the three powers, and peace was restored by the ratification of the treaty of Paris, dated February 10, 1763. By this treaty, England obtained possession of Canada and all the posts along the

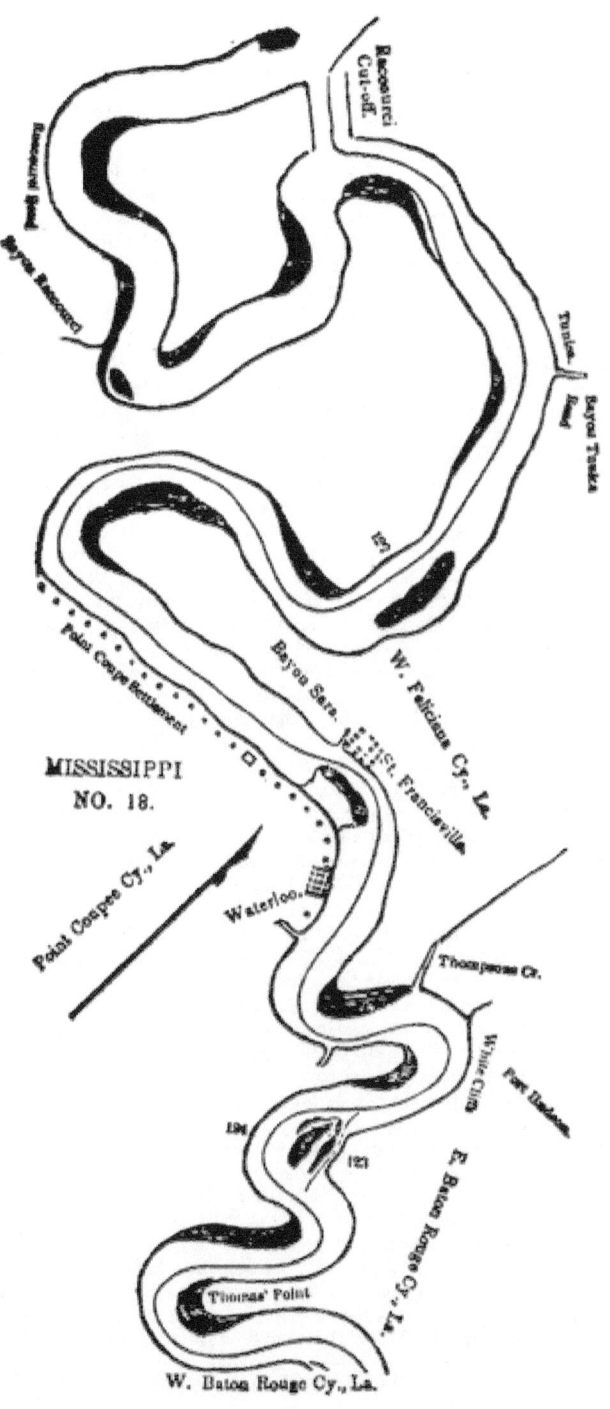

St. Lawrence. France also ceded to her all that portion of Louisiana, extending from the source of the Mississippi, on the east side, to the mouth of the Bayou Iberville; thence along the bayou, to Lake Maurepas; thence, along the center of the lakes, to the Gulf of Mexico, including the port and river of Mobile. The navigation of the Mississippi was to remain forever free to both powers. At the same time, the French King formed a secret treaty with Spain, by which he agreed to deliver to the Spanish government the remainder of Louisiana, including the Island of New Orleans. Two or three years elapsed before Spain took possession of this valuable territory. The French population were very much dissatisfied at the change; and, in order to prevent an outbreak, it was deemed necessary to keep a large military force constantly at New Orleans. The laws of Spain were very despotic and unpopular. Morales, the intendant, knowing that Spain could not long maintain her position on the Mississippi, determined to exercise his vindictive feelings against the Americans, by denying them the right to deposit goods and produce in New Orleans. This act so completely aroused the people of the western States, that it was with great difficulty that the general government was able to restrain them from the conquest of the country. This suspension of trade brought the people of New Orleans on the verge of famine. Accordingly, to modify the evil, without fully removing the cause, Morales issued an order, that Western people might have the privilege of sending flour into the territory, provided they paid a duty of *six per cent. ad valorum*, and shipped it in Spanish vessels. But the Americans respectfully declined to avail themselves of the privileges of this order. The King, however, so far revoked the acts of Morales, as to again restore, in 1795, for three years, the free navigation of the river, and the right to deposit at New Orleans, which continued till 1802.

After the overthrow of the Bourbon dynasty, the King of Spain formed a secret treaty with the First Consul, Oct. 1, 1800, by which he agreed to deliver within six months, the province of Louisiana to the French authorities. In consideration of this act of Spanish generosity, the French established on the throne of Tuscany, the Prince of Parma, son-in-law of the King of Spain. Napoleon now began to make extensive preparations to extend his authority over this rich and valuable territory. A large fleet and an army of 25,000 men were soon ready to sail for the Mississippi. After spending a year in the various ports of Holland, continually watched by the English, Napoleon determined to abandon the enterprise, and transfer, if possible, the territory to the United States. Near the close of the year 1802, he directed his minister, M. Talleyrand, to open negotiations with Mr. Livingston, United States Minister at Paris. While this correspondence was going on, Mr. Jefferson, then President, deeming the possession of New Orleans and Florida of vast importance to the whole Union, sent over Mr. Monroe, with instructions to make some arrangement, if possible, for its purchase. When Mr. Monroe arrived in Paris, he was somewhat surprised to find Napoleon so willing to part with Louisiana. The only thing then for the American Commissioners to arrange, was to fix the price to be paid. Napoleon wanted 125,000,000 francs; but the commissioners, thinking it by far too high, offered only 50,000,000. After some time spent in consideration, they agreed upon 80,000,000, deducting 20,000,000 for spoliation upon our commerce. Their course was fully approved by the President and his cabinet, and confirmed by the Senate of the United States On the 20th of December, 1803, the province of Louisiana was officially delivered over to the constituted authorities of the United States.*

The Spanish government were very much displeased at this transfer of Louisiana, but finally, in 1804, became reconciled. Spain, however, still retained possession of Florida till 1820, when it was purchased by the United States. Immediately after the United States obtained possession of Louisiana, it was formed into a territorial government. In 1811, the people were authorized by Congress to

---

*See American State Papers. Also, Martin's Louisiana.

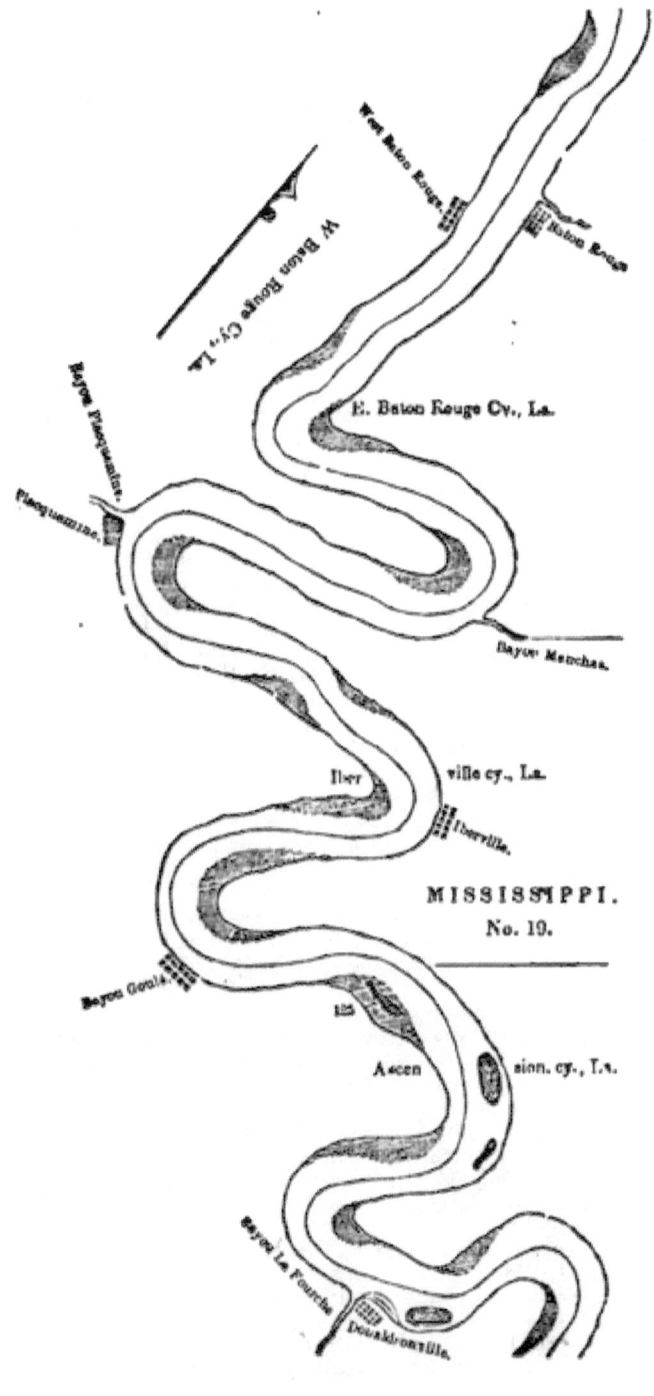

form a State constitution; and in 1812, Louisiana was admitted into the Union, with full privileges, as a sister State of this Great Western Republic. In 1812, war was declared between England and the United States, and the British Ministry, resolved, if possible, to possess themselves of New Orleans, and thereby control the entire navigation of the Mississippi. New Orleans was in imminent danger; the city was without defensca, and the Spaniards at Mobile and Pensacola, were ready to receive a British army with open arms. This state of things, was repeatedly urged upon the consideration of the President and his Cabinet, but nothing was done, till the arrival of General Jackson, in the autumn of 1814.

On the 12th of December, 1814, the British fleet made its appearance off Cat Island, near the entrance of Lake Borgne. Commodore Patterson dispatched a flotilla of 5 gun-boats, to observe the movements of the enemy, and check, if possible, his advance. On the 14th, the boats were attacked by a superior force of 43 barges, and 1200 men; and, after a gallant struggle of one hour, they were overpowered and compelled to surrender. In this engagement, the Americans lost but 6 killed and 35 wounded, while the British loss could not have been less than 300 in killed and wounded.

General Jackson, on reviewing the militia and defenses of the city, found it necessary to proclaim *martial law*, which no doubt saved the city. This measure was very much opposed at the time. Judge Hall took upon himself the responsibility to impose upon the General, after the battle, a fine of $1000, in consequence of the suspension of the *habeas corpus* act. The Judge undertook to interfere with the military arrests, and Jackson ordered him beyond the limits of the camp. This fine, which the General promptly paid from his own resources, was refunded by Congress with interest, a short time before his death.

On the 22d, a division of the British army, under General Keane, succeeded in passing from Lake Borgne into Bayou Bienvenu. The British, supposing themselves perfectly secure, concluded to encamp near the banks of the river. The American general determined to attack them in their new position. He accordingly collected his whole force, which was less than 2000, and marched to attack the English, who were not less than 3000 strong. The schooner Caroline, and the Louisiana, were sent down the river, with orders to commence the attack when the proper signal should be given. The action commenced at half-past seven in the evening, by a heavy discharge of grape and canister, which was the first warning the enemy had of the approach of the American army. Jackson commanded here in person; and so complete was the surprise of the enemy, that hundreds were cut down, without even an opportunity of offering any resistance. The British lost nearly 400, in killed, wounded, and prisoners.

General Jackson fell back within 5 or 6 miles of the city; where he commenced fortifying himself on a narrow strip of land, lying between a low swamp and the river. The General determined to build a breastwork of cotton-bales and earth, extending from the swamp to the river, a distance of nearly a mile. He accordingly ordered all the drays and wagons in the city, to haul the cotton from the warehouses; which orders they were compelled to obey, at the peril of their lives The front of this cotton breastwork was protected by a deep ditch, filled with water. On the 28th, a skirmish occurred a short distance from the American lines, which lasted several hours; in this the English lost about 250, and the Americans only 7.*

The British army under Packingham, encamped near the American lines, waiting several days for reinforcements. The Americans numbered 6000, and the British 15,000. At length the anxious night of the 7th had passed away, and the dawn of the glorious 8th, had just shed its mellow light on the extended

---

* See Breckenridge' History of the War.

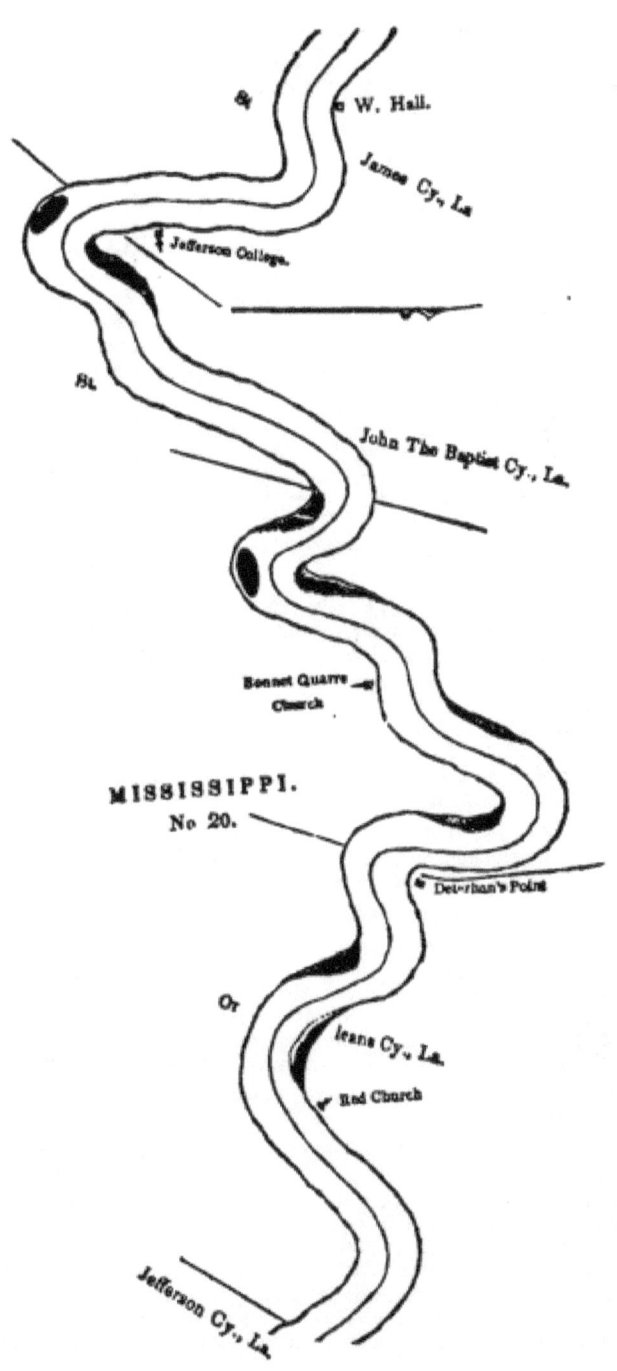

lines of the two reposing armies. Packingham, after sending 800 of his men, under Colonel Thorton, on the opposite side of the river, arranged the remainder of his army into two divisions, of 60 deep; the right under General Gibbs, and the left under Gen. Keane. The English moved slowly to the attack; but when within a short distance, the batteries along the American lines opened upon them such a destructive fire, that their ranks were broken almost as fast as they were closed up. But when they came within reach of the muskets, the whole American line opened upon them such a discharge of musketry, that they soon retired in confusion from the field. Packingham was killed in front of his troops, endeavoring to encourage them by his presence. The officers succeeded in bringing the troops to a second attack, but this was even more disastrous than the first. They soon gave way, leaving more than 2,000 lying on the field, killed and wounded. The American loss was only 7 killed and 6 wounded.

The battle of New Orleans, one of the most important in the history of our country, was the closing scene of the war of 1812.

Battle Ground, 6 miles below New Orleans.

Ducro's Landing, is 6 miles below. The Mexican Gulf Railway here diverges and crosses to Lake Borgne.

Fort St. Leon is on the Mississippi, 5 miles below.

English Turn, is a bend in the river, opposite Fort St. Leon. It is the point where the English vessels, sent to explore and take possession of the Mississippi, met the French, who informed them that they were in the dominions of his majesty, the King of France, and unless they retreated, the large force, which they alleged was but a short distance up the river, would be brought against them. The English reluctantly turned, and sailed down the river.

Forts St. Philip and Jackson, are on opposite sides of the Mississippi, 55 miles below English Turn.

The Mouths of the Mississippi, 30 miles below. We have now arrived at the point where this mighty river, separating into a number of branches resembling a large hand with extended fingers, discharges its waters into the Gulf. The sediment which is annually deposited in the Gulf of Mexico, is about $\frac{1}{1151}$ of the quantity of water by weight.

The North-east Pass, latitude 29° 7' N., and longitude 89° 10' W., is the principal pass. The word Balize, means a level. At the mouth of the pass, there is a small settlement of pilots, known as the Balize settlement. The other passes, are the Outlet Pass, the South-east, the South, the South-west, and the West.

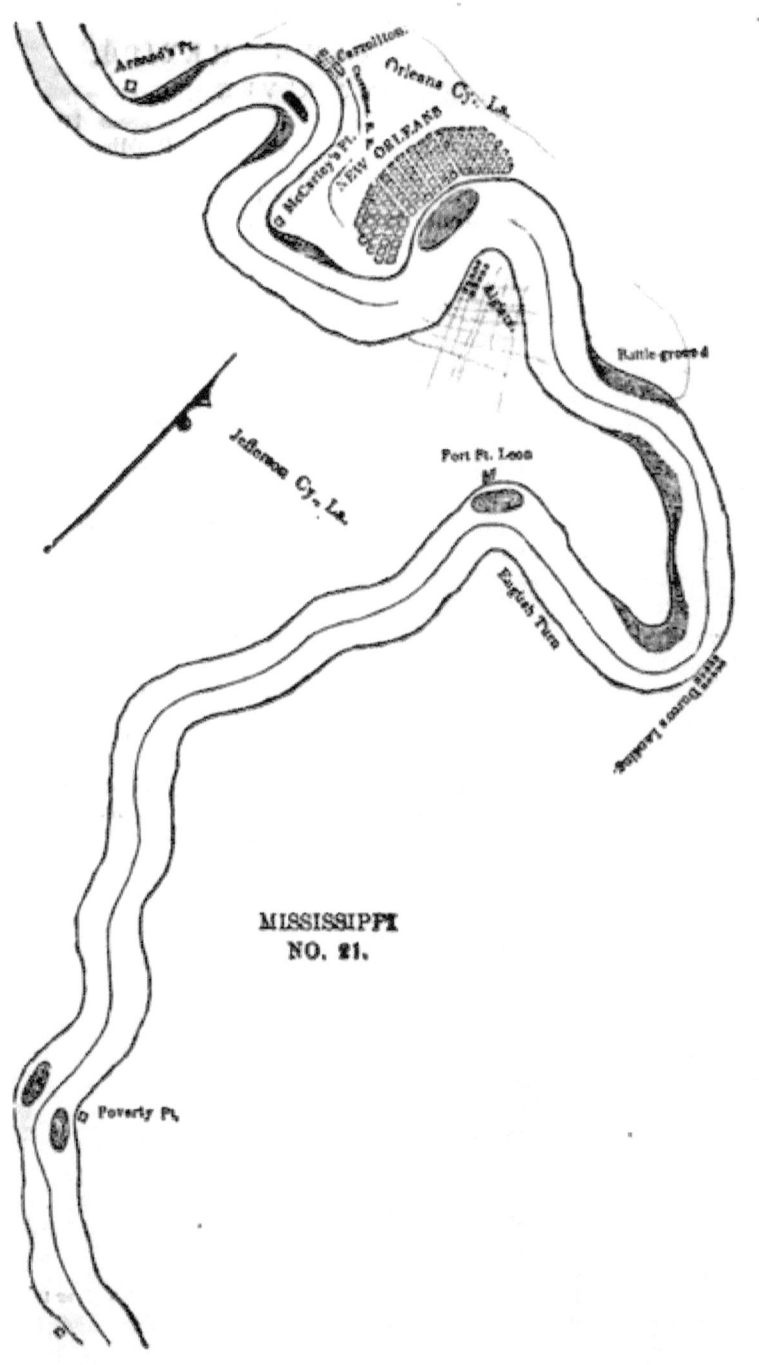

ROUTES ON THE GULF OF MEXICO.
THE ALABAMA RIVER

Is formed by the junction of the Talapoosa and Coosa rivers, about 10 miles above Montgomery, Ala. The Talapoosa takes its rise in Paulding co., Ga., about 250 miles from its mouth. It is navigable about 40 miles, for small steamers. The Coosa rises in Georgia, also; length some 350 miles, and navigable for small boats, about 175 miles from its junction with the Talapoosa.

The Alabama is a very crooked stream, but is navigable at all seasons for the largest class of boats, except in times of great drought. Its whole length is near 340 miles. The country through which it runs is exceedingly rich, occupied by extensive cotton plantations, and large tracts of valuable timber. It enters Mobile bay, at the city of Mobile, in lat. 30° 41'.

Montgomery, capital of the State of Alabama, and county seat of Montgomery co., is a thriving city, beautifully situated in a healthy and fertile region. It has an extensive trade, and fine facilities for reaching important points in the surrounding country. The terminus of the Montgomery and West Point Railroad is here. About 80,000 bales of cotton are annually shipped from Montgomery. Population about 7600.

Washington, 13 miles below, in Autauga co., is a small village.

Lowndesport, 10 miles below, in same co.

Vernon, In same co., 8 miles below.

Miller's Ferry, 9 miles below.

Benton, Lowndes co., 15 miles below, is a thriving town and has an active trade. Population about 500.

Selma, 26 miles below, in Dallas co., is a flourishing town, situated in a populous and fertile region, and has a large business. It contains 3 or 4 churches and a printing office. Population about 1600. The terminus of the Alabama and Tennessee Railroad is here.

Cahawba, 16 miles below, is the county seat of Dallas co., just below the mouth of Cahawba river, and a place of considerable trade. It contains the usual county buildings, several churches, 2 printing offices, and a U. S. land office. The Cahawba river is navigable for small steamers about 100 miles. It passes through the Alabama coal field.

Elm Bluff, 5 miles below.

Portland, 19 miles below, in Dallas co.

Bridgeport, 16 miles below.

Canton, Wilcox co., 5 miles below.

Prairie Bluff, 10 miles below, in same co.

Upper Peachtree Landing, 11 miles below.

Black Bluff Landing, 13 miles below.

Lower Peachtree Landing, 5 miles below.

Bell's Landing, Monroe co., 16 miles below, is a small village.

Claiborne, 22 miles below, is the capital of Monroe co.

Gosport, Clarke co., 7 miles below, is a small place.

Gainestown, 9 miles below, in same co., is a landing place.

French's Landing, 8 miles below.

James' Landing, 6 miles below.

Tombigbee River, enters the Alabama 40 miles below. This river takes its rise in the north-eastern part of Missisippi, and is over 400 miles in length. It is navigable for nearly 300 miles from its mouth. It flows, mostly, through a

level, fertile country, much of which is occupied by cotton plantations. There are many important towns on the Tombigbee River, a few of which are: *Fulton, Aberdeen,* and *Columbus,* Miss., and *Pickensville, Gainesville,* and *Demopolis,* Alabama.

Fort St. Philip, 22 miles below the mouth of Tombigbee river.

Mobile, capital of Mobile co., Ala., 22 miles below, at the mouth of the river, near its entrance into the bay of same name, 30 miles from the Gulf of Mexico, and 167 miles from New Orleans. Lat. 30° 41' north. It is the commercial capital of the State, and next to New Orleans, the greatest cotton market in the Union—nearly 600,000 bales have been exported in a single year. The situation is considered very healthy, being built on a plain that rises near 15 feet above tide water. The breezes from the sea render the atmosphere pure, which, together with the climate, make it the resort of a great number of invalids, from various parts of the world. The city is supplied with water brought from a neighboring hill, and distributed through the town in iron pipes. Mobile contains a naval hospital, city hospital, 3 or 4 banks, a theater, Burton Academy, several churches and 6 printing offices.

About 2 miles from Mobile, is SPRING HILL COLLEGE, incorporated in 1830.

The Bay of Mobile, is the outlet of one of the most prolific cotton-growing regions in the South.

Mobile is the terminus of the Ohio and Mobile Railroad. Population of the city in 1850, 20,515; 1870, 32,000.

Pensacola, capital of Escambia co., Florida, is situated on Pensacola bay, 10 miles from the sea, and 64 miles east from Mobile. The town is built on a sandy plain, about 40 feet above the waters of the bay. It is regularly laid out, and contains a court-house, custom-house, and 2 public squares. Population about 2600. 8 miles below the city, there is a United States Navy Yard, which covers 80 acres of ground.

THE SABINE RIVER

Takes its rise in Hunt co., Texas, and runs in a south-easterly direction, to the eastern boundary of the State, from which point it runs in a southerly course, being the boundary between Louisiana and Texas, and empties (through Sabine lake) into the Gulf of Mexico. Its whole length is about 500 miles. It is shallow at its mouth, but is navigable, during high water, for small boats, for some distance.

The principal towns on the Sabine river are *Logansport,* in De Soto parish, La *Hamilton,* below, in Shelby co., Texas. *Sabinetown,* Sabine co., Texas, (a shipping point for cotton, &c.) *Belgrade,* Newton co., Texas. *Salem,* in same co. *Madison,* Jefferson co., Texas, (near the head of Sabine lake.)

THE NECHES RIVER

Rises in Van Zandt co., Texas, and enters Sabine lake near its upper extremity It is navigable, for small steamers, about 100 miles, in high water.

Sampter is on the Neches river, in Trinity co., Texas. *Woodville,* below, is the capital of Tyler co., Texas. *Beaumont,* county seat of Jefferson co., Texas, and about 28 miles above the mouth of the Neches river. Immense numbers of cattle and horses range over the prairies in this part of Texas.

Sabine City, is situated on the west side of the outlet of Sabine lake about 6 miles from the Gulf of Mexico, in Jefferson co., Texas.

THE TRINITY RIVER

Rises in Cook co., Texas, in two branches—the *West Fork* and *Elm Fork*—which unite in Dallas co. Its course is south-easterly, and it empties into Galveston bay, near its upper end. The Trinity is nearly 600 miles in length, and is navigable, during high water, some 350 miles. It flows through a very

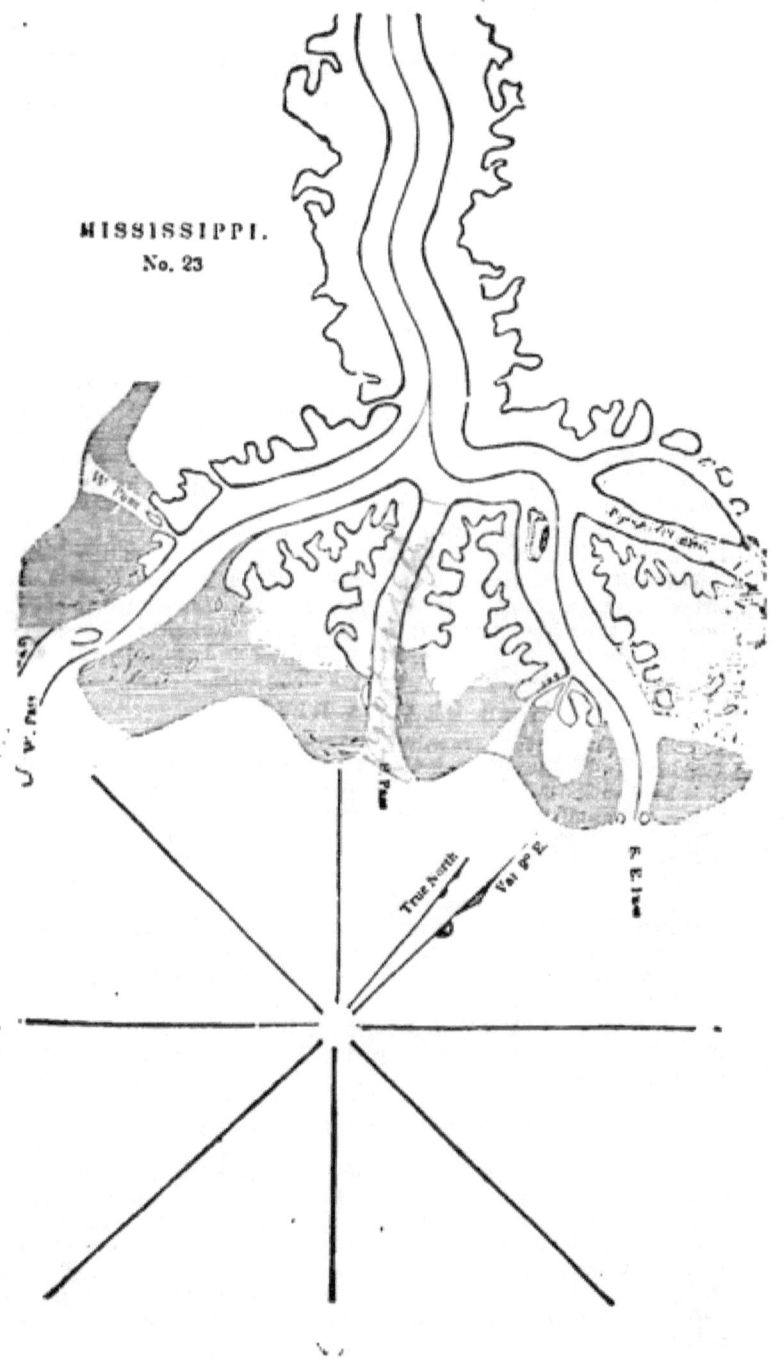

fertile region of country, producing cotton, corn, sugar, and rice, in great abundance. A great variety of timber is found along its course.

The principal towns on the Trinity are *Birdsville*, on the West fork, in Tarrant co. *Dallas*, in Dallas co., a short distance below the mouth of Elm fork. *Buffalo*, Henderson co. *Pine Bluff* and *Alabama*, Leon co. *Cincinnati*, Walker co. *Swartwout*, Polk co. *Smithfield*, in same co. *Liberty*, capital of county of same name.

Anahuac, in Liberty co., is on the east side of Galveston bay, opposite the mouth of Trinity river.

THE SAN JACINTO RIVER

Is a small stream which rises in Walker co., Texas, and empties into Galveston bay, about 25 miles north-east of Houston. It is navigable for 10 or 12 miles.

Houston, capital of Harris co., is situated on Buffalo bayou, about 44 miles from Galveston bay, at the head of steamboat navigation. Large quantities of cotton, corn, and sugar are shipped from this point. Houston contains 4 or 5 printing offices, an iron foundry, machine shop, &c. Population about 6000.

San Jacinto, on Buffalo bayou, Harris co., Texas, near Galveston bay, is celebrated on account of an important battle fought here in 1836, which resulted in the capture of Santa Anna and the independence of Texas. *Lynchburg*, Harris co., on Buffalo bayou, opposite San Jacinto.

Galveston, county seat of Galveston co., Texas, is situated on the eastern end of Galveston Island, at the entrance to the bay, in lat. 29° 17' north, and nearly 450 miles from New Orleans. It is the most important city of the State, and has a good harbor, with sufficient depth of water to float all ordinary vessels. Galveston has an extensive and active trade. It has 7 or 8 churches, 4 printing offices, several large hotels and a population of about 7500.

THE BRAZOS RIVER

Rises in the western part of Texas, and runs first easterly, then south-easterly, and enters the Gulf of Mexico about 45 miles south-west of Galveston. Its whole length is between 900 and 1000 miles, and it is navigable during *high* water, some 300 miles, the country along its course is generally very fertile, and produces large crops of cotton, sugar, and corn. There are extensive forests of red cedar and live oak on some parts of its course. The lower part of the Brazos flows through a level country, but slightly elevated above the sea.

The principal towns on this river are, *Waco Village*, McLennan co. *Nashville*, below, in Milam co. *Washington*, Washington co. *San Felipe*, Austin co. *Richmond*, capital of Fort Bend co. *Columbia*, Brazoria co. *Velasco*, in same co., at the mouth of the Brazos.

THE COLORADO RIVER

Takes its rise in the north-western part of Texas, and after a course of between 800 and 900 miles, empties into Matagorda bay. It is navigable for small steamers, during the rainy season, 200 or 300 miles. The lower part of its course, like the Brazos, flows through a rich alluvial plain, occupied by cotton, rice, corn, and sugar plantations.

The principal towns on the Colorado are, *Austin*, capital of the State, and county seat of Travis co. (Austin is delightfully situated in a fine region of country, and is a flourishing city. Population about 3500.) *Bastrop*, below, capital of Bastrop co. *La Grange*, Fayette co. *Columbus*, county seat of Colorado co. *Wharton*, capital of Wharton co. *Preston*, in same co. *Matagorda*, at the mouth of Colorado river, and on Matagorda bay, (this is a place of considerable business, population about 1500. There is a light-house at this point.)

THE LAVACCA RIVER

Is a small stream, which rises in Lavacca co, Texas. It is navigable to Texana, Jackson co., about 20 miles. It empties into Lavacca bay.

Port Lavacca, capital of Calhoun co., Texas, on the west side of Lavacca bay. *Indianola*, Calhoun co., on the same side of Lavacca bay as Port Lavacca.

La Salle, Calhoun co., Texas, on the south-west side of Matagorda bay.

Port Cavallo, in same co., on a point of land at the entrance of Matagorda bay, about 33 miles west of Matagorda. *Saluria*, same co., at the north-eastern end of Matagorda island, and entrance to the bay.

THE GUADULUPE RIVER

Takes its rise in Bexar co., Texas, and after a course of between 200 and 300 miles, enters the San Antonio some 15 miles from its mouth. The land on the course of this river is very rich.

The most important towns on Guadulupe river are, *Sisterville*, Comal co. *New Braunfels*, below capital of Comal co. *Gonzales*, capital of Gonzales co. *Clinton*, capital of De Witt co. *Victoria*, capital of Victoria co.

THE SAN ANTONIO RIVER

Rises in Bexar co., Texas, and enters Espirito Santo bay opposite Matagorda island.

The principal towns on San Antonio river are *Castorville*, capital of Medina co. *Helena*, capital of Carnes co. *Goliad*, capital of Goliad co.

THE MISSION RIVER

Is a small stream running through Refugio co., Texas, into Aransas bay. *Refugio*, capital of county of same name, is situated a short distance above the mouth of the river. *Lamar*, and *Copano*, are small villages on Aransas bay, in Refugio co.

THE ARANSAS RIVER

Is a small stream. It empties into the bay of same name.

THE NUECES RIVER

Rises in the western part of Texas, and after a very circuitous course of between 350 and 400 miles, it empties into the Corpus Christi bay, in latitude 27° 30 north. It is navigable for small steamers about 125 miles.

San Patrico, in county of same name, on Nueces river. *Baranca Blanca*, below, in Nueces co.

Corpus Christi, capital of Nueces co., Texas, is situated at the mouth of Nueces river, on Corpus Christi bay.

THE RIO GRANDE

Takes its rise in the Rocky Mountains, and, in its course, forms the boundary between Mexico and Texas. Its whole length is about 2000 miles. It enters the Gulf of Mexico in latitude 25° north. It is mostly a shallow river, and navigation is greatly obstructed by sand bars and rapids. It is navigable for small steamers, in the highest stages of water, for about 400 miles.

Some of the most important places on Rio Grande are, *El Paso*, Mexico, near the north-western boundary of El Paso co., Texas. *San Elazario*, below, in El Paso co. *Fort Leaton*, Presidio co., Texas. *McKinney*, McKinney co. *Kingsbury's Rapids*, in same co., (about 400 miles above the mouth of the river; stone coal is found a short distance above these rapids.) *Palafox*, Webb co. *Fort McIntosh*, and *Laredo*, in same co. *Alamo*, Starr co. *Mier*, in Mexico. *Roma*, in Starr co., Texas. *Rio Grande city*, capital of Starr co., (Population about 1000.) *San Francisco*, in Mexico, (opposite Rio Grande city.) *Edinburg*, in Hidalgo co., Texas. *Reinosa*, Mexico. *Santa Rita*, Mexico. *Matamoras*, Mexico.

Brownsville, opposite Matamoras, is the county seat of Cameron co., Texas, and one of the most important towns in the State. It has a large trade with Mexico. Population about 5000. An important battle was fought here, in 1846, between the Mexican and U. S. troops, in which the latter were victorious. Brownsville is situated about 38 miles above the mouth of the Rio Grande.

Point Isabel, same co., is situated on the shore of Laguna del Madre, about 30 miles east of Brownsville.

Vera Cruz, capital of the State of Vera Cruz, Mexico, is situated on the south-west shore of the Gulf of Mexico, in 19° 12' north latitude, and 96° 9' west longitude, and has an average annual temperature of 77°. It is the principal seaport of Mexico, and is one of the oldest Spanish towns on the continent. The present city of Vera Cruz was founded by Count de Monterey, near the close of the 16th century, and is situated about 15 miles from the old town, planted in 1519, by Cortes, who, guided by religious superstition, named it "LA VILLA RICA," or, *The rich town of the true Cross*. Before approaching the city, the lofty peak of Orizaba comes in view, with its cap of eternal snow, rearing its head far above the region of the drifting clouds, which hover around its summit.

The city is enclosed by walls, and the streets are wide, regular, well-paved, and lighted by 232 lamps. The houses are mostly two stories high, with flat roofs, and built of submarine stone, obtained from the sea-shore. The red and white cupolas, numerous towers, and battlements, present a beautiful appearance when viewed from the sea. The harbor is very insecure, on account of the rocky state of the coast and the severity of the gales, that prevail here during a large portion of the year. The public buildings consist of hospitals, churches, and convents, and a custom-house, all remarkable for their size and solidity, rather than for their architectural beauty. The climate of the city, owing to the reflected heat from the numerous sand hills without the walls, and the scarcity of water, is extremely unhealthy, especially to foreigners. It is, perhaps, more subject to yellow fever than any other place on the coast.

The country in the vicinity of Vera Cruz, produces every thing in abundance. Cattle roam in vast numbers over the plains, which, when properly cultivated, yield annually two abundant crops of corn, and tropical fruit of a superior quality. The table-lands vary so little in temperature, that they will produce most of the grains and fruits common to both temperate and torrid zones.

Vera Cruz has been besieged and taken near ten times—once by a band of robbers—twice by the independent and ministerial troops—three or four times by the Spaniards—once by the French—and lastly by the Americans, under General Scott. The castle of SAN JUAN DE ULLOA commands the entrance of the harbor, and is the most celebrated fortress in America. It was commenced in 1582, on a small island or bar, a little more than 1000 yards distant from the town. The cost of this great work, whose foundations, buried deep in the sea, have resisted for near three centuries the lashing of its waves, and the fleets of the most powerful nations, is estimated at forty millions of dollars. The walls are from four to five yards in thickness. There are seven large cisterns within the castle, which contain 93,767 cubic feet of water. Its full equipment of artillery pieces is 367.

The population of Vera Cruz is 15,000, and its commerce, very extensive. Most of the goods for the interior pass through this place. It is connected with the city of Mexico, by an excellent road, along which, stages and merchandise are constantly passing. A regular communication is kept up by sea, with the various United States and European ports.

Chagres and Panama, situated in the republic of New Grenada, on opposite sides of the Isthmus of Darien, are, from the great amount of travel to California, fast becoming important places. Chagres is on the Chagres river, 7 miles from its mouth, and is the landing place of all those who are going to California, by way of the Isthmus. The Chagres river is navigable as far as Cruses, which is but 15 miles from Panama. The passage across the Isthmus, formerly performed on mules, was, during the rainy season, extremely difficult. It is now crossed by the Panama Railway. The climate is very unhealthy, and few foreigners think of remaining long in the place.

ASPINWALL, Navy Bay, near Chagres, is the terminus of the Aspinwall and Panama Railroad—across the Isthmus, 46 miles—and the depot of steamers from New York.

PANAMA, on the Bay of Panama, Pacific coast, is a fortified town, having considerable trade.

The population of Chagres is 2000, and of Panama 10,000.

Being one of the regular stopping points of the New York, New Orleans, and Chagres steamers, we here insert a short description of

Havana, the capital of the island of Cuba, is situated in the north-western part of the island, in 23° 9' north latitude, and 82° 23' west longitude. This city has one of the most secure and commodious harbors in the world. Its entrance is through a small channel, admitting but a single ship; but within the basin it will contain a thousand ships. The harbor is sheltered from the wind by the surrounding heights, and the channel, which communicates with the sea, is eight or ten fathoms deep. On the hills opposite the city, there is a continuous row of forts, from whose outer parapet, elevated 150 feet above the level of the sea, a beautiful view of the city and its environs can be obtained. These works are said to have cost forty millions of dollars.

The greatest object of attraction in Havana, is the cathedral. It is built of coral rock, of a yellowish color, which gives it the appearance of great age. In this cathedral are deposited the remains of Columbus. His bones rest on the right hand of the altar, in a small recess in the wall. On the left hand side of the altar, hangs the painting which was the constant companion of Columbus during his eventful voyages. Columbus died at Valladolid, May 20. 1506, and his body was deposited in the Convent of St. Francisco. In 1513, his remains, and those of his son, were removed to Seville. In 1536, they were removed to Hispaniola, where they remained till 1795. His remains were then collected and carried in great pomp to Havana, where they now rest.

Moro and Punta castles are very strong works. The arsenal and dockyard are also on a grand scale. The city, when viewed from a distance, presents a most beautiful appearance. Population 140,000.

Vessels run regularly from Havana to New Orleans, and most of the Atlantic ports. Also, to all the important seaports of Europe.

THE ST. PETERS, OR MINNESOTA RIVER.

This river has a total length of nearly 450 miles, and is navigable for steamboats 50 or 60 miles. The principal towns on its banks are *South Bend City*, in Blue Earth co., Minn., (about 100 miles from Fort Snelling); *Mankato*, in same co., 3 miles below; *St. Peters*, in Nicollet co., 8 miles below; *Traverse Des Sioux*, 3 miles below, in same co.; *Le Sueur*, 8 miles below, in Le Seuer co.; *Henderson*, 6 miles below, in Sibley co.; *Chasca*, Scott co., 34 miles below; *Carver*, in same co., 2 miles below; *Hennepin*, 10 miles below, in Hennepin co.

The St. Peters empties into the Mississippi river at Fort Snelling, about 25 miles below Hennepin. (*See Mississippi river*.)

THE ST. CROIX RIVER.

Rises in the north-western part of Wis., near Lake Superior, and flows southward till it reaches the Mississippi in 44° north latitude. It is about 200 miles long, and navigable for steamboats about 60 miles. Large quantities of pine lumber are annually brought down the river and shipped to ports below.

St. Croix Falls, capital of Polk co., Wis., is at the head of steamboat navigation, on this river.

Osceola, 9 miles below, in same county.

Marine Mills, Washington co., Minn., 9 miles below.

Stillwater, county seat of Washington co., Minn., 15 miles below. It contains a court-house, land-office, penitentiary, saw mills, and other machinery propelled by water-power, 3 hotels, a number of stores and forwarding houses. Settled in 1843. Population about 2000. The surrounding country is diversified with timber and prairie, with a rich soil, watered by a number of small lakes and streams, abundantly supplied with fish. Stillwater commands a large portion of the lumber trade of the pineries on the upper waters of the St. Croix.

Hudson, county seat of St. Croix co., Wis., 5 miles below, at the mouth of Willow river, has considerable water-power, and contains 2 churches, a court-house, land office, and several stores and mills.

Lake St. Croix, commences just below Hudson, and extends to near the mouth of the river; it is a mere expansion of the river. Its width is from 3 to 4 miles. The St. Croix river enters the Mississippi 16 miles below Hudson, at Point Douglas. (*See Mississippi River*.)

THE CHIPPEWA RIVER

Rises in the northern part of Wis., near the head waters of the Montreal, and flows in a south-westerly direction. After a course of 300 miles, it joins the Mississippi near the termination of Lake Pepin. Its principal branches are the Clear-Water and Red Cedar rivers. It is navigable for steamboats 70 miles. The shores abound with pine forests. The mouth of this river is the southern boundary of that tract of land known as *Carver's Tract*. It lies principally in Crawford county, and contains an area of more than eight millions of acres. Captain Carver held this land by a deed obtained from the Indians, May 1, 1767. It commences at the Falls of St. Anthony and follows the Mississippi to the mouth of the Chippewa; thence east, about 100 miles; thence north 120 miles; and thence, in a direct line, to the Falls. *The Mississippi Land Company*, of New York, obtained, in 1824, a recognized deed before Judge Van Ness, of the U. S. District Court, New York.

Chippewa Falls, on the Chippewa river, is the capital of the county of same name, in Wis., at head of steamboat navigation. It has extensive water-power, and a number of mills. Population about 500.

THE WISCONSIN RIVER

Rises in some small lakes near the northern boundary of the State, and after a south and south-westerly course of about 600 miles, crossing the entire State of Wis., it enters the Mississippi in 43° north latitude, 3 miles below Fort Crawford. It is navigable for steamboats about 160 miles, to Portage city, where a short canal connects with Fox river, which enters Green bay at Fort Howard, opening navigation from the Mississippi to the northern lakes. There are numerous tributaries emptying into the Wisconsin all along its course, some of them quite large streams.

Wausau, or Big Bull Falls, on the Wisconsin river, in Marathon co., Wis., 170 miles north of Madison, capital of the State. Large quantities of lumber are annually sent down the river, in rafts, from this point. It contains a number of stores, flouring and saw mills, and a population of about 500.

Little Bull Falls, about 18 miles below, in same co.

Stephen's Point, 28 miles below, in Portage co., Wis., is a thriving village, with extensive water-power, and the adjacent country abounds in pines. The lumber business of this place is very extensive. It contains a number of stores, hotels, mills, and manufacturing establishments. Population about 700.

Plover, county seat of Portage co., Wis., 3 miles below, at the mouth of Plover river. The lumber trade, as in the towns above, is the chief business of Plover. Population about 500.

Portage City, county seat of Columbia co., Wis., 115 miles below, is the terminus of the Wisconsin Central Railroad; and a canal, a few miles long, connects the Wisconsin and Fox rivers at this point, as mentioned above. Portage city is a flourishing place, and increasing rapidly, it contains a large number of stores, hotels, manufacturing establishments, a bank, and 2 printing offices, and commands the trade of a large district of country. Population about 3000.

Prairie du Sac, Sauk co., Wis., 40 miles below.

Richland, 45 miles below, capital of Richland co., Wis., is situated on Pine creek, just above its junction with the Wisconsin, with abundance of water-power.

Brooklyn, Grant co., Wis, 65 miles below, and 7 miles from the mouth of the Wisconsin river.

ROCK RIVER

Rises in Fon du Lac co., Wis., near Lake Winnebago, and flows in a south-westerly course, about 325 miles, through Wis., and Ill., and enters the Mississippi, 2 miles below Rock Island. It is navigable for steamboats about 225 miles, during high water. The country through which this river passes, is remarkable for its fertility and beauty of scenery.

Watertown, Jefferson co., Wis., situated on Rock river, at the "Great Bend." The rapids near the town have a fall of about 25 feet, affording abundant water-power. Watertown contains 7 or 8 flouring and saw mills, 3 printing offices, several churches, a large number of stores and manufactories of different kinds. Population about 4500. It was settled in 1836.

Jefferson, capital of Jefferson co., Wis., is a flourishing village, 16 miles below Watertown, near the mouth of Crawfish river. It has fine water-power, contains a number of churches and mills. Population about 1500. The Rock River Valley Railroad passes through the place.   2176

Fort Atkinson, 8 miles below, is a thriving village in the same county, at the mouth of Bark river. It is situated in a rich farming region. Population about 600.   2010

Janesville, county seat of Rock co., Wis., 34 miles below, is beautifully situated, and contains 6 or 8 churches, a court-house, a female seminary, the State asylum for the blind, 4 printing offices, and factories and mills of different kinds. The Milwaukee and Mississippi Railroad passes through Janesville. Population about 6000. Settled in 1835.

Beloit, 18 miles below, in the same co., near the mouth of Turtle creek, has an active business and extensive water-power, it has several fine churches and seminaries. Beloit College is located here. Population about 4000. A branch of the Galena and Chicago Railroad extends to Beloit.   8759

Roscoe, Winnebago co., Ill., 8 miles below, is a flourishing village. It has good water-power, and a large woollen factory. Population about 500.

Rockford, 12 miles below, is the county seat of Winnebago co., Ill. A large business is transacted here, and the place is supplied with an abundance of water-power, the Chicago and Galena Railroad passes through it. Rockford contains 5 or 6 churches and 2 printing offices. Population about 4000.   11049

Byron, Ogle co., Ill., 12 miles below.

Oregon, 10 miles below, in the same co. Population about 600.

Dixon, county seat of Lee co., Ill., 20 miles below, has extensive water-power. It is on the line of the Galena branch of the Illinois Central Railroad. It contains several mills, a land office, 2 or 3 churches, and court-house. Population about 2500.   4055

Sterling, Whiteside co., Ill., 12 miles below, is beautifully located, with extensive water-power.

Lyndon, 16 miles below, in same co., is a flourishing village.

Prophetstown, 2 miles below, in same co., has good water-power.

Erie, 10 miles below, in same co.

Camden, 35 miles below, in Rock Island co., Ill., near the mouth of Rock river. It has an abundance of water-power, and a number of fine mills.

THE IOWA RIVER

Enters the Mississippi just below New Boston, 26 miles below Muscatine. It takes its rise in Hancock co., Io., and flows in a south-east direction. Its length is about 300 miles, and is navigable for small steamboats, about 80 miles, during high water.

Hardin, on the Iowa river, in Hardin co., Io., *Eldora*, below, in same co. *Marietta*, below, in Marshall co., Io. *Toledo*, below, in Tama co., Io. *Marengo*, below, in Io. co.

Iowa City, capital of the State, and county seat of Johnson co., is beautifully situated on a high bank of the Iowa river, 80 miles from its mouth. It was laid out in 1839. The state-house is a fine edifice, built of "Birdseye Marble," quarried in the neighborhood. The city contains 7 churches, 1 college, 1 academy, and 3 printing offices. The river affords abundant water-power for manufacturing purposes. Population about 4000. Johnson co. is in a rich agricultural region, well adapted to raising stock, wheat, corn, potatoes, &c.   5914

Port Allen, Louisa co., Io., 35 miles below Iowa city.

Concord, 10 miles below, in same co.

Wapello, county seat of Louisa co., Io., 12 miles below, it has fine water-power, and contains several mills, and a printing office. Laid out in 1839. Pop. about 1000. The Iowa river enters the Mississippi 23 miles below Wapello.

THE DES MOINES RIVER

Rises in the southern part of Minnesota, and, after a course of 400 miles, joins the Mississippi, 4 miles below Keokuk. It is navigable for steamboats about 200 miles. Its course is through an exceedingly rich and fertile region, with numerous prairies.

Fort Dodge, on the Des Moines river, about 300 miles from its mouth, in Webster co., Io. *Boonsboro*, below, in Boone co., Io., capital of Boone co. Population about 350.

3095 — Fort Des Moines, capital of Polk co., Io., on the Des Moines river, at the point where Racoon river enters it. It contains several schools and churches, a printing office, and a number of stores and manufactories. The rivers furnish extensive water-power. 12035 — East Des Moines is about 220 miles, following the course of the river, from the Mississippi. It was laid out in 1846. Population estimated at 1500, and increasing rapidly. The river is navigable to this place, for small steamboats, during high water.

Dudley, 14 miles below, in same co.

Lafayette, 5 miles below, in same co.

Bennington, Marion co., Io, about 10 miles below, is a small village.

Red Rock, 16 miles below, in same co., is a thriving place. Pop. about 500

Amsterdam, 12 miles below, in same co.

Bellefontaine, Mahaska co., Io., 12 miles below, is a small village.

Auburn, a small place, 12 miles below, in same co.

Des Moines City, 8 miles below, in same co.

Eddyville, 2 miles below Des Moines city, in Wapello co., is a flourishing village, with a number of churches and schools.

Chillicothe, in the same co., 8 miles below.

5214 — Ottumwa, county seat of Wapello co., Io, 12 miles below, is a thriving town, with abundance of water-power, and surrounded by a fertile country. It has several mills and manufacturing establishments.

Iowaville, Van Buren co., Io., 20 miles below, has 2 flouring mills and 1 distillery.

New Market, just below, in same co.

Portland, in same co., 6 miles below.

Philadelphia, 8 miles below, in same co.

Pittsburg, 7 miles below, in Van Buren co.

Keosauqua, capital of Van Buren co., Io., 5 miles below, is a thriving town. It contains a number of schools and churches, several grist and saw mills, a paper mill, and a number of manufacturing establishments. Pop. about 1200.

Pleasant Hill, nearly opposite Keosauqua, in same co.

Bentonsport, 8 miles below, in same co., is a flourishing village, with good water-power, and several mills and manufactories.

Vernon, just below, in same co., is also a thriving place.

Bonaparte, 5 miles below, in same co., has several grist and saw mills, and an extensive woollen factory.

Farmington, 8 miles below, in same co., is a flourishing town, containing several flouring and saw mills, a foundry, and an engine shop. Pop. about 1000.

Black Hawk, 3 miles below, in Clark co., Mo.

Croton, 3 miles below, in Lee co., Io.

Athens, 5 miles below, in Clark co., Mo., has good water-power, and several mills.

ILLINOIS RIVER.   71

Belfast, 6 miles below, in Lee co., Io.
Niagara, Clark co., Mo., 5 miles below.
St. Francisville, 5 miles below, in same co., is a thriving village.
Churchville, 14 miles below, near the entrance of the Des Moines, into the Mississippi river.

THE ILLINOIS RIVER

Is formed by the union of the Kankakee and Des Plaines rivers at Dresden, Grundy co., Ill. Above the mouth of Vermilion river, it is greatly obstructed by rapids; but below this point the current is gentle, and the river is navigable for steamboats during most of the year. The country bordering on the river, is very rich and productive, and the corn merce on it very large. Steamboats ascend the river about 250 miles, where, by the aid of the Illinois and Michigan Canal, a direct communication is opened with the lakes at Chicago. On the banks of this river, the French emigrants from Canada, settled themselves, and here was the scenery on which they founded their extravagant panegyrics upon the western country.

Dresden, is at the head of the Illinois river, as mentioned above, and about 325 miles from its entrance into the Mississippi. Population 300. The Illinois and Michigan Canal passes through the place.

Morris, 10 miles below, is the capital of Grundy co., Ill., and an important shipping point for produce. The Chicago and Rock Island Railroad passes through Morris. Population about 1000.

Clarkson, a small village in same county, 4 miles below. Pop. about 150.

Marseilles, 17 miles below, in La Salle co., is a thriving town. The Grand Rapids of the Illinois at this place, affords an immense water-power. There are a number of mills of various kinds, and a population of 500. The Illinois and Michigan Canal passes here.

Ottowa, 9 miles below, is the capital of La Salle co., Ill., situated on both sides of the river, and on the Illinois and Michigan Canal, near the mouth of Fox river. The Chicago and Rock Island Railroad passes through the town. Fox river, furnishes an immense water-power by a fall of about 30 feet. Stone coal is found near Ottowa. It contains a number of churches, mills, and factories, and 2 printing offices. Population about 3800.

Utica, 10 miles below, in same co., is a thriving village.

La Salle, 5 miles below, in same co., is a flourishing town at the terminus of the Illinois and Michigan Canal. The river is navigable for steamboats to this point. A large manufacturing and commercial business is carried on here. The neighboring country is exceedingly rich and productive. The Galena branch of the Illinois Central Railroad passes through La Salle. Population about 3500.

The Illinois & Michigan Canal.—This important work was commenced in the year 1836, and finished in 1848. Its length is 100 miles, is 60 feet wide at top, and 36 at bottom, and is 6 feet deep. There are 17 locks, each 110 feet long, and 18 feet wide, being large enough for vessels of 120 tuns burden. The entire cost of the work was $6,000,000.

Peru, 2 miles below La Salle, in same co., is a place of active business, and improving rapidly. It has fine water-power advantages. There are rich veins of stone coal in the vicinity. The Central Railroad, and Chicago and Rock Island, intersect here. Population nearly the same as La Salle.

Hennepin, county seat of Putnam co., 17 miles below, in the Great Bend of the Ill. river. The location is a beautiful one, being elevated by a gradual and gentle ascent, to a height of about 25 feet above the river. This town was named in honor of Louis Hennepin, a Franciscan friar, and one of the early explorers of the north-west. It contains a court-house, jail, 2 churches, a number of stores, and about 800 inhabitants. Hennepin has an active trade in shipping and receiving produce and merchandise.

THE ILLINOIS RIVER.

West Hennepin, Bureau co., nearly opposite.

Henry, Marshall co., 13 miles below, is a flourishing village. Large quantities of produce are shipped from Henry. Population 1000.

Lacon, 6 miles below, is the capital of Marshall co. It is a thriving town, and has an active trade. Population 1000.

Chillicothe, Peoria co., 13 miles below, at the head of Peoria lake, is a shipping point of importance. Population about 700.

Peoria Lake, is an expansion of the Illinois river, commencing at the town of Chillicothe, and extending in a southerly direction for a distance of 22 miles. It has very little current, and the water is beautifully clear and transparent, so much so, that the fish, of which there is a great abundance, can be distinctly seen swimming about, and performing their various evolutions, far beneath the surface.

Rome, 4 miles below Chillicothe, in same co., on the west bank of Peoria lake.

Spring Bay, 4 miles below, on the opposite side of the lake, in Woodford co., is a flourishing village doing an active shipping business.

Detroit, 7 miles below, in Peoria co.

Little Detroit, 2 miles below, in Woodford co.

Peoria, 5 miles below, county seat of Peoria co., is handsomely situated at the southern end of Peoria lake. The town lies on two tables of land, the first being about 12 feet above the water's edge, and the second 5 or 6 feet higher, and extending back some distance to the bluffs, in the rear of the town, which rise 100 feet above the general level. It contains, besides the county buildings, 10 or 12 churches, 6 printing offices, a number of schools and seminaries, mills and manufacturing establishments, and has a very large trade in pork, grain, lumber, &c. The Peoria and Oquaka Railroad has a terminus here. Pop. 23,000

Wesley City, 4 miles below, in Tazewell co., is a thriving village.

Pekin, 7 miles below, in same co., is an important town, and has an active trade. It contains 2 or 3 printing offices, and several schools, churches, and steam mills. Population about 3000.

Liverpool, Fulton co., 28 miles below. Population about 800.

Havana, 9 miles below, capital of Mason co., opposite the mouth of Spoon river, is a flourishing town and finely situated on a high ridge, 50 feet above high water mark. Population about 1100.

Bath, in same co., 12 miles below, is surrounded by a rich country.

Sangamon River, enters the Illinois, 18 miles below.

Fredericksville, 3 miles below, in Schuyler co., is a thriving village, doing a large business in the shipping of produce.

Beardstown, 4 miles below, on the east bank of the river, is the county seat of Cass co. It has an active trade, and 2 or 3 churches, a printing office, the usual county buildings, and a population of about 600.

La Grange, Brown co., 8 miles below, is a small village.

Merodosia, 9 miles below, in Morgan co., is pleasantly situated on the east bank of the Illinois, on a fine elevation. It contains 2 steam mills, a number of stores, and a population of 400.

Naples, 7 miles below, in Scott co., on the east bank of the river, is a pleasant and thriving town. It contains 2 churches, 3 steam mills, a number of stores, a printing office, and a population of about 1000. The Morgan and Sangamon Railway terminates here, which connects Naples with *Springfield*, the State capital, about 55 miles east. Large quantities of produce are shipped from this point.

Florence, Pike co., 10 miles below, has a good landing.

Montezuma, 6 miles below, in same co., is a good shipping point.

Bridgeport, Green co., 6 miles below, is a small village, and good shipping point for produce.

Newport, 8 miles below, in same county, is a small place.

Hardin, county seat of Calhoun co., 14 miles below. Population about 650.

Guilford, 4 miles below, in same co., is a small village.

Monterey, in same co., 4 miles below, and 13 miles above the mouth of the Illinois river, which empties into the Mississippi, 18 miles above Alton.

THE MISSOURI RIVER

Rises in the Rocky Mountains, and takes its name after the union of three branches, the Jefferson, Gallatin, and Madison. The springs which give rise to the Missouri river, are not more than a mile distant from some of the head waters of the Columbia river, which run, in a contrary direction, into the Pacific ocean.

At the distance of 441 miles from the extreme point of the navigation of the head branches of the Missouri, are what are denominated the "Gates of the Rocky Mountains," which present an exceedingly grand and picturesque appearance. For the distance of about 6 miles, the rocks rise perpendicularly from the margin of the river, to the height of 1200 feet. The river is compressed to the breath of 150 yards, and for the first 3 miles, there is but one spot, and that only of a few yards, on which a man can stand between the water and the perpendicular ascent of the mountain. At the distance of 110 miles below, and 551 miles from the source of the river, are the "Great Falls", 2,575 miles from the egress of the river into the Mississippi. At this place the river descends, by a succession of rapids and falls, a distance of 357 feet in 16¾ miles. The lower and greater fall has a perpendicular pitch of 98 feet, the second of 19, the third of 47, and the fourth of 26 feet. Between and below these falls are continual rapids of from 3 to 18 feet descent. These falls next to those of Niagara, are the grandest on the continent. Above the falls, the course of the river is northwardly.

The length of the Missouri river, from its source to its entrance into the Mississippi, is 3,096 miles, which, with the addition of 1,353 miles, the distance from the mouth to the Gulf of Mexico, makes a total length of 4,449 miles, being the longest river in the world. Through its whole course, there is no substantial obstruction to the navigation, before arriving at the "Great Falls." Its principal tributaries are each navigable from 1 to 800 miles. Through the greater part of its course, the Missouri is a rapid and turbid stream, and in the upper part it flows through an arid and sterile country. It is over half a mile wide at its mouth, and is generally nearly a mile in width. Notwithstanding it drains such an extensive region of country, and receives so many large tributaries, it is, at certain seasons of the year, quite shallow, not affording sufficient water for steamboat navigation, owing to its passage through a dry and open country, and being subject to more than usual evaporation.

The Missouri river trade has became a very important one, and the annual business between St. Louis and the towns on the river, and with Santa Fe, through Independence, is increasing with an amazing rapidity.

The Missouri river enters the Mississippi, 18 miles above St. Louis, by a mouth much wider than the upper Mississippi. It is the opinion of many geographers, that the Missouri river is the main river, and should be considered as one river from its head to the Gulf of Mexico. The reasons in support of this opinion are, that below the mouth of the Missouri, the Mississippi has the same turbulent appearance as the Missouri; while the upper Mississippi is remarkable for its clearness and transparency.

There are some peculiarities of the Missouri river, which it is highly important for emigrants, who design settling on its banks, to understand. The river has no permanent and settled channel, and it is on this account that steamboats are generally compelled to lay up in the night, it not being considered safe to run unless with the light of day to guide them. Many persons who have purchased farms on the banks of this river, not understanding the nature of the current, have lost acre after acre by the washing away of the soil. Not only have farms suffered in this way, but whole towns have been laid waste, and swept off with the resistless current of this mighty river, compelling the inhabitants to seek other, and more permanent places of abode.

The channel is rendered intricate by the great number of islands and sand bars; and in many places the navigation is made very hazardous by the rafts, snags, banks, &c. The river begins to rise in March, and continues till July, when the summer floods of its remote tributaries come in. During this period, there is sufficient depth of water for steamboats of almost any class; but during the remainder of the year, it is hardly navigable for any distance, for the smallest vessels that float upon the western waters.

"The bottoms of this river have a character very distinguishable from those of the upper Mississippi. They are higher, not so wet, more sandy, with trees which are not so large, but taller and straighter. Its alluvions are some thing narrower; that is to any, having for the first 500 miles a medial width of some thing more than 4 miles. Its bluffs, like those of the other river, are generally limestone, but not so perpendicular, and have more tendency to run into the *mamelle* form. The bottoms abound with deer, turkeys, and small game. The river seldom overflows any part of its banks in this distance. It is little inclined to be swampy. There is much fewer lakes, bayous, and small ponds, than along the Mississippi. Prairies are scarcely seen on the banks of the river, within the distance of the first 400 miles of its course. It is heavily timbered; and yet, from the softness of the wood, easily cleared. The water, though uncommonly turbid with a whitish earth, which it holds in suspension, soon and easily settles, and is then remarkably pure, pleasant, and healthy water. The river is so rapid and sweeping in its course, and its bed is composed of such masses of sand, that it is continually shifting its sand bars. A chart of the river as it runs this year, gives little ground for calculation in navigating it the next. It has numerous islands, and generally near them is the most difficult to be stemmed. Still more than the Mississippi below its mouth, it tears up one place and deposits in another, and makes more frequent and powerful changes in its channel than any other western river. * * * * * * * * *
Above the Platte, the open and prairie character of the country begins to develop. The prairies come quite into the banks of the river, and stretch from it indefinitely, in naked grass plains, where the traveler may wander for days without seeing either wood or water The 'Council Bluffs,' are an important military station, about 600 miles up the Missouri. Beyond this point, commences a country of great interest and grandeur in many respects, and denominated, by way of eminence, the Upper Missouri. The country is composed of vast and almost boundless grass plains, through which, stretch the Platte, the Yellow Stone, and the other rivers of this ocean of grass. The savages of this region have a peculiar physiognomy and mode of life. It is a country where commence new tribes of plants. It is the home of buffalos, elk, white bears, antelopes, and mountain sheep. Sometimes the river washes the bases of the dark hills of a friable and crumbling soil Here are found, as Lewis and Clarke, and other respectable travelers relate, large and singular petrifactions, both animal and vegetable. On the top of one of these hills, they found the petrified skeleton of a huge fish, 45 feet in length. The herds of the gregarious animals, particularly the buffalos, are innumerable. Such is the general character of the country, until we come in contact with the spurs of the Rocky Mountains." (*Flints' Geo. and Hist. of the Mississippi Valley.*)

From the source of the Missouri and tributaries, to Sioux City, Io., the lands along the river are almost entirely void of human habitations. There are some United States' military posts along the banks of the river, among which, are Fort Benton, Fort Berthold, Fort McKenzie, Fort Union, Fort Mandan, Fort Clarke, Fort St. Pierre, and a few others.

Sioux City, is at the junction of Big Stone river, with the Missouri, in Woodbury co., Io.

Tekama, county seat of Burt co., Nebraska, about 60 miles below, is finely situated on a high bank, in a good farming region.

De Soto, 30 miles below, in Washington co., Nebraska, is also finely situated in a rich country, well timbered.

Fort Calhoun, 15 miles below, in Washington co., Nebraska.

Florence, 10 miles below, in Nebraska.

Council Bluff's City, 10 miles below, capital of Pottawattomie co., Io., is finely situated on a high bluff, with a beautiful view of the surrounding country, which is a rich farming region, well timbered. Council Bluff's is on one of the emigrant routes for California and Oregon. It contains a land office, 2 churches, 3 schools, a number of stores, and mechanic's shops. Population about 4500.

Omaha City, capital of Nebraska, in Douglass co., opposite Council Bluff's City, is beautifully situated, on a plain about 50 feet from the bed of the river The eastern terminus of the Union Pacific Railroad is here. Population about 5,000.

Council Point, 5 miles below, in Pottawattomie, co. Io., is the landing point for a Mormon town, named KANESVILLE, about 4 miles in the interior.

THE MISSOURI RIVER.

Traders' Point, 3 miles below, in the same co., is a small French settlement, established to facilitate trade between the various Indian traders. It contains about 100 inhabitants.

Bellevue, 2 miles below, in Nebraska. It is the residence of the agent employed by the United States, to attend to the government business, with the tribes inhabiting this territory. It has a good landing, and is pleasantly situated on a high plain. The first newspaper published in Nebraska was commenced here in 1854. This point was first visited by Lewis and Clarke, in 1804, and soon after, the American Fur Company established a trading post here.

St. Mary's, 5 miles below, in Mills co., Io.

California City, 2 miles below, in same co., opposite the mouth of Nebraska or Platte river.

Platte, or Nebraska River, rises in the Rocky Mountains, by two branches, termed the North and South Forks. After an easterly course of nearly 2000 miles, it empties into the Missouri at this point. It is about a mile wide at the mouth; but is, as its name indicates, exceedingly shallow, and is not navigable, except in times of the great spring freshets.

Platteville, Mills co., Io., 2 miles below the mouth of Platte river.

Plattsmouth, capital of Cass co., Nebraska, 1 mile below, is beautifully located on a high bank, in the vicinity of fine timber and stone coal.

Bethlehem, 1 mile below, in Mills co., Io.

Kenosha, Cass co., Nebraska, 10 miles below.

Nebraska City, county seat of Otoe co., Nebraska, 10 miles below.

Brownsville, county seat of Nemehaw co., Nebraska, thirty miles below, is finely situated in the region of stone coal and good timber.

Iowa Point, 40 miles below, in Holt co., Mo., is the landing point for the town of Oregon, county seat of Holt co., situated 10 miles in the interior. Oregon contains a population of about 500.

Nodeway City, 30 miles below, in Andrew co., Mo., is a small village containing a few stores, and about 200 inhabitants. It is the landing point for Savannah, a town of about 800 inhabitants, situated a few miles off the river, the county seat of Andrew co.

St. Joseph, 25 miles below, county seat of Buchanan co., Mo., is a thriving and important town. It was laid out in 1843, and named in honor of Mr. Joseph Rubidoux, who resided here upward of 40 years. St. Joseph is the largest town in western Missouri, and one of the points of departure for emigrants to California and Oregon. It is situated in an exceedingly rich region of country, producing large quantities of hemp, wheat, and tobacco. It contains 7 or 8 churches, 5 steam flouring mills, several saw mills, a bagging factory, various manufacturing establishments, 3 printing offices, a large number of stores and warehouses, and a population of 13,000. The western terminus of the Hannibal and St. Joseph Railroad is here.

Leachman, 25 miles below, in same co.

Doniphan, 8 miles below, in Kansas.

Atchinson, 9 miles below, in Kansas.

Kickapoo City, 12 miles below, in Kansas, is well situated for trade. It has one newspaper office, and is improving rapidly.

Weston, 10 miles below, in Platte co., Mo., is a fine flourishing place, and is rapidly improving. Many of the emigrants make this a stopping place, for laying in supplies, previous to starting out on the plains. It contains several churches, 2 printing offices, a large number of stores, &c. Pop. about 3500.

THE MISSOURI RIVER.

Fort Leavenworth, 4 miles below, in Kansas, is on a high bluff. The situation is remarkably fine, the bluff being about 150 feet in height, and composed principally of white limestone. There is an excellent landing for boats, and many other superior advantages at this point. It is the rendezvous for all United States' troops destined for Santa Fe, Oregon, and the frontier stations. One of the principal routes to California commences at this place.

Little Platte River, rises in Clarke co., Io., and pursuing an almost direct southward course for a distance of about 200 miles, empties into the Missouri, 20 miles below Fort Leavenworth. This river is exceedingly shallow, and difficult to navigate.

Parkville, 2 miles below, in Platte co., Mo., is a fine flourishing village. It was named in honor of one of the early settlers of this region, by the name of Park. It is an important shipping point for produce. Population about 1,000.

Wyandotte City, 12 miles below, in Kansas, at the junction of Kansas river with the Missouri, is one of the starting points for emigrants.

Kansas River.—This is one of the largest tributaries of the Missouri. It rises in the Rocky Mountains, and flows eastward through the entire breadth of the Indian territory, and empties into the Missouri, 12 miles below Parkville. Its entire length is about 1200 miles, for 900 of which, it might be navigated. It is 340 yards wide at the mouth, and discharges an immense amount of water; many of its tributaries being nearly as large as itself. Solomon's fork, is 700 miles long; Smoky Hill fork, 800 miles.

Kansas, near the mouth of Kansas river, in Jackson co., Mo., is pleasantly situated, standing on a high bank of the river, and commanding a view of the surrounding country for many miles. It is thought by many, to possess the finest situation of any town on the river. The business is very extensive, there being an almost constant stream of emigrants passing through it. Pop. 32,200.

Randolph, 5 miles below, in Clay co., Mo., is a handsome village, finely situated on a commanding eminence. It contains 2 churches, several stores, and a population of 300.

Wayne City, 7 miles below, is the principal landing point for goods and merchandise destined for Independence, and is connected with it by the Independence Railroad.

The INDEPENDENCE RAILROAD DEPOT is about one mile from Wayne city. There is generally quite an air of business about this place, from constant arrival of goods and emigrants on their way to Independence. The road is 4 miles long.

Independence, county seat of Jackson co., Mo., about 4 miles back of Wayne city, is a place of great importance and growing rapidly. The country around is exceedingly fertile, and well adapted to cultivation. The business done is very large. It contains a court-house and county buildings, 3 hotels, 7 churches, a large number of wholesale and retail stores, and a population of about 5000. There is a large trade carried on between this place and Santa Fe. The goods are transported across the country in wagons, built very large and strong, and usually drawn by oxen, from 16 to 20 of which are attached to each wagon. It is the western terminus of the St. Louis and Pacific Railroad.

Independence derives much of its importance from being the point where many of the emigrants for California and Oregon, get their last supplies.

Liberty Landing, 5 miles below Wayne City, in Clay co., is a landing point for the town of Liberty, 4 miles from the river.

Livingston, Jackson co., 5 miles below, is a small village, formerly a landing place for Independence.

Owen's Landing, 1 mile below, in same co.

Richfield, Clay co., 10 miles below, is a small village.

THE MISSOURI RIVER. 77

Sibley, 10 miles below, is a thriving village, in Jackson co.. It occupies the former site of Fort Osage. It contains 2 churches, a number of stores, and about 800 inhabitants.

Napoleon, 6 miles below, in same co.

Camden, 6 miles below, in Ray co., is a flourishing town. Population 500.

Wellington, 7 miles below, in Lafayette co., is a small village.

Lexington, county seat of Lafayette co., 8 miles below. It is a fine, thriving town, having the highest location of any town on the river, being about 300 feet above high water mark. The first house built here was in the year 1830; and it now contains a court-house, jail, and county offices, 7 churches, a seminary, a land office, 2 printing offices, and a large number of stores. Population about 5200. Extensive veins of stone coal are found near Lexington.

Crooked River, enters the Missouri from Ray co., 6 miles below Lexington.

Walconda, 15 miles below the mouth of Crooked river, in Carroll co.

Waverly, 3 miles below, in Lafayette co., is a flourishing village. Population about 2,000.

Hill's Landing, Carroll co., 10 miles below, is a small village.

Miami, 20 miles below, in Saline co.

De Witt, Carroll co., 6 miles below.

Grand River, rises in Madison co., Io., and flows in a southwest direction for a distance of 240 miles, and enters the Missouri 5 miles below De Witt, forming the boundary line between Carroll and Chariton counties. It is navigated by boats about 100 miles.

Brunswick, 2 miles below the mouth of Grand river, in Chariton co., is an enterprising town. It is situated on a beautiful level prairie, and contains several churches, a large number of stores, and business establishments. Population about 2500.

Old Jefferson, 25 miles below, in Saline co., is a small village. There was formerly a place by this name, a short distance down the river, opposite Glasgow; but the remorseless river swept it off, and the inhabitants were compelled to seek for other lodgings.

Cambridge, 2 miles below, in same co.

Chariton River, rises in Lucas co., Io., and after a course of 150 miles, in a southerly direction, enters the Missouri 5 miles below Cambridge. It is not navigable for more than about 30 miles.

Glasgow, 3 miles below, in Howard co., is a thriving town. It has an active trade, and is a shipping point of produce, &c., for the surrounding country. It has two printing offices, a female seminary, several churches, and a large number of business houses. Population about 1500.

Bluffport, 5 miles below, in Howard co., is a small village.

Arrow Rock, 10 miles below, in Saline co., is finely situated about 150 feet above the river. It derives its name from the fact that the Indians used pieces of the rock found here, for making arrow heads. Population about 700.

La Mine River, rises in Lafayette and Johnson counties, and empties into the Missouri 10 miles below Arrow Rock. It is navigable for about 30 miles. The water of this river is remarkably clear.

Booneville, 6 miles below the mouth of La Mine river, is the county seat of Cooper co. It is situated on a bluff, elevated about 100 feet above high water mark, and received its name in honor of the celebrated Colonel DANIEL BOONE. It contains 3 or 4 printing offices, 2 academies, several churches, a court-house, and a large number of stores and business houses. Booneville is in the midst of a rich farming country. Much attention is paid to the cultivation of the grape. Bituminous coal, iron, lead, &c., are found in the vicinity. Population about ?500.

Old Franklin, Howard co., opposite Booneville.

Rocheport, Boone co., 12 miles below, at the mouth of Moniteau creek. Stone coal is found in the vicinity. Population about 500.

Mt. Vernon, Moniteau co., 8 miles below.

Providence, 6 miles below, in Boone co., is the landing place for Columbia, situated a few miles in the interior.

Nashville, 2 miles below, in the same county, is a small village.

Moniteau, 3 miles below, in county of same name.

Marion, Cole co., 6 miles below. Population about 50.

Stonesport, 10 miles below, in Boone co., is a small village.

Jefferson City, 6 miles below, is the capital of the State of Missouri, and county seat of Cole co. The situation is high, and commands a fine view. It contains a State house, the Governor's house, State penitentiary, court-house, 8 printing offices, a number of churches, and a large number of stores and commission houses. The St. Louis & Pacific Railroad passes through Jefferson City. Population about 8500.

Hibernia, opposite Jefferson City, in Callaway Co., is a small village.

Formosa, 9 miles below, in Cole co., near the mouth of the *Osage river*.

Osage River rises in the Indian territory, and after a meandering course of about 500 miles, empties into the Missouri at this point. It is 400 yards wide at the mouth, and is navigable for steamboats about 200 miles. The land bordering on this river is exceedingly fertile, and yields abundant crops of all the products of the West.

Cote Sans Dessein, 5 miles below the mouth of the Osage river, in Callaway co., is a small village.

Smith's Landing, 8 miles below, in same co.

Portland, 16 miles below, in same co.

Gasconade River rises in Wright co., Mo., and taking its course in a northerly direction for a distance of 200 miles, enters the Missouri 10 miles below Portland. It is not navigable to any extent, but affords a vast amount of water-power to the numerous mill-seats along its banks.

The St. Louis & Pacific Railroad crosses this river near its mouth, which was the scene of a terrible and heart rending calamity, at the celebration of the opening of the road to Jefferson City, in November, 1855, by which about 30 of the most prominent citizens of St. Louis lost their lives, and hundreds of others were seriously maimed. Just as the locomotive had crossed the first span, the bridge gave way, and 9 of the 13 cars in the train, crowded to overflowing with people, were, with the locomotive, precipitated to the bed of the river, with an awful crash, into a mass of ruins.

Hermann, 6 miles below, is the capital of Gasconade co. It is a thriving place. Population about 2000. The St. Louis & Pacific Railroad passes through Hermann.

Bridgeport, 1 mile below, in Warren co.

Pinckney, in same county, 12 miles below, is a small village.

Griswold, nearly opposite Pinckney, in Franklin co.

Washington, 16 miles below, in same co., is a flourishing town.

Bassora, 1 mile below, in same co.

South Point, 2 miles below, also in same co. The St. Louis & Pacific Railroad passes through Griswold, Washington, Bassora, and South Point.

Portmuna, 6 miles below, in St. Charles co.

Mt. Pleasant, in same co., 1 mile below Portmuna.

St. Albans, Franklin co., 8 miles below.

Missouriton, 1 mile below, in St. Charles co.

Johnson's Ferry, 2 miles below, in same co., is a small village.

Port Royal, opposite Johnson's Ferry, in Franklin co.

Pittman's Ferry, 5 miles below, in St. Charles co.

St. Charles, 13 miles below, is the capital of St. Charles co., and a flourishing place. It is handsomely situated on elevated ground, and commands delightful views. There are fine quarries of limestone, and sandstone in the vicinity; also mines of stone coal. The river at this point is over a mile wide. St. Charles contains a college, 7 or 8 churches, a court-house, and a number of stores. Population about 5000.

Jamestown, 16 miles below, in St. Louis co.

Bellefontaine, in same co., 2 miles below.

Columbus, 4 miles below, at the mouth of the Missouri, and junction with the Mississippi.

THE KASKASKIA RIVER

Rises near the center of Illinois, in Champaigne co., and empties into the Mississippi, 76 miles below St. Louis. It is navigable for steamboats about 150 miles, its whole length is some 300 miles.

Shelbyville, Ill., on the Kaskaskia river, is the county seat of Shelby co. It contains a court-house, several churches, and a number of stores. The Alton and Terre Haute Railroad passes through Shelbyville.

Vandalia, about 50 miles below, (following the river course,) is the county seat of Fayette co., and was the former capital of the State. It is on the line of the Illinois Central Railroad. Population about 3500.

Keysport, Clinton co., 27 miles below, (by the river,) is a small village.

Carlyle, capital of Clinton co., 12 miles below, contains several mills, the county buildings, and a number of stores. The Ohio and Mississippi Railroad passes through the place.

Covington, 14 miles below, in same co.

Fayetteville, St. Clair co., 26 miles below, is a small place.

Athens, 9 miles below, in same co.

Lively, in same co., 2 miles below.

Tamarawa, 3 miles below, in Monroe co.

Evansville, Randolph co., 20 miles below.

Kaskaskia, county seat of Randolph co., 8 miles below, was founded shortly after the visit of La Salle to the Mississippi, in 1683, by Father Gravier, a Catholic missionary among the Illinois, and was the capital of the Illinois country, so long as the French continued in possession of it. In 1763, it was ceded by France to Great Britain. In 1778, the fort, on the east side of the river, was taken by Col. George Rogers Clark. Kaskaskia contains a court-house, a land office, and a population of about 1000, mostly of French descent. The Kaskaskia river enters the Mississippi 7 miles below the town.

WHITE RIVER

Rises in the Ozark Mountains, and runs first north easterly into Mo., and then into Ark., in a southwardly direction to its entrance into the Mississippi, 16 miles above the Arkansas river. Black river is its largest tributary. Its whole length is between 750 and 800 miles. It is navigable for about 400 miles. The country through which it passes, is generally fertile, producing fine crops of cotton and corn, and some portions rich in minerals. Pine forests abound on its upper waters, and cypress swamps, toward the mouth.

Worth, is a small village in Marion co., Ark., on White river, near the boundary line of Mo.

Johnson, 55 miles below, (by the river course,) in same co.
Liberty, 28 miles below, in Izard co.
Athens, in the same co., 25 miles below.
Mt. Olive, 6 miles below, is the capital of Izard co.
Sylamore, in same co., 6 miles below.
Batesville, 45 miles below, capital of Independence co., and a thriving town. Small steamers can reach this place at nearly all seasons. It contains several churches, the usual county buildings, and 2 printing offices. The surrounding country is fertile, with fine water-power. Population about 1800.
Jacksonport, Jackson co., 35 miles below, at the mouth of *Black river*, which is navigable for small steamers, some distance.
Elizabeth, 10 miles below, is the county seat of Jackson co. This is a thriving place, and exports large quantities of timber.
Augusta, 65 miles below, in same co., is a flourishing village, finely situated in a rich region of country.
Des Arc, Prairie co., 35 miles below, in a fertile cotton, and sugar growing country; oak, cedar, and cypress timber, is abundant in the vicinity. Pop. 500.
Clarendon, 38 miles below, in Monroe co.
Crockett's Bluff, in Arkansas co., 33 miles below.
Cass Coe, 8 miles below, in same co., 50 miles from the Mississippi river, by the meanders of the stream.

THE ARKANSAS RIVER

Rises in the Rocky Mountains, near the boundary between the Indian Territory and Utah, and after pursuing an easterly course of over 2000 miles, empties into the Mississippi in latitude 33° 54' north. It pours a broad and deep stream from the mountains upon the arid and sandy plains below. The sand and the dry atmosphere absorb the water to such a degree, that it may often be forded many hundred miles below the mountains. Some of its tributaries are so impregnated with salt, as to render even the waters of the main stream unpotable. To the distance of about 400 miles from its mouth, it has many lakes and bayous. In high water, it is navigable for steamboats as far up as Fort Gibson, at the mouth of Grand river, by water, 750 miles. Next to the Missouri, this is the largest tributary of the Mississippi, though not the most important. Below Van Buren, the land along the river is productive, and well timbered. The territory drained by this river and its tributaries is estimated to contain 178,000 square miles. Between Fort Smith and Little Rock, bituminous coal is frequently found along its banks.

Fort Gibson, a military station, in the Indian territory, on the Neasho river, just above its entrance into the Arkansas. The *Illinois* and *Canadian* rivers empty into the Arkansas, some distance below Fort Gibson.
Fort Coffee, 100 miles below, and west of the boundary of Arkansas.
Fort Smith, 20 miles below, on the western boundary of the State, in Sebastian co., is a thriving town. It carries on an extensive trade with the Indians. The U. S. Government has a military post here. It contains the government buildings, a printing office, a church, and a population of about 1400.
Van Buren, capital of Crawford co., 10 miles below, is a thriving place, pleasantly situated. It has a large trade with the surrounding country. The place contains a cotton factory, a steam flouring mill, 4 or 5 handsome churches, 2 printing offices, and a population of about 2000.
Ozark, county seat of Franklin co., 60 miles below, is a small village.
Roseville, 12 miles below, in same co.
Patterson's Bluff, a small place, 20 miles below, in Johnson co.
Spadra Bluff, in same co., 15 miles below.
Pittsburg, 5 miles below, in same co.

St. Martin's, Pope co., 10 miles below.

Scotia, 2 miles below, in same co.

Norristown, in same co., 20 miles below.

Dardenelle, opposite, in same co.

Lewisburg, Conway co., 40 miles below.

Greene Grove, 18 miles below, in same co.

Little Rock, 40 miles below, capital of the State of Arkansas, and county seat of Pulaski co., is situated on a high rocky bluff, the first above the mouth of the river, commanding a beautiful and extensive view of the adjacent country. The city contains the State House, a fine brick building, a U. S. arsenal, the State penitentiary, 7 or 8 churches, 2 printing offices, and a population of about 3000. Slate, and a species of granite are found in the vicinity, also good clay for making brick.

Straw Hat, 70 miles below, in Jefferson co.

Pine Bluff, 20 miles below, county seat of Jefferson co., is a flourishing place, in a fertile cotton raising region. Large quantities of cotton are annually shipped from this point. Population about 600.

Rob Roy, in same co., 12 miles below.

New Gascony, 10 miles below, in same co.

Richland, 8 miles below, in same co.

Swan Lake, Arkansas co., 5 miles below.

Niccattoo, 10 miles below, in same co.

South Bend, 30 miles below, in same co.

Arkansas Post, 25 miles below, capital of Arkansas, co., is the oldest town in the State. It was founded by the French in 1685. It is located on a high bluff; but, in the rear of the town, the land is low and frequently inundated. It contains a court-house; jail, and printing office. Population about 500.

Red Fork, Desha co., 10 miles below.

Wellington, 20 miles below, in same co.

The Arkansas river enters the Mississippi, 30 miles below Wellington.

THE YAZOO RIVER

Rises near the central part of the State of Mississippi. It is formed by the union of the Tallahatchee and Yallabusha, which are navigable rivers. After receiving the Sunflower which runs nearly parallel with the Mississippi, and is navigable for 80 miles, it empties into the Mississippi, 300 miles from its source. The country bordering on this river is very rich, and produces cotton in great abundance. From Greenwood, at the mouth of the Tallahatchee, several large steamboats run regularly to New Orleans, during the cotton season. The number of bales of cotton that annually float down this river, is estimated at 150,000. It is a sluggish stream, and navigable throughout its whole length.

Yazoo City, county seat of Yazoo co., Miss., some 160 miles below Greenwood, is a flourishing town, in the midst of a rich cotton growing country, and has considerable trade. A large amount of cotton is forwarded from this point to New Orleans. It has 2 or 3 printing offices, a number of churches, and a population of about 2000.

Liverpool, and Satartia, below, in same co.

Cardiff, about 15 miles from the mouth of the river, in Warren co., Miss.

RED RIVER

Rises in a chain of hills near Santa Fe, in New Mexico, called the Caous mountains, and after pursuing an easterly course of some 1500 miles, empties into the Mississippi 215 miles above New Orleans, and 776 below the mouth of the Ohio. It receives, in its course, the waters of a number of rivers, the largest of which, are the Blue river and False Washita, or Rio Negro. After leaving the mountains, it flows through extensive prairies of rich, red soil, which impart their color to the water. From this circumstance it received the name of *Red* river. The margin of the river is covered, in many places, with grass and fine vines, which bear delicious grapes. The bottoms are from one to ten miles wide, and are well timbered with willow, locust, cotton-wood, pawpaw and buckeye. On the uplands, elm, ash, hickory, mulberry, and black-walnut grow in great abundance. The width of its channel, for 400 miles from its mouth, does not correspond with its length, or the immense mass of waters which it collects in its course from the Rocky mountains. In high waters, it is often divided into two or three channels, and spreads into a line of bayous and lakes, which take up its superabundant waters, which are a considerable time in filling, and prevent the river from displaying its breadth and amount of waters, as it does in the high-lands, 500 miles above. About 100 miles above Natchitoches, commences what is called the *Raft*, which is nothing more than an immense swampy alluvial of the river, to the width of 20 or 30 miles. The river here, spreading into a vast number of channels, frequently shallow, of course, has been for ages, clogging up with a compact mass of timber and fallen trees, wafted from the regions above. * * * The river is blocked up with this immense mass of timber, a distance, by its meanders of 70 miles. There are places where the water can be seen in motion under the logs. In other places, the whole width of the river may be crossed on horse-back. Weeds, flowering shrubs, and small willows, have taken root upon the surface of this timber, and flourish above the waters. It is an impediment of incalculable injury to the navigation of this noble river, and the immense extent of country above it. There is probably no part of the United States, where the unoccupied lands have higher claims from soil, climate, intermixture of prairies and timbered lands, position, and every inducement to population, than the country above the Raft; where the river becomes broad, deep, and navigable for steamboats, in moderate stages of water, for several hundred miles."—(*Flint's Geo. and His.*)

The bottom land along the river is very fertile, producing corn, cotton, tobacco, and sugar cane in great abundance. If the navigation of this river could be permanently opened, the fertile lands that now lie in waste would soon be under cultivation; and boats, laden with the rich products common to the West and Southwest, would glide smoothly along its *reddened* waters, to the great commercial depot of the South. The United States Government cut a channel through the raft, at an expense of $300,000, but another has since formed. Along the river, the trees grow very tall and thick; in some places their branches nearly meet across the stream.

Lanesport, is situated in the southwestern corner of the State of Arkansas, Sevier co., on Red River, which is here, and for some distance above and below, the northern boundary of the State of Texas.

Fulton, about 100 miles below, by the meanders of the river, in Hempstead co., Ark., is an important point.

Conway, about 100 miles below, in Lafayette co., Ark.

Shreveport, about 90 miles below, is the capital of Caddo parish, La. It is finely located for business, being surrounded by an exceedingly fertile planting region, and about 30 miles below the great raft. Some 50,000 bales of cotton, and a very large number of cattle, from Texas, are annually shipped from this point. The town contains a large number of stores, several churches, and steam mills, a printing office, and a population of about 3000.

Natchitoches, about 100 miles below, is the capital of Nachitoches parish, La. It was first settled by the French, under a grant to St. Dennis, who, in 1713, established a trading post here. In 1732, it was attacked by the Natchez Indians, who had been driven from their own country, after the great massacre of the 28th of November, 1729. After a hard fought battle, which lasted several hours, the Indians were repulsed, leaving ninety-two of their bravest warriors on the field. With this battle, ended the existence of the Nachez as a distinct nation. Those who were taken prisoners were conveyed to the West Indies. Nachitoches contains a printing office, a U. S. land office, and several churches, and has an active business. Population about 1500.

"Two or three leagues west of Nachitoches, is the ancient Spanish town of ADAYES. We can see no where in the United States so fair a sample of an ancient Spanish town, as this. The houses are of the construction of a hundred years ago. A little old church, with three or four bells, some of them cracked,

OHIO—No. 1.

and some coarse paintings, give the church an air in keeping with the town. The inhabitants are all Spanish."

Alexandria, 80 miles below Nachitoches, and 150 from the entrance of Red river into the Mississippi, is the capital of Rapides parish, La. The location of the town is very beautiful. The surrounding country is quite level, producing cotton in great abundance. Population about 800.

THE MONONGAHELA RIVER

Rises in Randolph co., Va., and after a northern course of 300 miles, unites with the Alleghany at Pittsburg. It is navigable for steamboats as far as Brownsville, 40 miles above Pittsburg; and for keelboats, near 200 miles from its mouth. Its principal branches are the Cheat and Youghiogheny rivers. Large quantities of excellent coal, are annually brought down this river. The navigation of this river has been greatly improved, and made permanent, by the erection of 8 or 10 substantial locks, between Brownsville and Pittsburg.

Clarksburg, county seat of Harrison co., Va., is situated on the west fork of the Monongahela, 70 miles from the Ohio river. There are excellent coal mines in the vicinity of this place. Iron and salt are also found to some extent. It is a flourishing place, and contains several large mercantile houses, 4 churches, 2 academies, and 2 printing offices. The North-Western Railroad, (a branch of the Baltimore and Ohio R. R.,) passes through the town.. Pop. about 1500.

Fairmount, capital of Marion co., Va., is situated on the Monongahela, 22 miles north of Clarksburg. The surrounding country is hilly, and the soil productive. The forests are filled with excellent timber, and the earth is well stored with iron and coal, which are largely exported. Population about 1300. A splendid wire suspension bridge connects the town with Palatine, on which, the Baltimore and Ohio Railroad crosses.

Palatine, Marion county, opposite Fairmount. It is a thriving village, containing 10 stores, several mills, &c. Population 600.

Morgantown, county seat of Monongalia co., is a flourishing and wealthy village, situated on the Monongahela, about 60 miles south of Pittsburg. The town was laid out in 1785. It contains a number of stores and mills, 3 printing offices, 1 academy, and 4 churches, &c. The surrounding country is very fertile, and abounds in coal and iron. Population about 1000.

New Geneva, Fayette co., Pa., is pleasantly situated on the right bank of the Monongahela, at the mouth of George's creek. It contains about 100 dwellings, a large steam flour mill, and a glass factory.

Brownsville, Fayette co., Pa., at the intersection of the National Road, and the Monongahela river. It occupies an important point as a place of business, enjoying the advantages of the National Road, and the improved navigation of the river.

The inexhaustible beds of coal in the vicinity, must eventually make it a great manufacturing place. The town contains a bank, 7 churches, several foundries, and machine shops, a number of mills, glass, and other factories, of various articles. There is a splendid bridge over the Monongahela, built in 1832, 630 feet long, and cost $50,000. Brownsville was incorporated in 1815, and now contains a population of about 5000.

Monongahela City, Washington co., Pa., on the Monongahela, at the mouth of Pigeon creek. Iron, coal, and salt, abound in the surrounding country. This town is noted as being the place where the insurgents held a great meeting in 1794, during the *Whisky Insurrection*. Since the year 1830, it has increased rapidly. It contains 2 glass factories, 3 saw mills, 2 carding machines, and 6 churches. Population about 1800.

Elizabeth, Alleghany co., Pa., is a beautifully located manufacturing town, on the Monongahela, 16 miles above Pittsburg. The town was laid out in

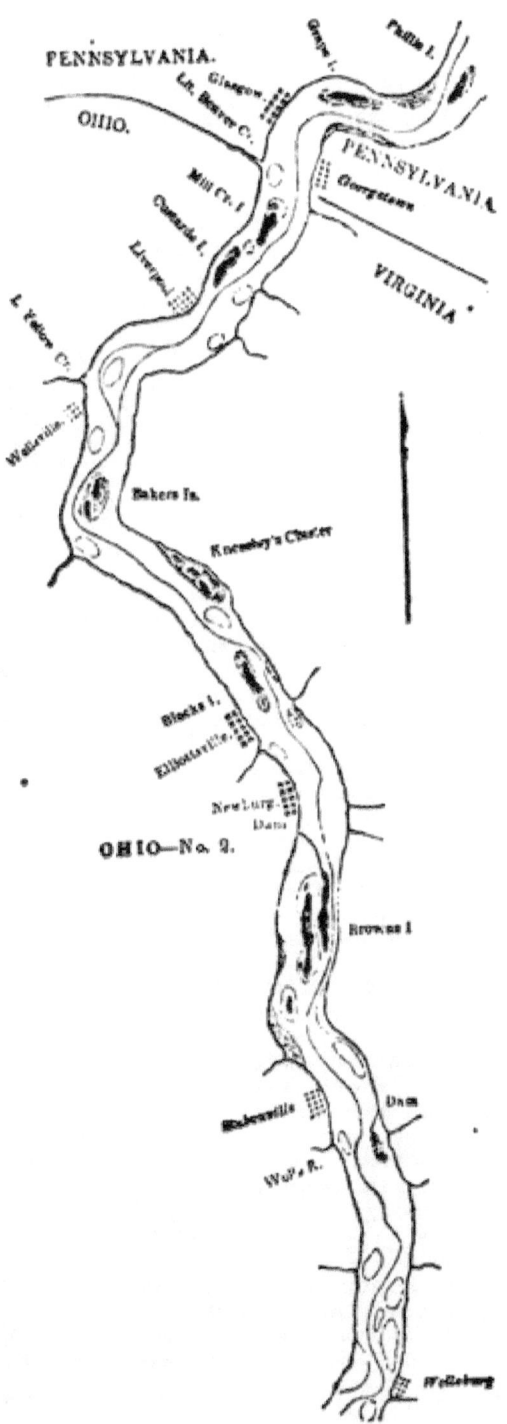

1787. The completion of the Monongahela slack water navigation, has greatly increased the commercial advantages of this place. The town contains 4 churches, 3 ship yards, several saw mills, and glass, woolen, and other manufactories. Pop. 2800.

Braddock's Field, is in Alleghany county, on the banks of the Monongahela, 10 miles above Pittsburg. This field will long be remembered and visited, as it is the spot where Washington first displayed those high qualities of a man, and a general, which, in after life, entitled him to the respect of his country.

Birmingham, is a large manufacturing town, situated on the south side of the Monongahela, 1 mile from the center of Pittsburg. It has 3 churches, 1 market house, and several large glass factories, and iron foundries. A very large capital is employed here, in the various manufactories. Population, 4000.

THE ALLEGHANY RIVER

Rises in the northern part of Pennsylvania, and flows in a north-westerly direction through the southern part of New York, thence returning to Pennsylvania; and after pursuing a general south-west direction of 400 miles, unites with the Monongahela at Pittsburg. The waters of this river are pure and clear, while those of the Monongahela, are colored by the soil through which it flows. Vast quantities of lumber are sawed along this river, and floated in rafts to Pittsburg and towns below. It is navigable for keel boats, about 250 miles. The country between the Alleghany and Monongahela rivers, is the richest coal region in the Union.

Olean, Cattaraugus co., N. Y., on the Alleghany river, at the junction of Olean creek. This is a flourishing village. The Genessee Valley Canal, which connects it with Rochester, terminates here. The line of the Erie Railroad, which connects New York and Dunkirk, on Lake Erie, passes through the place. The width of the Alleghany, is 20 rods, and its channel free from obstructions. It is estimated that more than 200,000,000 feet of lumber, of excellent quality, is annually sent to various places along the river. Population about 1000.

Warren, county seat of Warren co., Pa., on the right bank of the Alleghany river, and on the Sunbury and Erie Railroad, near the mouth of Conewango creek. During the spring, the town is alive with the bustle and activity of lumber merchants, preparing to depart for below, with their long train of rafts. Population about 1200.

Franklin, county seat of Venango co., Pa., on the Alleghany, near the mouth of French creek. It was laid out in 1795, and contains the usual county buildings, and 6 churches. There are several large mills and furnaces in the vicinity, from which, the town derives an extensive trade. During high water, the Alleghany is navigable from Pittsburg to this place, a distance of 124 miles. The dams on French creek afford immense water-power for mills. There is a splendid bridge across the river here. Population about 1200.

Kittanning, seat of justice of Armstrong co., Pa., on the left bank of the Alleghany, near the center of the county, was formerly the site of an old Indian town of the same name. It was laid out in 1804. It contains the county buildings, an academy, a female seminary, and several churches. Population 2100.

Freeport, Armstrong co., Pa, is a flourishing town on the right bank of the river, and Pennsylvania Canal. Many salt wells are now in successful operation. Freeport contains a number of woolen factories and mills. Pop. 1200.

Sharpsburg, is pleasantly situated on the right bank of the Alleghany, 5 miles above Pittsburg. It is a flourishing village. It has several large ship yards, from which a number of steam and keel boats are annually launched. Population, about 2000.

Lawrenceville, named in honor of Captain Lawrence, of the U. S. Navy, is pleasantly situated on the left bank of the Alleghany, 2½ miles above Pittsburg. In the center of the town, there is an U. S. Arsenal, at which are stored all sorts of military equipments, which are shipped west and south, as occasion

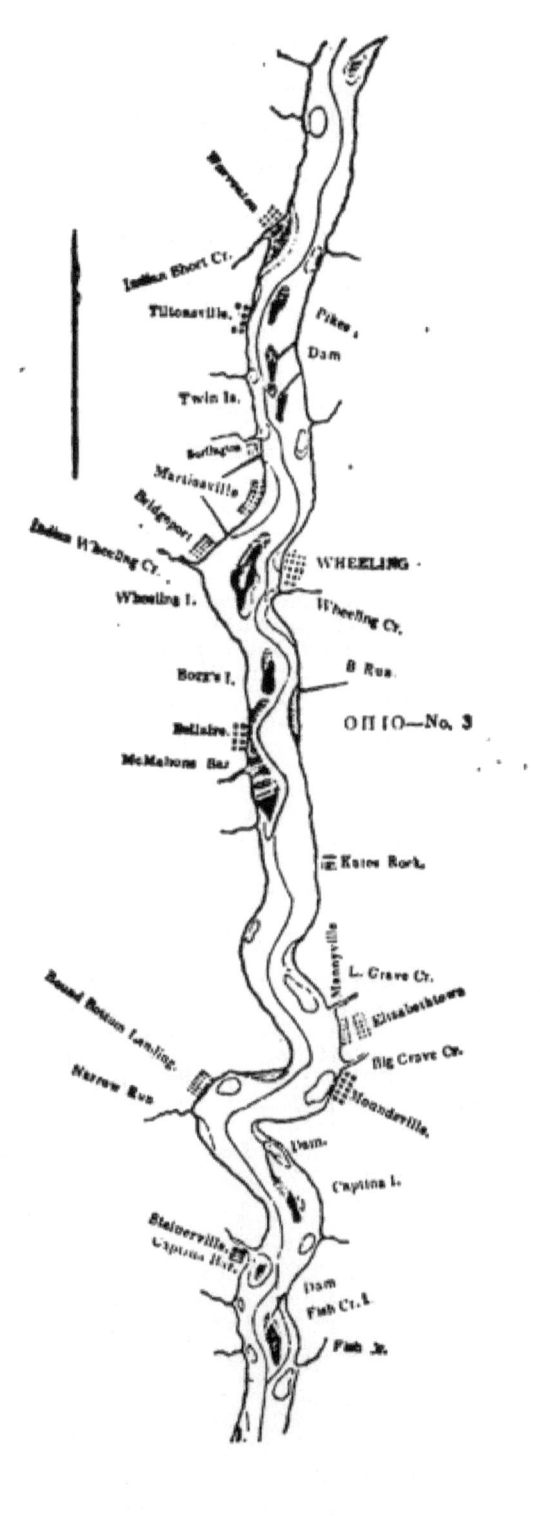

requires. The town contains 4 churches, and a lyceum. It was at this place General Washington, in 1753, came near losing his life, by attempting to cross the river on a raft, when it was filled with floating ice. Population 1800.

Alleghany City, is situated on the right bank of the Alleghany river, opposite Pittsburg. This city is strictly a part of Pittsburg, though under a different corporation. Many of the business men of Pittsburg reside here. It has considerable commerce, and does a large manufacturing business; employing a heavy capital. The city contains 20 churches, of various denominations, 3 academies, 15 schools, and a population of 53,000.

The Western Theological Seminary, of the Presbyterian Church, was located here, in 1827. This institution has connected with it, a workshop for manual labor, and a library of 9000 volumes.

Behind Seminary hill, is the Western Penitentiary, an immense castle-built building, of the ancient Norman style. It was completed in 1827, at a cost of $183,002.

THE OHIO RIVER

Is formed by the junction of the *Alleghany*,* and *Monongahela* at Pittsburg, in Lat. 40° 32' N., and after a meandering course of 1007 miles, enters the Mississippi in Lat. 37° north, 172 miles below St. Louis, and 990 miles above New Orleans. Tributary rivers and creeks, to the number of 75, empty into the Ohio, between Pittsburg and its mouth, the principal of which, are described in their proper places, in this work. And there are, at least, 100 considerable Islands, besides a great number of *tow heads* and sand bars. Some of these Islands are of exquisite beauty, covered with trees of the most beautiful foliage.

No river in the world, rolls for so great a distance, such a uniform, smooth, and placid current. Its banks are generally high, and precipitous, rising into bluffs, cliffs, and hills, sometimes to the height of 400 to 500 feet. Between these hills and the river, there is generally a strip of land, of unequal width, called *bottom*. These hills and bottoms, are mostly covered with a dense growth of gigantic forest trees, exhibiting a wild and picturesque grandeur. The scenery along the Ohio, although not possessing the savage grandeur of parts of the Mississippi, and Missouri, is of surpassing loveliness and beauty; especially in the spring, when the trees, vines, and other plants are putting forth their exuberant foliage and blossoms. The graceful curves and bends of the river, exhibiting, in the distance, one range of hills, laped on to another, with beautifully rounded tops, and covered with the verdure of an almost unbroken forest, produce a series of splendid views rarely found.

The Ohio river flows through a greater extent of rich Iron and Coal regions than any other river, probably, in the world. Building stone, of fine quality, and great variety, is found in exhaustible quantities, on and near its banks. And most of the tributaries, also, extend into and run through regions of country, containing vast mineral wealth. And for agricultural purposes, and timber in great variety, the extent of country drained, (more than 200,000 square miles) is unequaled in richness and fertility.

The medial width of the Ohio, during ordinary stages of water, from Pittsburg to its mouth, is about half a mile; but in some places it expands to a mile and more, and at other points, it contracts to *less* than half a mile. The average range between high and low water, is nearly 50 feet, but during the highest floods, it has risen, at Cincinnati, to the height of 63 feet above low water mark.

---

* "In tracing the Ohio to its source, we must regard the Alleghany as its proper continuation, * * * * a boat may start with sufficient water, within seven miles of Lake Erie, in sight, sometimes, of the sails which whiten the approach to the harbor of Buffalo, and float securely down the Conewango, or Cassadaga, to the Alleghany, down the Alleghany to the Ohio, and thence uninterruptedly to the Gulf of Meixico."—*Ellet on the Mississippi and Ohio rivers*.

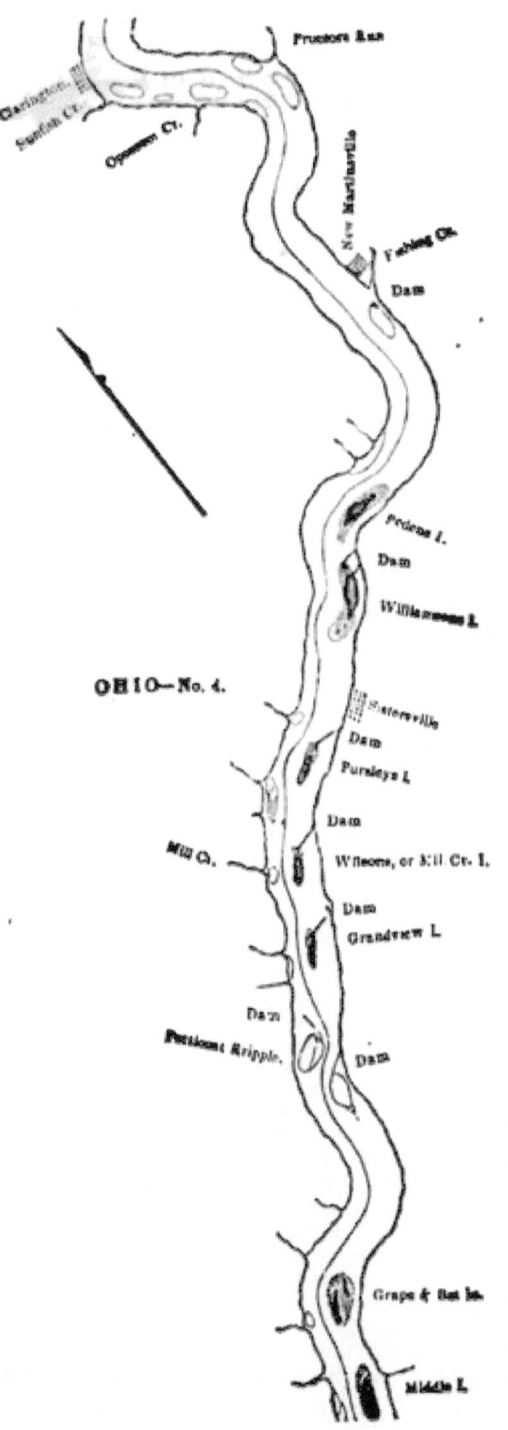

THE OHIO RIVER.

The Ohio is generally navigable for steamers of the largest class, from Pittsburg to its mouth, at all seasons, except for a short period during dry summer months, and sometimes a few weeks obstruction by ice, in severe winters. The smaller boats are never stopped running by low water.

Pittsburg, the principal city of Western Pennsylvania, is situated on a

PITTSBURG.

point formed by the junction of the Alleghany and Monongahela rivers. It is 251 miles west of Harrisburg, the capital of the State, and 357 miles west by north from Philadelphia. Perhaps its site is unrivaled in the world — surrounded by inexhaustible beds of iron, coal, &c., and with a navigation of about 50,000 miles, which gives it access to the richest and most fertile regions of the globe. Its early history is very interesting. The Governor of Canada (then under dominion of the French) having formed the design of connecting that province with Louisiana, by a line of defenses extending from the Lakes to the Mississippi, had established a post at the mouth of French creek, and was about to take possession of "the Forks," as the site of Pittsburg was then called. Gov. Dinwiddie, of Virginia, dispatched George Washington, in October, 1753, to demand of the French commander his designs. On his route, he stopped at "the Forks," and, thinking it a proper place for the erection of a fort, communicated it to the Governor. The following spring, the Virginia Ohio Company commenced erecting fortifications on it. While engaged in doing so, on the 17th of April, 1754, Monsieur de Contricœur, a French officer, arrived with 300 canoes, containing 1000 French and Indians, and 18 cannon, and compelled them to surrender. This was the commencement of the French and Indian wars, which continued 9 years. The French gave to the fort the name of Fort Duquesne, and occupied it until the 24th of November, 1758, when Gen. Forbes, of Pennsylvania, and Col. George Washington, having marched against them, they set fire to, and evacuated it. Gen. Forbes took possession the next day, and called it Fort Pitt, in honor of the Earl of Chatham. Little improvement was made until after the Revolution. In 1775, the number of houses did not exceed 30. In 1786, the first newspaper was printed here. After 1795, the city improved rapidly.

In 1801, James Berthone & Co., commenced the building of ships, and in 3 years, 5 or 6 ships and schooners were finished and sent to sea.

Pittsburg is now the great mart for the western part of New York, Virginia, and Pennsylvania. It is connected with Philadelphia and the Atlantic cities by the Pennsylvania Railroad, and, during the canal-boating season, by the Pennsylvania Canal for the carriage of heavy freight. The population of the city proper, is about 87,000. On the opposite side of the Alleghany, is Alleghany City, with a population of about 63,000, connected with Pittsburg by three bridges, a canal, and aqueduct. On the opposite side of the Monongahela, is Birmingham, also connected with the city by a splendid bridge. This place has a large number of manufactories, and is rapidly increasing. Adjoining it, is South Pittsburg. The district within 5 miles of the center of Pittsburg, embracing Alleghany city, Manchester, Birmingham, Sligo, Minersville, East Liberty, Scottsfield, South Pittsburg, &c., is estimated to contain a population of 175,000.

The city suffered very seriously in 1845, by one of the largest conflagrations that has been known in America. The fire broke out on the 11th of April, on the corner of Third and Market streets, and swept over a space of about fifty-six acres — twenty squares, and several parts of squares, consuming 1000 brick buildings,

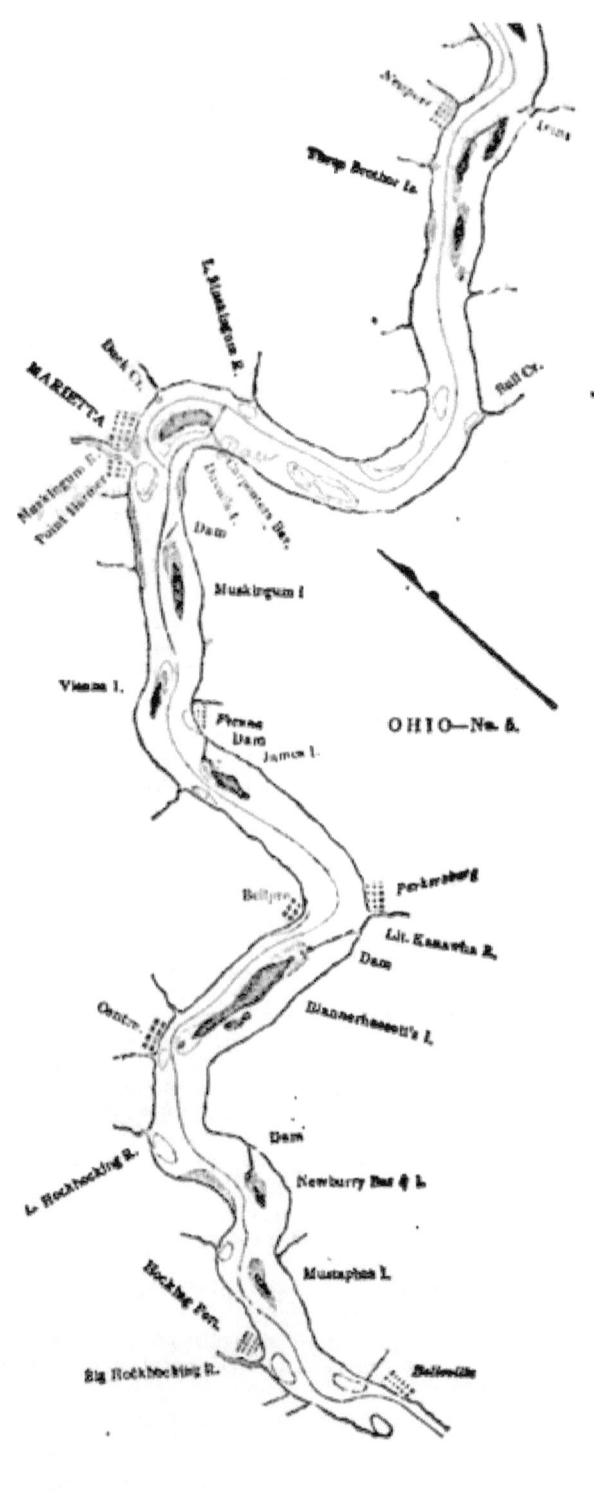

many of them running from street to street. This was the most wealthy and business portion of the city. Many large stores, foundries, manufactories, dwellings, churches, hotels, and the bridge across the Monongahela were entirely consumed. The destruction of property was estimated at between $9,000,000 and $10,000,000.

Pittsburg is a great manufacturing city. Iron casting, and iron mongery of every description, steam engines, cutlery, nails, glass, paper, wire, steamboat building, and many other branches, are carried on here to a large extent It has about 60 churches, a theological seminary, and a university, a merchants' exchange, a number of fine schools, a museum, a theater, and one of the finest court-houses in the United States. There is also an arsenal, consisting of an inclosed plot of 31 acres, containing a magazine of arms, a powder magazine, &c. The Western Penitentiary of the State is also located here. The city is supplied with clear and wholesome water, raised from the Alleghany by steam power, to a reservoir on Grant's hill, 395 feet above the level of the Ohio. The basin is 11 feet deep, and will contain 1,000,000 gallons. The water is conducted through the city in iron pipes.

Manchester, Pa., 2 miles below, is a flourishing manufacturing town. Population about 2000. The United States Marine Hospital is just below this.

Middleton, Pa., 9 miles below, is a small village in Alleghany co.

Sewickleyville, Pa., 2 miles below. Population about 1000. A seminary for boys is located here.

Economy, Pa., 6 miles below, is a settlement made by George Rapp, a German, who, with a number of his countrymen, of the religious order called Harmonists, first settled in Butler co., Pa. From thence, they all removed to the Wabash, and built the village of New Harmony. They numbered, then, about 800. New Harmony was purchased, in 1814, by Robert Owen, and Rapp and his followers established themselves at Economy. The Harmonists hold their property in common. They have a number of good mills here, and are noted for their industry and sobriety. The population of Economy is about 1400.

Mr. Rapp died in 1847, at a very advanced age. He was highly respected, and ably qualified for the station he occupied as the head of this community.

Baden, Pa., a small village, 4 miles below.

Freedom, Pa., is a small village, 2 miles below. Population about 600.

Rochester, Pa., 4 miles below, at the mouth of Beaver river. The Ohio and Pennsylvania Railroad passes along the bank of the Ohio, from this point to Pittsburg. Population about 1200.

Beaver, 1 mile below, in Beaver co., Pa., at the mouth of Beaver river, is a thriving town, possessing great water-power advantages, derived from the Falls of Beaver. A branch of the Ohio Canal extends from Akron, in Summit county, Ohio, to the Beaver division of the Pennsylvania Canal, near Newcastle, in Mercer county—length, 88 miles. The Beaver division of the Pennsylvania Canal runs from Beaver to the head of slack-water navigation on the Shenango—distance, 31 miles. Numerous mills and manufacturing establishments are in operation in and around Beaver, and several small villages are scattered along the river, within a short distance of it. Population about 2300.

Jacobsburg, Pa., opposite Beaver.

Georgetown, Pa., 14 miles below, and 1 mile above the Ohio line, is a small village. Population about 300.

Glasgow, Pa., opposite Georgetown. Here is the terminus of the Sandy and Beaver Canal.

Liverpool, 4 miles below, is a pleasant village in Columbiana co., O. Population about 2000. An extensive business is carried on here, in the manufacture of earthenware.

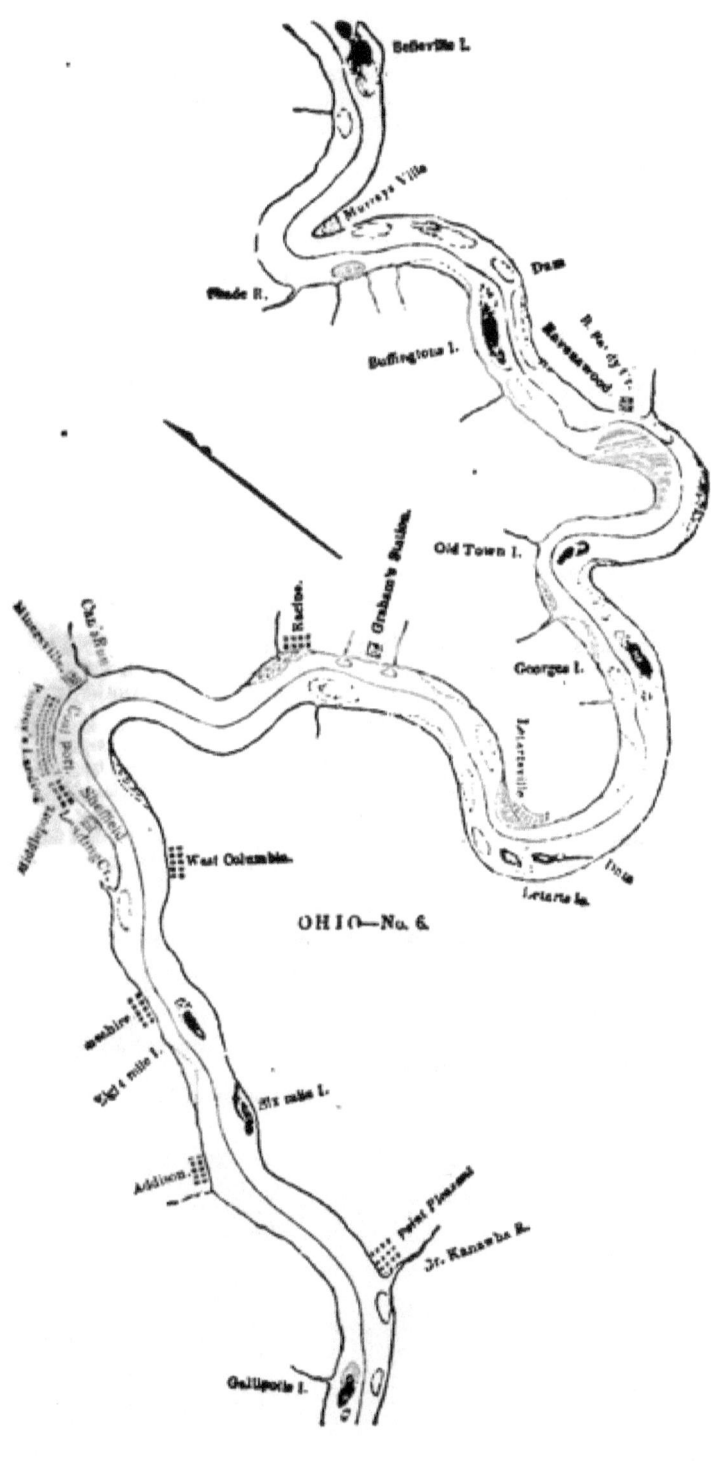

Wellsville, O., 4 miles below, in the same co., is the terminus of the Cleveland and Pittsburg Railroad. This town was laid out by Wm. Wells, in 1824, and now contains a population of about 2400. The landing for steamboats is good. It is an important point for the shipment of produce—the surrounding country being fine for agricultural purposes, and the county the best in Ohio for wool-growing.

Nearly opposite this place, the well-known desperate battle between Adam Poe, his brother, and a party of Indians, is said to have taken place; and 2 miles below, near the mouth of Great Yellow creek, the locality of the murder of the family of Logan, the Mingo Chief.

Elliottsville, Jefferson co., O., 8 miles below.

Newburg, O., 2 miles below, in the same co.

Steubenville, 9 miles below, is the county seat of Jefferson co., O. Fort Steuben was erected here in 1789, on the spot now occupied by the Female Seminary. It was guarded by a company of troops commanded by Col. Beattie. At the period of Wayne's victory it was deserted.

Steubenville is beautifully situated on an elevated plane, and contains a population of about 10,000, 12 churches, 5 public, and 4 select schools, 1 male academy, and a splendid female seminary. In the town and vicinity, there are a number of large flouring mills, a paper mill, 5 woolen factories, one of them manufacturing into cloth 60000 pounds of wool annually, 2 cotton, and 2 glass manufactories, 3 iron foundries, a steam saw-mill, 2 breweries, and several manufactories of copperas in the vicinity. In the neighboring country, much attention is paid to the rearing of Merino and other superior breeds of sheep. Through a great portion of this region, there are inexhaustible beds of stone-coal.

Three miles below Steubenville, was the former site of the old Mingo town, and residence of Logan, the celebrated Indian chief. It is now occupied as farms. The Pittsburg, Cincinnati and St. Louis Railroad (Panhandle route) crosses the river, on a fine bridge, at this point.

Wellsburg, 7 miles below, formerly called Charleston, is the county seat of Brooke co., Va., 373 miles from Richmond, the capital of the State. It was laid out in 1789, and is beautifully situated on an elevated bank of the river. It contains 6 churches, 2 white flint glass manufactories, 1 glass-cutting shop, 1 paper mill, 1 cotton factory, 5 large warehouses, 6 flouring mills, 1 woolen factory, 2 printing offices, 1 bank, and a population of about 3000. The manufacturing of earthen and stone ware is carried on here extensively. Extensive coal mines are worked in the vicinity.

Warrenton, sometimes called Warren, 7 miles below, in Jefferson co., O., is a small village, containing about 300 inhabitants.

Tiltonsville, O., 3 miles below, in Jefferson co.

Burlington, O., 4 miles below, in Belmont co.

Martinsville, 1 mile below, in the same co., is a flourishing village, containing 3 churches, and about 500 inhabitants.

Wheeling, 1 mile below, is the county seat of Ohio co., Va. It is 264 miles from Richmond, and 351 from Washington city. It lies on both sides of Wheeling creek, over which, there is a beautiful stone bridge. The city stands on a high bank of the river, surrounded by bold hills, in which abundance of stone-coal is found. It

WHEELING.

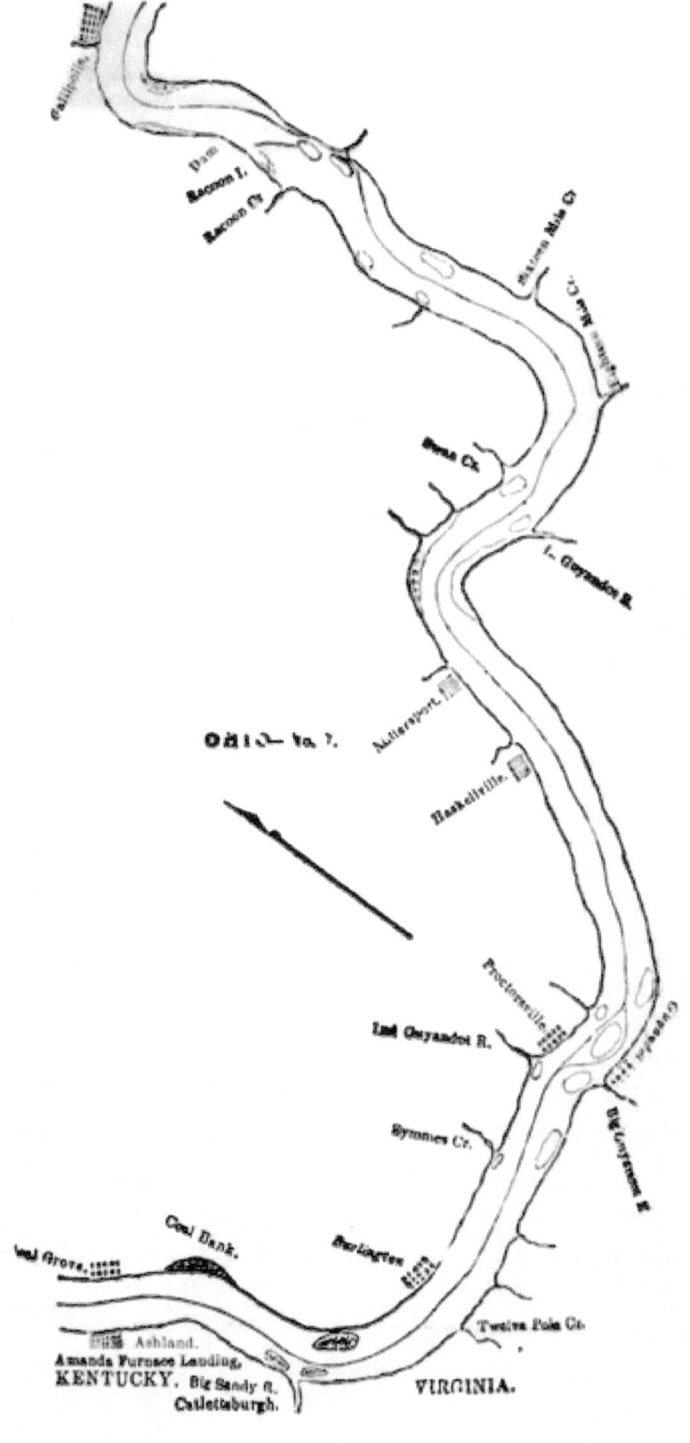

contains a population of about 14,000, has 14 churches, 2 academies, 3 banks, and a savings institution, a large number of stores and commission-houses, iron foundries, steam-engine factories, glass houses, woolen and cotton factories, paper mills, saw-mills, white and sheet lead and copperas factories, 6 or 8 printing offices, and many flourishing mills in its vicinity. A large number of steamboats are owned here. The National Road passes through Wheeling. The city is supplied with water from the river, raised by machinery.

Wheeling is the western terminus of the Baltimore and Ohio Railroad, also of the Hempfield Railroad, connecting with the Penn. R. R. at Greensburg, Pa.

The splendid wire suspension bridge, over the Ohio, at this place, built at a cost of over $200,000, was blown down during a gale, in May, 1854.* The following description of this bridge is from a former edition of the River Guide.

"The span is the longest in the world, being 1010 feet. It is 92 feet above low water mark, 21 feet wide, and supported by 12 wire cables, each 1380 feet long, and 4 inches in diameter, and each containing 572 strands of No. 10 wire. There is a carriage way of 17 feet, and 2 foot-paths, each 3½ feet wide. The towers on the Wheeling side are 153½ feet above low water mark, and 60 feet above the abutment on which it stands; on the other side they are 21 feet lower. This stupendous structure was built by a company of capitalists, who obtained a charter in 1847."

Fort Henry, at the mouth of Wheeling creek, the first settlement was formed here in 1769, by 3 brothers of the name of Zane, together with a small party of emigrants. The fort, however, was not built till 1774, and was at first called Fincastle · but in 1776, the name was changed to that of Henry, in honor of Patrick Henry, the eloquent and patriotic Governor of Virginia. During Dunmore's war it was a place of refuge for settlers.

Bridgeport, opposite Wheeling, in Belmont co., O., is a depot of considerable importance, from which goods are forwarded through that part of Ohio, by the National Road. It contains 1 church, several mills, and warehouses, a branch of the State Bank of Ohio, and a population of about 500.

Bellaire, O., 4 miles below, in Belmont co. This is the terminus of the *Central Ohio Railroad*. Population 4.000.

Mannyville, Va., 8 miles below, at the mouth of Little Grave creek.

Elizabethtown, Va., 1 mile below, is the county seat of Marshall co. It is situated on the upper side of Big Grave creek. On the lower side of the creek is MOUNDSVILLE. United, they contain a population of about 1200, a printing office, several stores, an academy, and a steam flouring mill. The Baltimore and Ohio Railroad passes through the place.

Big Grave Creek, affords some matter of curiosity to the traveler. A short distance up the creek is the largest Indian mound, perhaps, in the United States. It is between 30 and 40 rods in circumference at the base, and about 75 feet high. Its sides are covered with aged trees. The mound may be seen from steamboats passing along the river. Grave creek was settled in 1770 by Joseph Tomlinson, who, with a small party, emigrated from Maryland.

Opposite Grave creek, in Ohio, in 1790, stood Fort Dillies.

Steinerville, 8 miles below, is a small village in Belmont co., O., at the mouth of Captina creek. Near this place, a most bloody contest took place between the Americans and Indians, in May, 1794, known as the battle of Captina.

Clarington, 7 miles below, is a small village in Monroe co., O., at the mouth of Sunfish creek. Population about 400. The county is generally hilly, and the western part abounds in iron ore and coal. A large amount of tobacco is grown here.

---

* Rebuilt soon after.

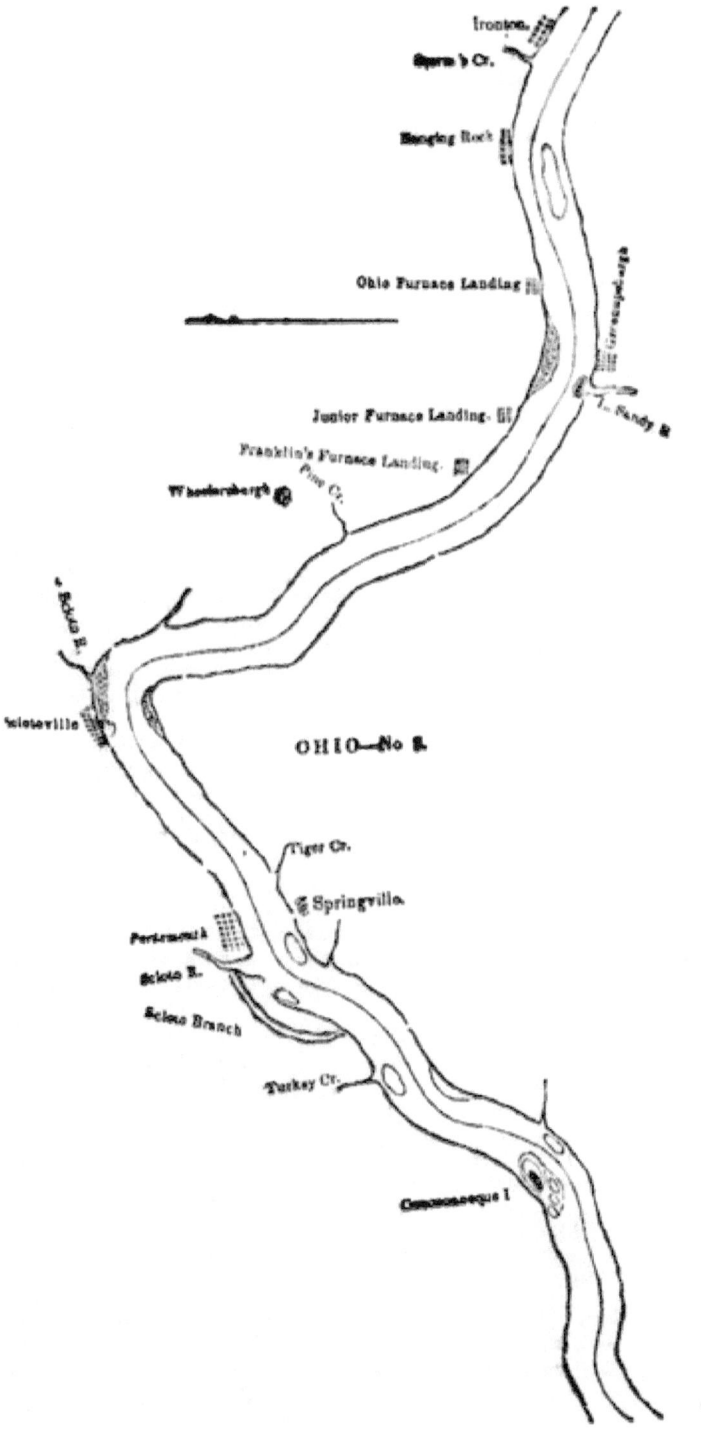

New Martinsville, capital of Wetzel co., Va., 8 miles below, at the mouth of Fishing creek, contains a court-house, a number of stores, and about 300 inhabitants.

Sistersville, Va., 9 miles below, in Tyler co. It has a good landing for steamboats, and is the terminus of several turnpike roads. Coal and iron are found near. Population about 1100.

Newport, 12 miles below, in Washington, co., O. Population about 2,000.

Marietta, 19 miles below, at the mouth of the Muskingum river, is the county seat of Washington co., O., and a place of considerable importance in the history of the State. Near this spot, on the right bank of the Muskingum, at its junction with the Ohio, the second military post in the State, was built in the autumn of 1785, by a party of troops, under the command of Major John Doughty. They erected a fort called Fort Harmar. On the 7th of April, 1788, a party of 47 men, under the direction of General Rufus Putnam, landed here, having been sent out by the Ohio Company to form a permanent settlement on its purchase. This was the first permanent settlement in Ohio. General St. Clair, who had been appointed Governor, not having arrived, temporary laws were formed for the government of the settlers, and published by nailing to a tree. Return Jonathan Meigs was appointed to execute them. Many of these settlers were men of high character; some of them had served in the severe toils of the revolution. General Washington said of them, "There never were men better calculated to promote the welfare of such a community." On the 2d of July, a meeting was called on the bank of the Muskingum, and the name of Marietta given to the place, in honor of Maria Antoinette, Arch-Duchess of Austria. On the 2d of September, the first court was organized with great solemnity, at Campus Martius Hall, (as the stockade was called,) Rufus Putnam and Benjamin Tupper, judges. This settlement experienced great privations and trials, during its early history, but improved rapidly.

Marietta is built on a level plot of ground, and part of it is liable to be overflowed by the floods of the Ohio. It contains 8 churches, 2 academies, a college, 2 public libraries, 1 bank, 2 printing offices, and a number of extensive manufacturing establishments. Population about 5500.

Marietta is the terminus of the *Marietta and Cincinnati Railroad*.

Harmar, is on the south side of the Muskingum, opposite Marietta. It is favorably situated for manufacturing purposes, having the double advantage of 2 rivers and the dam of the Muskingum. Steamboat building is carried on to a considerable extent, and there are several mills, and manufactories of different kinds. Harmar has a fine large hotel, a male and female academy, and about 1600 inhabitants.

Muskingum River, (*See page* 124.)

Vienna, Va., 6 miles below Marietta, nearly opposite an island of the same name.

Parkersburg, 7 miles below, is the county seat of Wood co., Va., and is at the mouth of Little Kanawha river. It is a place of considerable business, and contains 4 churches, 1 printing office, 1 bank, 4 steam mills, 2 tanneries, and 1 carding factory. Population nearly 4,000. A splendid iron bridge, built by the Baltimore and Ohio Railroad Co., crosses the river at this point, connecting that road with the Cincinnati and Marietta Railroad, at Belpre, O.

Little Kanawha River, rises in Braxon co., Va., and after a course of 150 miles, empties into the Ohio at Parkersburg. Extensive veins of stone coal, and a number of salt springs, are in the country through which it flows. It is navigable but a few miles.

Belpre, opposite Parkersburg, in Washington co., O. Population 2,000.

Blannerhassett's Island, 2 miles below, is celebrated as having been the residence of Herman Blannerhasset, an Irish emigrant of distinction, who,

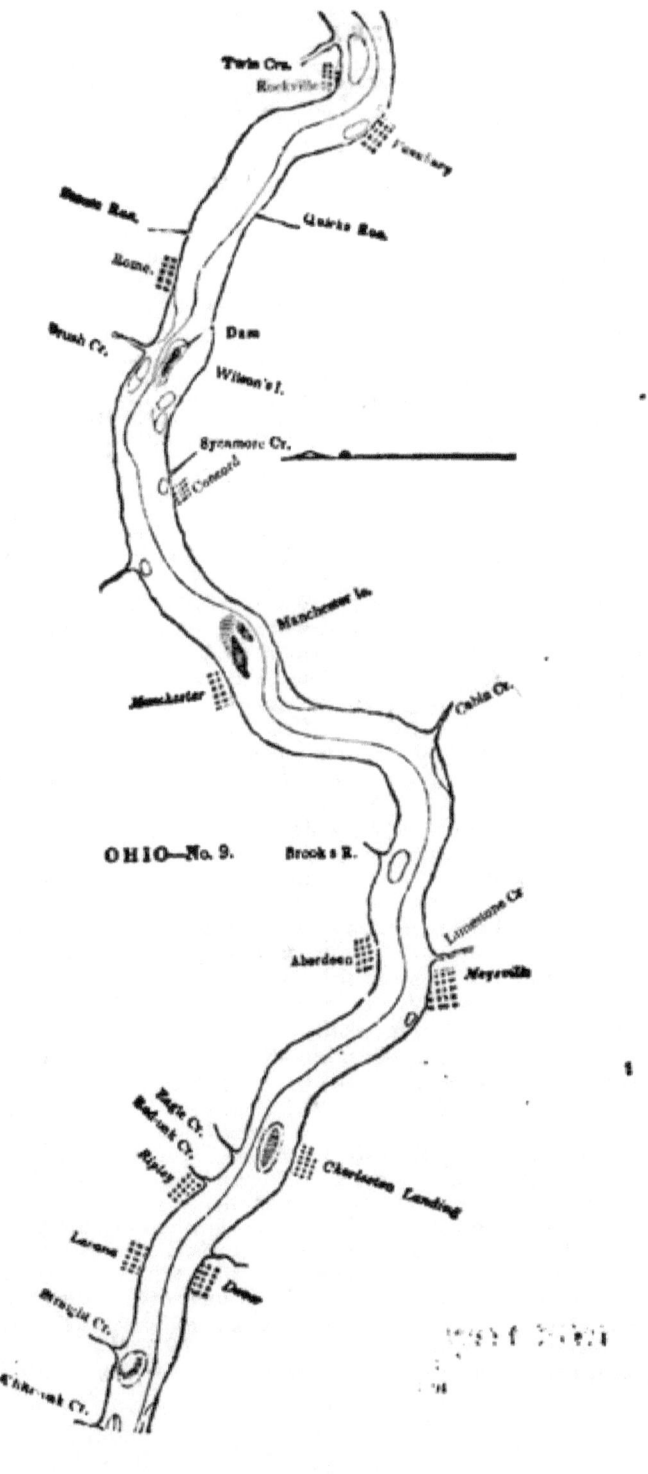

about the year 1798, commenced improving it, and built a splendid mansion. His lady was a highly accomplished woman, and his house was the resort of the most literary and refined society. When Aaron Burr was projecting his famous expedition, he called on Blannerhasset, induced him to join in the conspiracy, and embark all his wealth in the scheme. They were detected, arrested, and tried for treason. Although not convicted, Blannerhasset was ruined. His splendid mansion was deserted and went to decay, and his pleasure grounds overrun with brush and weeds.

Centre, O., is a small village, nearly opposite the foot of the island.

Troy, or Hockingsport, 12 miles below, in Athens co., O., is a small village, at the mouth of the Hockhocking river. Population about 850.

The Hockhocking River, rises in Fairfield co., O., winds through a hilly country about 80 miles, and enters the Ohio river at Troy. The name of the river is that given to it by the Delaware Indians, and signifies a *bottle*.

This river is navigable for small crafts to Athens, the county seat. 7 miles from Lancaster, it falls over a ledge of rocks, about 40 feet perpendicular. Above the falls it resembles a bottle in shape, which probably gave rise to the name. The whole country along it is full of wild and picturesque scenery. Numerous ancient mounds and fortifications, are found north of Athens, some of them built of stone—differing entirely from any found in the vicinity. Some of them are of an extraordinary size; in one was found a thousand perch of stone, out of which, a dam was constructed across the river. At Athens there is a flourishing university endowed with 2 townships of land.

Belleville, 4 miles below Troy, in Wood co., Va., at the mouth of Lee's creek, was settled in 1785, by a party of emigrants from Pittsburgh, under the direction of Joseph Wood, Esq. In 1786, extensive blockhouses, surrounded by pickets, were erected, to prevent the incursions of the Indians, from whom the settlers suffered severely. It was the scene of many tragical events.

Murraysville, 5 miles below, in Jackson co., Va. The business of steamboat building is carried on here to some extent.

Shade River, 1 mile below, on the Ohio side, is a small stream which empties in the Ohio here. Its mouth was formerly called the "Devil's Hole." This was the point at which the Scioto Indians usually crossed the Ohio, after their predatory incursions into Virginia.

Ravenswood, 11 miles below, in Jackson co., Va., has a population of about 350, 2 churches, 2 school houses, a number of stores, and a large saw and grist mill. The country is hilly but generally very productive, and is finely adapted for grazing, and many sheep and cattle are raised here.

Letartsville, 23 miles below, is a small town in Meigs co., O. It is situated just at the falls, and at the foot of the Island bearing that name.

Graham's Station, 6 miles below, in Meigs co., O., a small place containing about 150 inhabitants.

Racine, O., 1 mile below, is a small village.

Minersville, O., 6 miles below, immediately above Pomeroy. *pop 1,000*

Pomeroy, 1 mile below, the county seat of Meigs co., O., is a flourishing town. It was settled in 1816, and the coal mines opened in 1832. In 1841, Pomeroy was made the county seat. It is situated on a narrow strip of land, running some distance along the river. Immediately back of it is a rough, precipitous hill, and the country in the interior is wild and romantic. It abounds with stone coal of a good quality, and large quantities are furnished to steamboats and shipped to points below. In 1851, a company was formed here for the manufacture of salt, and an extensive business is now carried on in that article. There are a number of large manufactories, foundries, mills, &c., established here, employing a heavy capital and a large number of hands. Population 5800.

Coalport, 1 mile below, is the principal mining point of the Pomeroy company. Railways are here built for the purpose of running down the coal from the mines to boats in the river.

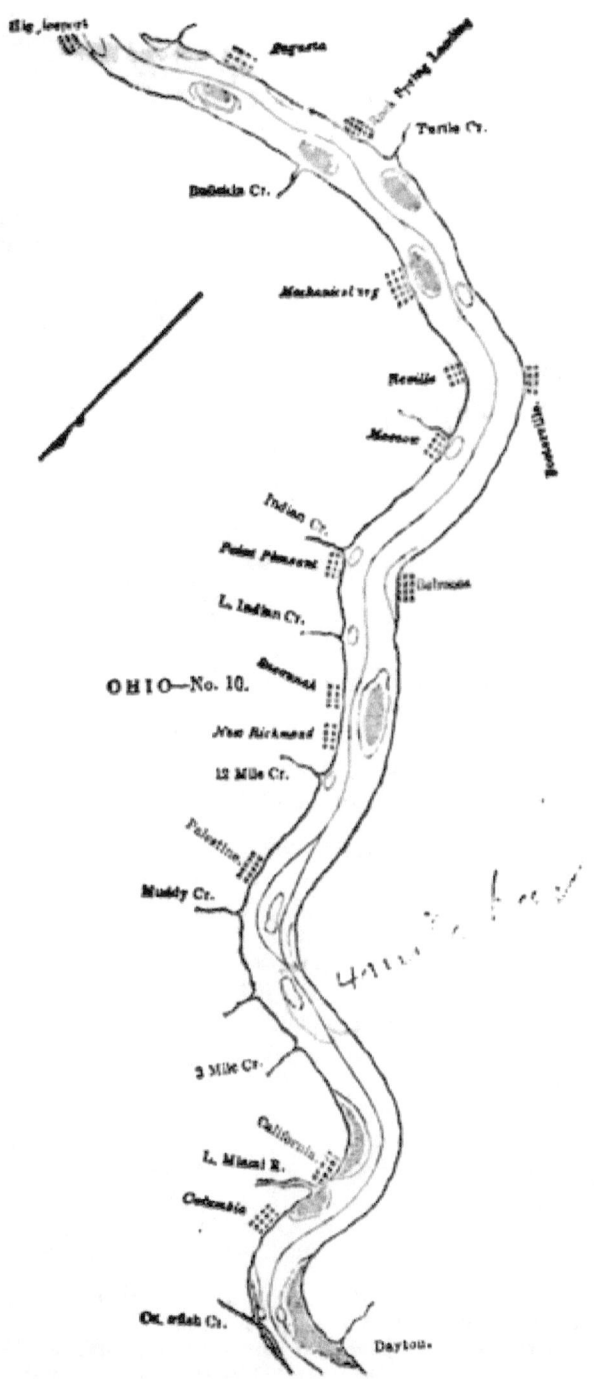

OHIO—No. 10.

Middleport, 1 mile below Coalport. These towns owe their increase to the coal trade, which is becoming more extensive every year.

Sheffield adjoins Middleport, and is a flourishing village.

West Columbia, 1 mile below, in Mason co., Va., is a thriving village. The manufacturing of salt is carried on here to considerable extent.

Cheshire, 3 miles below, in Gallia co., O.

Addison, O., 3 miles below, in same co.

Point Pleasant, 4 miles below, at the mouth of the Great Kanawha river, is the county seat of Mason co., Va. It is the site of the bloodiest battle ever fought with the Indians in Virginia—the "battle of Point Pleasant," on the 10th of October, 1774, when about 1100 Americans were attacked by a large body of Indian warriors, comprising the flower of the Shawanee, Delaware, Mingo, Wyandotte, and Cuyahoga tribes, led on by that famous warrior, Cornstalk. The battle continued all day, when the Indians finding themselves about to be completely surrounded, retreated across the Ohio, to their towns on the Scioto. Point Pleasant contains 2 churches, several stores, a court-house, 2 mills, 2 tanneries, and about 600 inhabitants.

The Great Kanawha River, is the principal stream of Western Virginia. It rises in the Alleghany mountains, and, after winding through a highly picturesque and mountainous region, enters the Ohio at Point Pleasant. It is navigable for small steamboats, to the Kanawha Salines—a distance of 60 miles from its mouth—where are the most extensive salines in the western country. The quantity of salt manufactured annually is about three millions of bushels.

The scenery along the Kanawha is unsurpassed by any in the west. From the mouth of the river to Charleston, the county seat of Kanawha county, a distance of 55 miles; it is pleasingly variegated by fertile fields and rough mountain landscapes. Above the salines, the river is broken by falls, and the country becomes more mountainous. In the neighborhood of the falls are many places of great interest. Among others, the "Hawk's Nest," or, as it has sometimes been called, "Marshall's Pillar," a bold projecting mountain peak, that rises to the height of 1000 feet above the river.

Gallipolis, 4 miles below, is the county seat of Gallia co., O. It is pleasantly situated on a high bank. It was originally settled in 1791, by a party of French emigrants. It is a forwarding point for a large amount of produce. Population about 3700.

Big Racoon Creek, enters the Ohio from Gallia co., 5 miles below Gallipolis.

Blandenburg, O., 6 miles below, in same co., is a small village.

Millersport, 14 miles below, is a small village in Lawrence co., O. Population about 150.

Haskellville, O., a small village, 3 miles below, in same co.

Guyandotte, 10 miles below, in Cabell co., Va., at the mouth of Guyandotte river, is the most important point of steamboat embarkation in Western Virginia, except Wheeling. The great stage route along the Kanawha to Winchester commences here. It is a flourishing place. Population about 2200.

Guyandotte River, rises in Logan co., Va. It is a small stream.

Proctorsville, a small village in Ohio, nearly opposite Guyandotte.

Burlington, 8 miles below, is the county seat of Lawrence co., O. Population about 800.

The country around Burlington, abounds in iron ore. There are a large number of furnaces in operation. It is situated in the most southern extremity of the State.

Big Sandy River, enters the Ohio, 4 miles below Burlington, and is the boundary between Ky., and Va. It is formed by the junction of the *east and west forks* at *Louisa*, Lawrence co., Ky., about 50 miles from its mouth. The east fork rises in Tazewell co., Va.; the west fork in Russell co., Va. The east branch is some 150 miles in length. The Big Sandy, and branches, flow through very extensive beds of bituminous coal, from which large quantities are annually mined and shipped to towns below, on the Ohio. It is navigable for small steamers during high water, about 100 miles.

Catlettsburg, at the mouth of the Big Sandy river, in Boyd co., Ky., forms the extreme north-eastern point of the State.

Coal Grove, Lawrence co., O., a small village, 4 miles below.

Ashland, Boyd co., Ky., nearly opposite Coal Grove.

Ironton, Lawrence co., O., 5 miles below, was commenced in June, 1849, by the "OHIO IRON AND COAL COMPANY." It is located on a bank of the river, above the highest freshets, in the midst of the richest iron and coal region of Ohio and Kentucky. A large

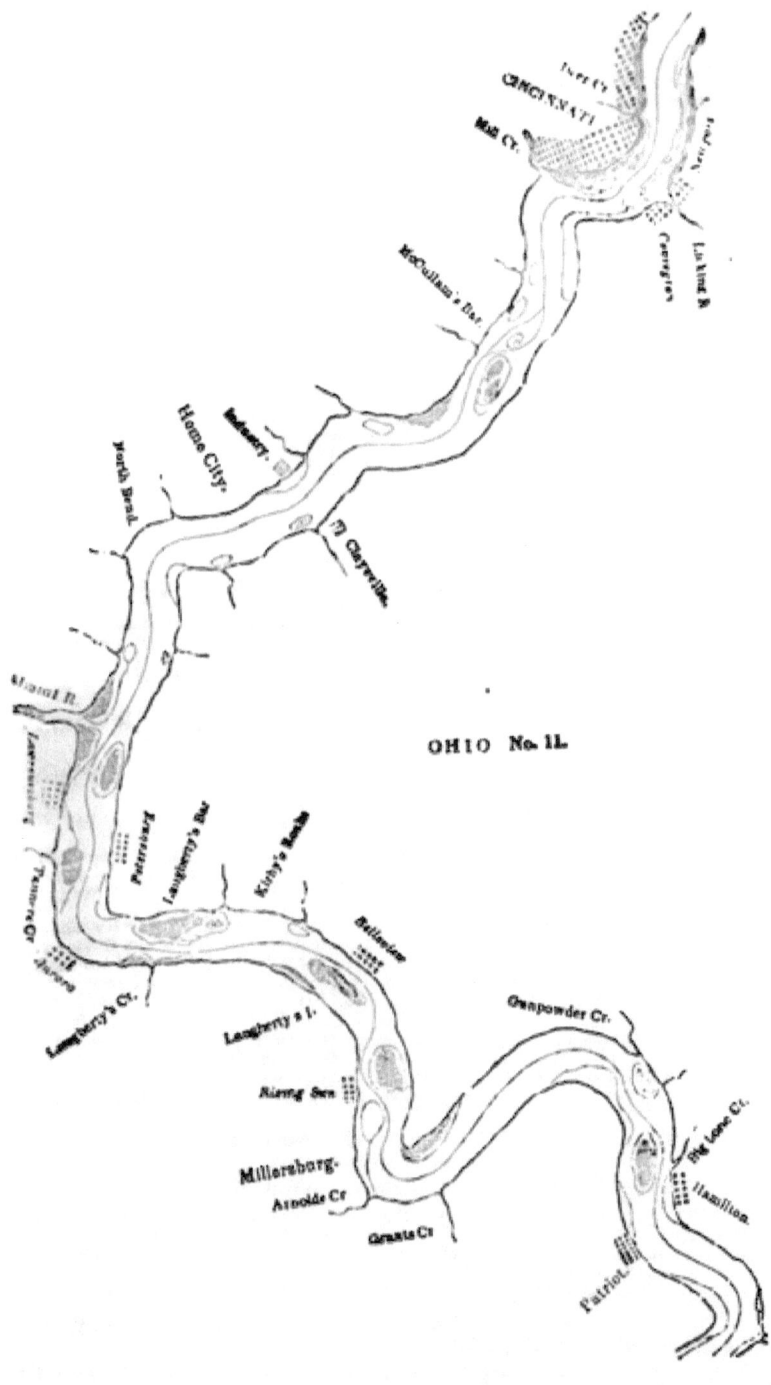

number of blast furnaces are in the vicinity. It is connected by the Iron Railroad with the mineral regions on the north. Steam engines, locomotives, railway cars, machinery, stoves, hollow ware, axes, &c., are manufactured extensively. There are, also, foundries, rolling mills, planing mills, &c. Population about 6000.

Hanging Rock, 4 miles below, in Lawrence co., O., derives its name from a cliff of rocks about 400 feet high, in the rear of the town. It is the principal shipping point for the iron manufactured in that region. The different mines in the vicinity are connected with this point by means of Railroads. Population about 2000.

Greenupsburgh, 6 miles below, is the county seat of Greenup, co., Ky. It is situated at the mouth of Little Sandy river. Population 1,000.

Wheelersburgh, 8 miles below, in Scioto co., O., is a flourishing town, with a population of 1,050.

Sciotoville, O., a small village, 3 miles below, in Scioto co.

Portsmouth, 9 miles below, county seat of Scioto co., is situated on a high bank, on the upper side of the mouth of the Scioto river, and at the terminus of the Ohio Canal. It is 90 miles south of Columbus, the capital of the State. Portsmouth is a point of considerable importance. A vast deal of business is transacted here, and the town is in a flourishing condition. It contains 8 or 10 churches, a fine court-house, a bank, a number of stores, rolling, flour, and oil mills, carding machine, forge, nail factory, and several foundries, and 4 printing offices. Iron ore, coal, and fine building stone, are abundant in the vicinity. The population is about 10,500 The Scioto and Hocking Valley Railroad terminates here.

Scioto River, (*See page 124.*)

Springville, Greenup co., Ky., opposite Portsmouth, contains a foundry, several manufactories, and a population of about 600. This county abounds in fine beds of iron ore. There are 10 blast furnaces in operation in it.

Alexandria, 3 miles below, in Scioto co., O., is a small village.

Bradford, 3 miles below, in same co.

Rockville, 11 miles below, in Adams co., O., is a small village. It has mills for sawing stone, quarried in the vicinity.

Vanceburg, 2 miles below, in Lewis co., Ky., is a small village. Pop. 200.

Rome, 7 miles below, in Adams co., O., is a small place.

Concord, 7 miles below, a small village in Lewis co., Ky. Pop. about 200.

Manchester, 7 miles below, a thriving village in Adams co., O., contains several flouring mills, and factories ; population about 600. The first settlement within the Virginia military district was made at this point, in 1795, by Gen. Nathaniel Massie.

Maysville, 12 miles below, county seat of Mason co., Ky. It was for many years known as "Limestone," from the creek of that name, which here enters the Ohio. It was settled in 1784, under the auspices of Simon Kenton. Col. Daniel Boone resided here in 1786. Maysville stands on a high bank, and presents quite a beautiful appearance from the river. It is surrounded by a range of bold and verdant highlands. It is the depot for goods and produce in the northeastern part of the State, and is the largest hemp market in the United States. Maysville was incorporated in 1833. It is a compactly built city, containing a number of fine edifices ; a handsome city-hall, a substantial stone jail, 8 or 9 churches, a hospital, 2 banks, 2 large seminaries, public and private schools, a number of printing offices, 2 steam cotton factories, 1 bagging factory, a wool-carding factory, 2 foundries, 5 rope walks, 2 steam saw mills, a large flouring mill, and divers other factories ; a large number of stores, and commission houses, pork-houses, lumber yards, &c. Population about 7000.

Aberdeen, on the opposite side of the river from Maysville, in Brown co., O., is a thriving village, containing a population of about 900.

Charleston, 7 miles below, in Mason co., Ky., is a small village.

Ripley, 2 miles below, in Brown co., O., is a flourishing business town. It was laid out in 1812, and was called Staunton ; it was changed to Ripley in honor of Gen. Ripley, a military officer, highly esteemed by the settlers at this place It contains 1 bank, 6 churches, a newspaper printing office, and about 2000 inhabitants.

Lavana, 2 miles below, is a small village in the same co.

Dover, opposite Lavana, in Mason co., Ky., is a thriving village, in the center of the tobacco region. Population 650.

Higginsport, 4 miles below, in Brown co., O., is a flourishing village. Population about 650.

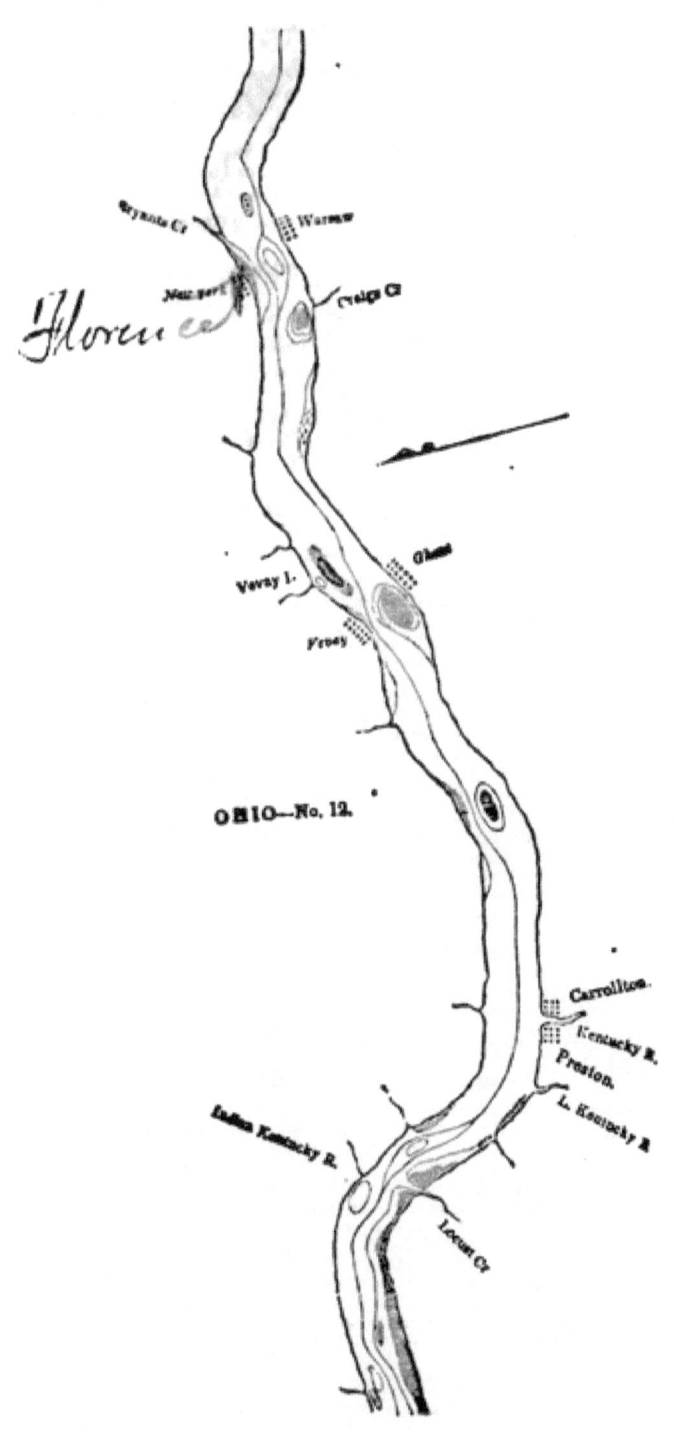

THE OHIO RIVER.

Augusta, 4 miles below, in Bracken co., Ky., is handsomely situated. There have been numerous human bones excavated from the earth in Augusta, proving it to have been a burial place in times long since gone by. A resident of this town mentions having found 110 skeletons in digging a cellar 60 by 70 feet.

Augusta contains about 1200 inhabitants. Augusta college was founded in 1822, by the Methodist Episcopal Church, being the first college ever instituted by that Church.

Rockspring, Ky., is a landing point, 4 miles below.

Mechanicsburgh, 4 miles below, is a small village in Clermont co., O. Population about 200.

Neville, 3 miles below, is a village of considerable enterprise, in the same co. Population 350.

Fosterville, a small village opposite Neville, in Ky.

Moscow, O., 2 miles below Neville. Population about 300.

Point Pleasant, 3 miles below, a village in Clermont co. Population 200. There are 2 large pork-packing establishments here.

Belmont, opposite Point Pleasant, in Ky., is a small village.

New Richmond, 5 miles below, in Clermont co., O., is a thriving business town, and the largest and most important one in the county. It contains about 2500 inhabitants.

Palestine, 4 miles below, in the same co., is a place of considerable business. There is an extensive brick-yard here. The brick are made by machinery and shipped to Cincinnati by flat-boats. Population about 350.

California, Hamilton co., O., is a small village near the mouth of the Little Miami.

The Little Miami River enters the Ohio, about 15 miles below New Richmond, and 6 miles above Cincinnati. It flows through a very fertile country, adorned with fine farms. There are upwards of 50 mill-seats on its banks. In the neighborhood of Yellow Springs, about 70 miles from its mouth, is a place called "Clifton," which affords some of the most beautiful scenery in the west. Here the river, in the distance of a few miles, falls 200 feet. These falls have cut a narrow channel to a great depth, through solid rocks of limestone. The banks are covered with hemlock, cedar, and other evergreens. In some places, the stream is so narrow that a person can leap from bank to bank. The Little Miami abounds in excellent fish. Toward the mouth of the stream, the land bordering on it is low, and is known by the name of the "*Miami Bottoms*," which are exceedingly fertile, subject to overflow, during *floods* in the Ohio, by "*back water*." It is not navigable.

Columbia, 2 miles below, was originally designed for the great emporium of the west. It was laid out by Major Benjamin Stites, in 1780, and a plat extends for more than a mile along the Ohio, reaching back about three-fourths of a mile. The site not being found sufficiently high above the floods of the river, the project of a city was abandoned. The first church in Ohio was built here.

Dayton, Ky., opposite the upper part of Cincinnati; formerly Jamestown and Brooklyn. Population about 2,000.

Cincinnati, the county seat of Hamilton co., and the largest city in the Western States, stands on the north bank of the Ohio river, directly opposite the mouth of Licking river, in N. Lat. 39° 6' 30", and west Long. from Washington, 7° 24' 45". It is 476 miles by the river, from Pittsburg, 142 above Louisville, 500 from Washington City, 531 above the mouth of the Ohio, and 1517 from New Orleans. It is situated in a beautiful valley of about 12 miles in circumference, surrounded by hills. This valley is divided nearly in the center by the Ohio. The first settlement was made here on the 24th of December, 1788, by a party of men sent out under Matthias Denman, Col. Israel Ludlow, and Robert Patterson, to improve a portion of the purchase made by Hon. John Cleves Symmes. This purchase embraced a tract of 311,682 acres in the southwest quarter of the State, lying between the Great and Little Miami rivers. It extends along the Ohio river a distance of 27 miles. One square mile in each township was reserved for the use of schools, and section 29 in each township for the support of religious societies.

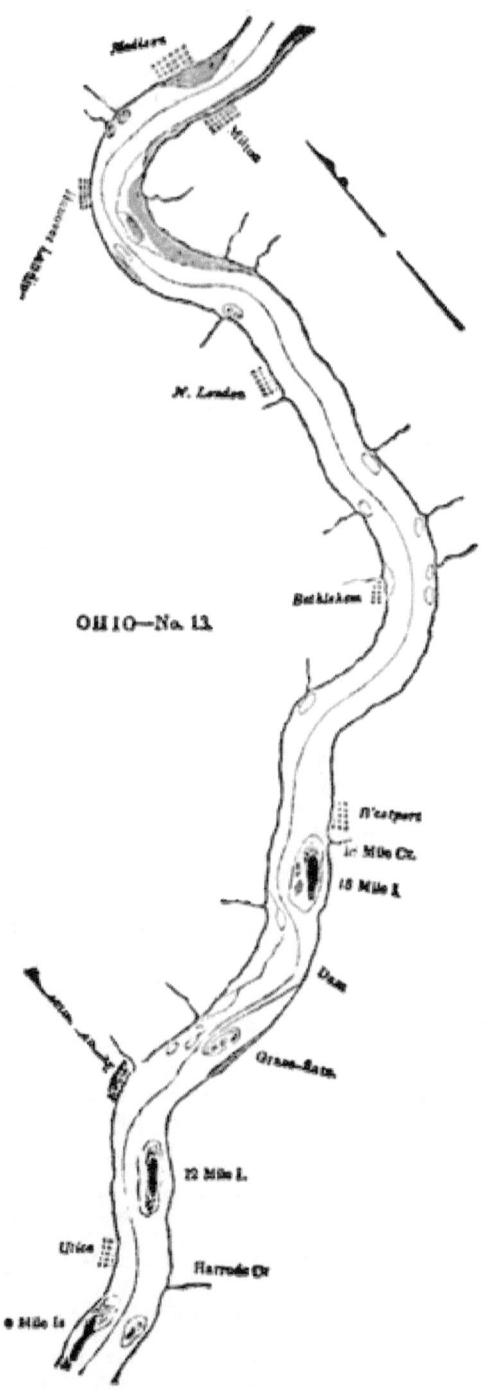

The party landed opposite the mouth of the Licking, and laid out a town called Losanti-ville. This name was, however, abandoned in a short time, and the name of Cincinnati given to it. In February 1789, a party under the immediate direction of Judge Symmes landed at what is now called North Bend, 15 miles below Cincinnati, and there laid out what was intended to be a large city, called Symmes. In March, a detachment of soldiers arrived at the Bend, to protect the settlers. There now existed considerable rivalry between the three places—Columbia, Cincinnati, and North Bend, as to which would eventually become the chief seat of business. This rivalry was terminated in favor of Cincinnati, by the arrival of Major Doughty, from Fort Harmar, who built *Fort Washington*, to which, the troops from the Bend, were subsequently removed. In January 1790, Gen. Arthur St Clair organized Hamilton county. In the same year, Gen. Harmar marched from Fort Washington against the Indians. In the next year, Gen. St. Clair started from the same place on his ill-fated expedition. On his return, Major Ziegler was appointed to the command of the Fort, and, in a short time after, was succeeded by Col. Wilkinson, who was, in 1794, succeeded by Capt. William Henry Harrison, (afterward President of the United States,) who retained it till 1793.

In 1792, the first church was erected. Rev. James Kemper was the first pastor of it, and Dr. Joshua L. Wilson, the second, who filled that station upward of 40 years, until his death, which took place in 1847. In 1793, William Maxwell established the first paper north of the Ohio river, at Cincinnati, called the "Sentinel of the Nortwestern Territory." On the 11th of January, 1794, two keel-boats, with bullet-proof covers and port-holes, and provided with cannon and small arms, sailed from Cincinnati to Pittsburg, each making a trip once in four weeks. During this period the town progressed but slowly.

The population in 1795, was about 500 ; in 1800, 750 ; in 1810, 2540. From 1800 to 1812, it progressed pretty rapidly, and considerable trade was carried on with New Orleans, in keel-boats, which returned, laden with foreign goods. The passage to New Orleans, occupied 25 days, and the return, 65. In 1819, it was incorporated as a city, and in 1820, contained a population of 10,000 ; in 1830, 24,831 ; in 1840, 46,338 ; in 1847, 90,000 ; in 1850, 115,438 ; in 1870, 220,000.

The city now occupies every portion of that part of the valley lying north of the Ohio river. It is laid out with considerable regard to regularity ; the streets in the center of the city being broad, and intersecting each other at right angles. Many of the hills surrounding the city are adorned by stately and elegant mansions, with ornamental grounds attached ; while some of them are yet covered with groves of ancient forest trees.

In point of commercial importance, Cincinnati occupies a front rank in the West. The numerous railroads which center here, and the many steamers on the river, connect the city with all the available points of importance in the country. Foreign importation and exportation are both extensively done. Pork packing is one of the most extensive branches of business in the city, and the manufacture of tobacco and cigars is largely carried on.

Cincinnati is the center of many extensive railway lines ; the ones having their termini here are : the Little Miami and Columbus and Xenia, connecting with many important roads in various directions, (New York, Philadelphia, Baltimore, Washington, etc.) The Cincinnati, Hamilton and Dayton, having also many important connections, east, north, and north-west. The Ohio and Mississippi, The Indianapolis and Cincinnati, The Marietta and Cincinnati, and the Covington and Lexington, with lines penetrating the Southern States ; the Louisville, Cincinnati and Lexington, (Short Line). Many extensive lines, doing a vast amount of business, enter the city over these roads, as the Hamilton, Eaton and Richmond ; Atlantic and Great Western, the Erie Railroad, the Cincinnati and Muskingum Valley Railroad, the Cleveland and Columbus, the Baltimore and Ohio, the New York Central, the Pennsylvania Central, etc., etc.

The Miami Canal, extending to Lake Erie at Toledo, has its terminus here.

Manufacturing is entered into here with great energy, and employs a vast amount of capital, ranking, in amount annually produced and in capital invested, the third city in the Union. Numerous mills and factories are in operation, besides founderies, planing mills, saw mills, rolling mills, flour mills, type founderies, machine shops, distilleries, etc. Nearly all kinds of machinery is driven by steam. Steamboat building is an extensive and important branch of industry.

The Fire Department of Cincinnati is second to none in the Union in point of efficiency ; steam fire engines are employed, and the pay system adopted. The Fire Alarm Telegraph is in use, by means of which all the fire bells of the city are rung simultaneously.

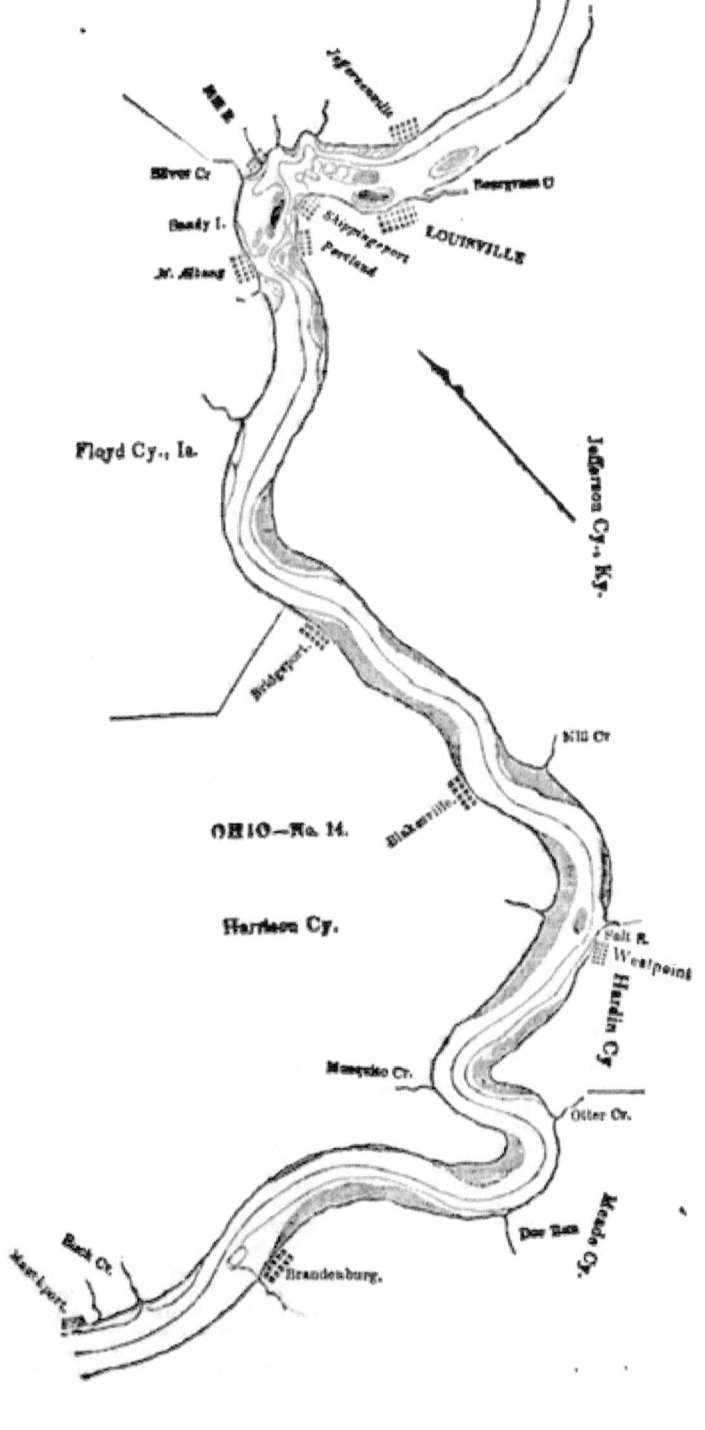

The Public Buildings of Cincinnati are numerous, and many of them handsome specimens of architecture.

The *Cincinnati Observatory* was built by public contribution, and is a fine, stone building situated on a beautiful hill to the east of the city, called Mount Adams, in honor of the late ex-president, who officiated on the occasion of laying the corner-stone, on the 9th of November, 1843. The telescope is from the manufactory of Mentz & Mahler, of Munich. It is an excellent instrument, of fine finish and vast power. Its cost was $10,000.

The following are noticeable for their prominence and fine architectural display: Cincinnati Hospital; Mechanics' Institute Building; Cincinnati College edifice, in which is located the Young Men's Mercantile Library Association; the Hamilton county Court-house; the Custom-house and Post Office building; the Masonic Temple; the Ohio Medical College; the Wesleyan Female College; St. Xavier's College; the Woodward and Hughes' High Schools; the Public Library Building; the House of Refuge; the City Work-house, and, just beyond the city limits, the Longview Lunatic Asylum, etc., etc.

The Churches of the city are numerous and handsome. The following are among the most conspicuous, viz: St. Paul's (Methodist Episcopal), St. Peter's Cathedral, the Central Christian Church, the Jewish Synagogue, etc. There are many private schools and seminaries, which hold a prominent place in the esteem of the citizens; but there are none which are looked on with so much pride as the COMMON or DISTRICT SCHOOLS. The city is divided into school districts, each having a school-house capable of accomodating from 700 to 1,200 pupils.

The Water-works of Cincinnati is an object of some interest. The water is forced, by means of powerful steam engines, from the river on to a hill, about 50 rods distant, and near 200 feet above the level of the lowest part of the city; it is then conducted, by means of iron pipes, through the city; thus affording a full supply of excellent water to every inhabitant.

The city is lighted with gas by the Cincinnati Gas Light and Coke Company.

There are several fine parks: Lincoln Park, Washington Park, etc. The largest—Eden Park—overlooking the river, contains 160 acres. In it is a large reservoir for the water-works, covering 14 acres.

About 6 miles from the Custom-house, to the north-west of the city, is *Spring Grove Cemetery*. It is a beautiful place, well laid out and adorned with shade trees and shrubbery, and comprising about 443 acres.

The longest wire suspension bridge in the world spans the Ohio between Cincinnati and Covington. Its length, including approaches, is 2,252 feet. Height above low water mark 100 feet. Circumference of cables 3 feet. Total cost, $2,000,000. There is also a bridge across the Ohio between Cincinnati and Newport. It accommodates foot passengers and wagons in addition to the railroad for which it was constructed especially.

Newport, on the south bank of the Ohio river, at the mouth of Licking river, opposite Cincinnati, in Campbell co., Ky. Newport is rapidly increasing in population and wealth. The town contains a number of churches, several schools, a large number of stores, mills, factories, &c. Population about 10,000.

At the mouth of Licking is an old United States' recruiting station, the buildings belonging to the station were, some years since, rebuilt in a neat and handsome manner.

A steam ferry plies from Cincinnati every few minutes in the day. A beautiful wire suspension bridge, across the Licking, connects Newport with Covington.

Licking River.—This is a very remarkable stream, and with but little expense could be made of immense value to the State. It is usually from 50 to 100 yards wide, with high steep banks, and in many places, even in low water, is more than 30 feet deep. The average depth for 60 miles above its mouth, during two-thirds of the year, except on the ripples, will no doubt exceed 6 feet. It is generally muddy, with but very little current. The shores are covered with large forest trees, whose gigantic limbs almost touch each other. The State commenced some years since to improve, by means of locks,

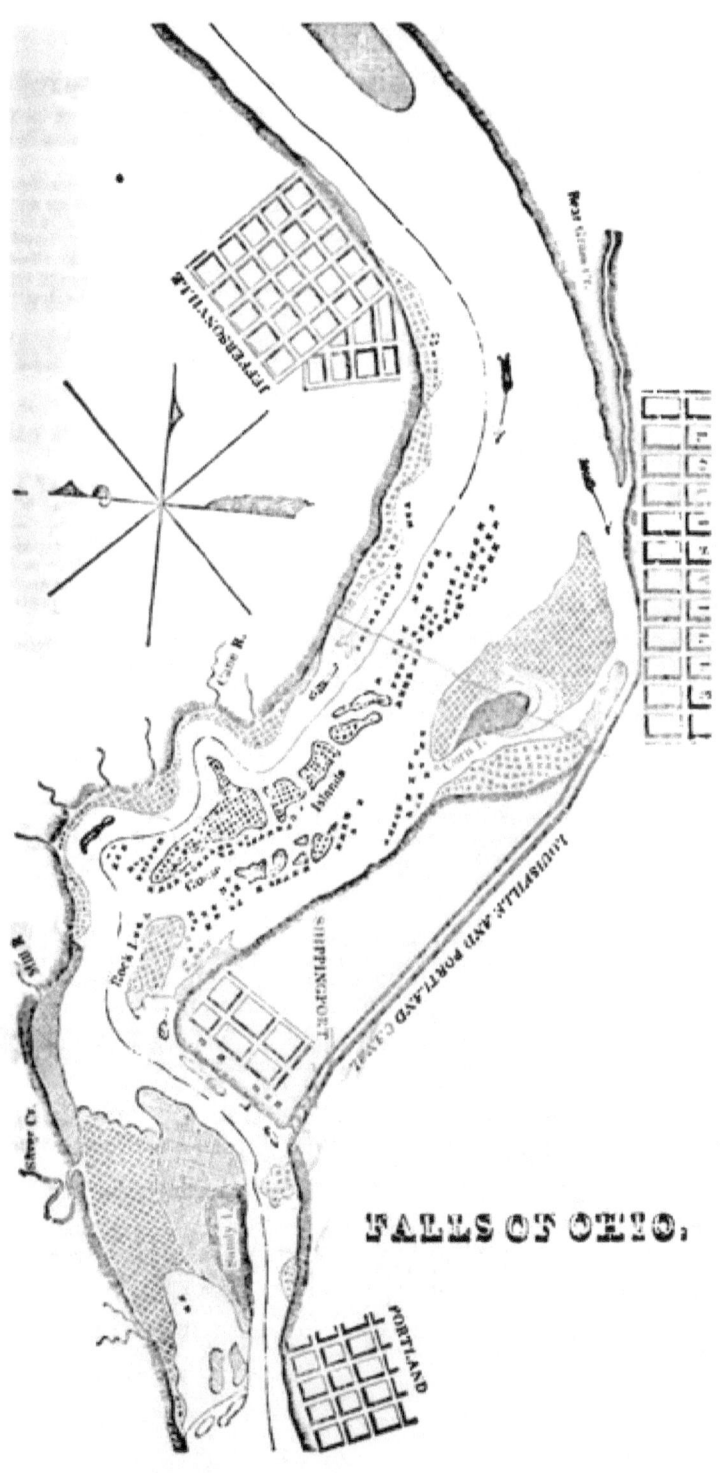

(a thing which could easily be accomplished,) the navigation of this river, but the project was abandoned.

During high water, light draught steamboats can, without difficulty, ascend 50 or 60 miles. This river rises in the Cumberland mountains, Floyd co., Ky., and after pursuing a north-westerly course of 180 miles, empties into the Ohio opposite Cincinnati.

Covington, on the lower side of the mouth of the Licking, in Kenton co., Ky., is built on a beautiful plane. Population about 25,000. The streets are laid out so as to appear from the hills back of Cincinnati as a continuation of that city. Covington is in a highly flourishing condition, and bids fair to become a very large city the bridge makes intercourse between it and Cincinnati easy. It contains a fine city-hall, 10 or 12 churches, a very richly endowed theological college, belonging to the Baptists, and a large number of manufactories of different kinds. Covington is the terminus of the Covington and Lexington Railroad.

Industry, 10 miles below Cincinnati, in Hamilton co., O., a small village. It contains a large stove foundry, owned by an association of journeymen stove-molders. Population about 200.

Claysville, Ky., a small place nearly opposite Industry.

Home City, 2 miles below Industry, in the same county, laid out for a town by an association styled "THE CINCINNATI BUILDING ASSOCIATION."

North Bend, 4 miles below, in Hamilton co., O., near the mouth of the Great Miami River, was the place originally laid out by Judge Symmes for the great city of the West. It is a small town, population about 200, and noted as the former residence and grave of the lamented President Harrison. On a beautiful knoll, just below, his remains are interred. A plain built brick vault is erected over them, and is visible for several miles up and down the river. Standing by its side, the eye of the observer takes in a beautiful view of parts of Ohio, Indiana, and Kentucky. About 30 rods west of it, is the grave of the Hon. John Cleves Symmes.

The Great Miami River rises in Hardin co., O., and after a south-west course of about 100 miles, empties into the Ohio, 4 miles below North Bend, at the State line between Indiana and Ohio. The country through which it flows is highly cultivated and exceedingly fertile; it is termed the "Great Miami Bottoms," in contradistinction to the "Little Miami Bottoms." There is a great amount of water-power obtained from this stream, which renders it of immense importance to the inhabitants of the region through which it passes. Several important towns are situated on the banks of this river; among which are Hamilton, Dayton, Troy, and Piqua. It is not navigable.

Lawrenceburg, county seat of Dearborn co., Ia., 2 miles below the mouth of the Great Miami, is a flourishing business place. Population about 4000. That part of the town near the river, being low, is liable to inundations by *floods* in the Ohio. It contains a court-house, 6 churches, an extensive distillery, 8 mills, a carding machine, and 3 printing offices. The Ohio and Mississippi Railroad, the Cincinnati and Indianapolis Railroad, pass through the town.

Petersburg, 2 miles below, in Boone co., Ky., is a small village. Population 250. Many curious remains of an ancient race have been found here, in digging wells and cellars. Near the town, are the remains of an ancient fortification, evidently the work of a more civilized people than our North American Indians appear to have been.

Aurora, at the mouth of Hogan creek, 2 miles below, in Dearborn co., Ia., is a flourishing place. It was laid out in 1819, and incorporated as a city in 1848. A large pork business is done here, besides distilling and various other branches of business. Population 3300. The Ohio and Mississippi Railroad passes through Aurora.

Belleview, 6 miles below, in Boone co., Ky., is a small village.

Rising Sun, county seat of Ohio co., Ia., 3 miles below, is a flourishing town. It contains a court-house, 3 churches, 3 mills, a large cotton and woolen factory, an extensive distillery, 2 printing offices, and a population of about 1800.

Millersburg, Ia., 3 miles below, in same county, a landing point for several of the interior counties.

Big Bone Lick Creek, 9 miles below, in Boone co., Ky., about 2 miles from the mouth of this creek is the place celebrated as the Big Bone Lick Springs. The water is impregnated with sulphur and salt, and the place derives its name from the immense number of bones of the Mastodon, or Mammoth, and the Arctic Elephant, formerly found scattered all over the surface of the earth, here.

Hamilton, a small village, just below the mouth of Big Bone Lick creek, in same co. Population about 200.

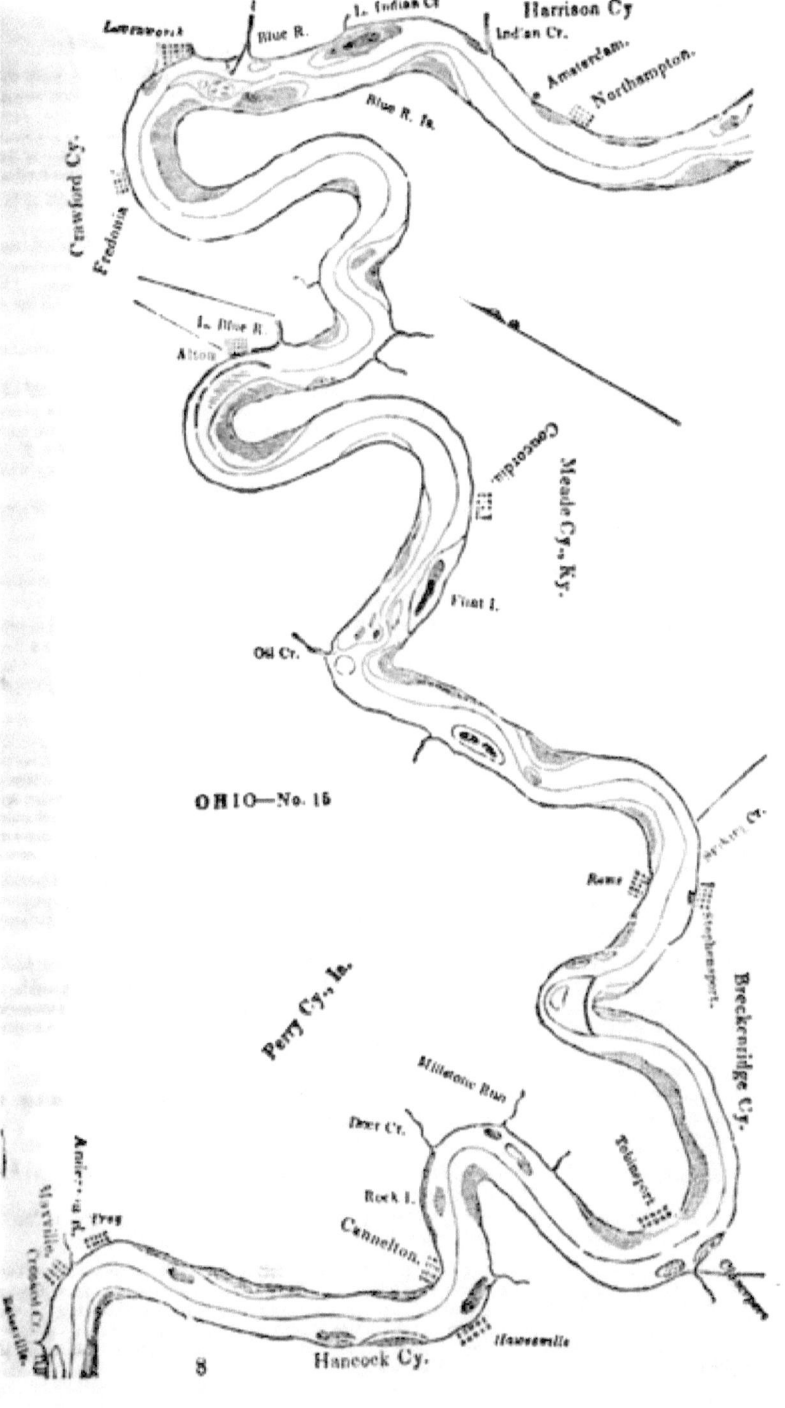

Patriot, 2 miles below, in Switzerland co., Ia. Population about 600.

Warsaw, 11 miles below, is the county seat of Gallatin co., Ky., and was formerly known as Fredericksburg. It contains a court-house and county buildings, 2 churches, 3 schools, 1 printing office, 2 pork-houses, 1 tobacco factory, 1 flouring mill, and a distillery. Population about 1000. This is a place of considerable trade, and exports large quantities of corn, tobacco, and various other kinds of produce. The surrounding country is hilly but very productive—raising fine crops of corn, wheat, and tobacco. It also abounds in fine timber.

New York, sometimes called Florence, 1 mile below, in Switzerland co., Ia., is a small village. Population about 200.

Vevay, 10 miles below, is the county seat of Switzerland co., Ia. Population about 2000. It was settled in 1804, by a number of Swiss families, to whom Congress made a favorable grant of land for the purpose of commencing the cultivation of the grape. The grape found to succeed best is the Cape grape, from which a considerable quantity of wine, resembling claret, is made.

Ghent, opposite Vevay, in Carroll co., Ky., is a handsome village. Population about 350.

Carrollton, formerly called Port William, 10 miles below, at the mouth of the Kentucky river, is the county seat of Carroll co., Ky. This point was first settled by a Mr. Elliot, in 1784. In March, 1785, his house was attacked by a body of Indians and burned, and himself killed. In 1786, Capt. Ellison erected a block-house, but was driven from it by the Indians. In 1789, Gen. Charles Scott, erected a block-house, and fortified it by pickets. It was occupied until 1792 when the present town was laid out.

Carrollton contains a court-house and public buildings, 1 academy, 3 churches, 2 corn mills, 1 steam saw mill, 1 carding factory, 1 rope-walk, and a population of 1000.

Kentucky River, (*See page* 125.)

Preston, a small village, just below the mouth of the Kentucky river, named in honor of Col. Preston, of Virginia. Population about 150.

Madison, county seat of Jefferson co., Ia., 10 miles below, is one of the largest and most important commercial cities in the State. It is beautifully located in a valley, about three-fourths of a mile in width and 3 miles in length, lying in a bend of the river, and surrounded by steep and rugged hills, from 4 to 500 feet in height. The principal part of the city is situated more than 30 feet above the highest floods of the Ohio river.

The trade of Madison is quite extensive, and the manufactures are very important. The principal part of the trade of the city is in wheat and pork, those articles being the chief products of the State. Population about 11,000. There is a fine hotel here, built at a cost of $30,000. The other buildings of note in the city, are the court-house, jail, and county offices, 2 market-houses, a bank, 2 schools, and about 15 churches. Several of these buildings are handsome and costly edifices. Madison contains several mills of various kinds, founderies, factories, and a large number of stores, many of which are wholesale houses, and do an extensive business. The Madison and Indianapolis R. R., completed in 1849, terminates here.

Indianapolis, capital of the State of Indiana, and seat of justice for Marion county, is situated on the West Fork of White river. It lies on a beautiful plain, nearly in the center of the county 108 miles N. W. from Cincinnati, and 86 from Madison. The city was laid out in 1820. Population now about 42,000.

Milton, Trimble co., Ky., is a small village nearly opposite Madison. Pop. 150.

Hanover Landing, 6 miles below Madison, in Jefferson co., Ia. South Hanover is a few miles in the interior. The town was first settled in 1810, and now contains about 600 inhabitants. South Hanover College, established in 1820, by Rev. J. F. Crowe, D.D., and the Hon W. Dunn, is a literary institution of the highest order.

New London, 6 miles below, in the same co., is a small village.

Bethlehem, 6 miles below, in Clark co., Ia., is a small town, containing a church, several stores, and about 300 inhabitants.

Westport, in Oldham co., Ky., 6 miles below. Population about 300.

Charleston Landing, Clark co., Ia., 12 miles below, is the landing point for the town of Charleston, 2½ miles from the river.

Utica, 5 miles below, in the same county, is a small village. Population 350. The article known as "*Louisville* Lime," is manufactured here in large quantities.

Jeffersonville, 9 miles below, in the same county, nearly opposite Louisville, with which, it is in constant communication by means of steam ferry boats. Population about 7500. The Indiana State Penitentiary is located here. It is a fine, large building. The terminus of the Jeffersonville & Columbus Railroad, connecting with the Ohio & Mississippi R. R. at Seymour, Ia., and the Madison & Indianapolis, R. R. at Columbus, Ia., is at this point. The river is here over a mile wide.

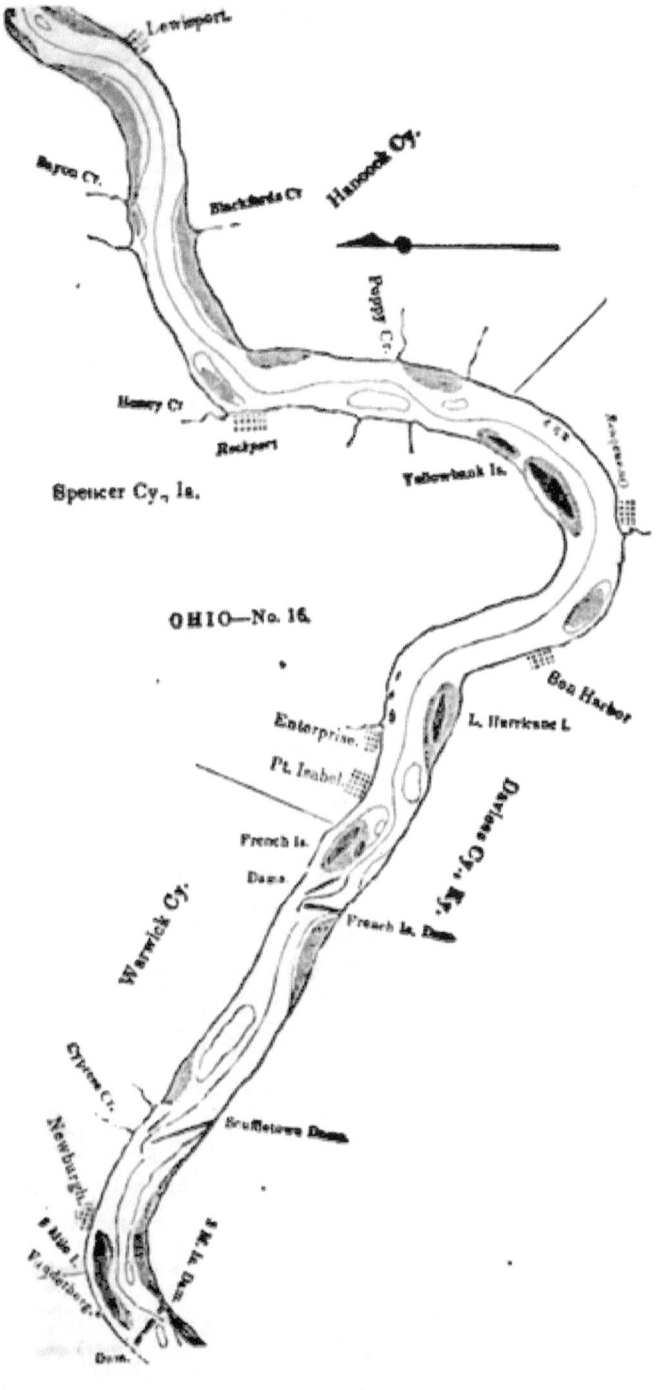

Louisville, 1 mile below, is the county seat of Jefferson co., Ky It is

situated at the head of the Falls of the Ohio, 618 miles from Pittsburg, and 1376 from New Orleans. It was laid off by Capt. Thomas Bullitt, of Va., in August, 1773, but no settlement was made until 1778, when a small party arrived here, with George Rogers Clark, and settled on what is now called Corn Island, close to the Kentucky shore. After the posts occupied by the British on the Wabash had been taken by Gen. Clark, they removed to the spot on which Louisville now stands, in the fall of the same year. They built a block-house here, which was subsequently removed and a large fort erected in 1782, called Fort Nelson. In 1780, the town was established by an act of the Legislature of Virginia, under whose jurisdiction Kentucky then was. At this time, the population was only 30. In 1800, it was 600; in 1810, 1300; in 1820 4,000; in 1830, 10,090; in 1840, 21,000; in 1843, 28,000; in 1845, 32,000; in 1850, 43,217; in 1870, 100,750. It is now the most important commercial city in Kentucky, and one of the most important in the West. It is built on a spacious sloping plane, 70 feet above low water mark. The streets are broad and beautiful, and laid out at right angles with each other. It contains a city-hall and court house, a medical institute and university, two hospitals, an asylum for the blind, 30 churches, 28 schools, two orphan asylums, a work-house, and a large number of religious, literary, and benevolent institutions. There are 4 daily, 4 tri-weekly, and 10 weekly newspapers, 1 monthly, and 1 quarterly periodical published here. There are, also, a large number of foundries, rolling mills, flouring mills, and factories of different kinds, all in successful operation. The packing of pork forms a large item of the business of the city. Louisville is the terminus of the Louisville and Lex. R. R.

The falls of the river just below Louisville, obstruct navigation entirely at low stages of water. The descent is 23 feet in 2 miles. To obviate this, a canal was cut around them, to Shippingsport, a distance of 2½ miles. It was a work of stupendous labor, being cut, a greater part of its length, through solid rock. It is, in some places, 40 feet deep, and of sufficient width to pass steamboats through, and affords fine water-power for the mill-seats below the locks.

On the 24th of September, 1816, the steamboat Washington, under the command of Capt. Shreve, made the first voyage ever made by a steam vessel from Louisville to New Orleans. On the 3d of March, 1817, she started on another trip, and made the time to New Orleans and back in 41 days; the ascending voyage being made in 25 days. A public dinner was given to the Captain by the citizens of Louisville, at which he predicted that the day was not far distant when the trip would be made in 10 days. It has since been made in *less than 5 days*.

A splendid bridge crosses the river, at the head of the falls, between Louisville and Jeffersonville.

Shippingsport, 2 miles below Louisville, in same county, at the foot of the canal, is a small village. Population about 200.

Portland, 1 mile below, in same county, is a place of importance. Large steamers generally make it a stopping place, not being able to get through the canal. There is a Railroad between Portland and Louisville, the cars running every 10 or 15 minutes during the day. It is connected with New Albany, on the opposite side, by a ferry boat, which plies almost constantly. Portland contains a number of very good buildings. Population about 700.

New Albany, county seat of Floyd co., Ia., opposite Portland, is one of the most important towns in the State. It was laid out in the year 1813, by 3 brothers of the name of Scribner. It is the southern terminus of the New Albany & Salem R. R., connecting the Ohio river with Lake Michigan, at Michigan city; and crossing and intersecting the numerous roads passing through Indiana.

The business of steamboat building is carried on here to a greater extent than any other place in the State. Other branches of mechanics are also in a flourishing condition.

In 1830, the population of New Albany was 2,000; in 1840, 4,235; in 1850, 9,785; 1870 16,200.

Bridgeport, Harrison co., Ia., 9 miles below, is a thriving village, boat building is carried on here to a considerable extent. Population about 200.

Blakesville, 6 miles below, in same county, is a small village.

Salt River, 4 miles below, rises in Boyle co., Ky., and, pursuing a north westerly course of 200 miles, empties into the Ohio at the line between Jefferson and Hardin counties. Its mouth is 200 yards wide. It derived its name from the numerous salt licks along its banks. The district of country through which Salt river runs, comprises some of the most

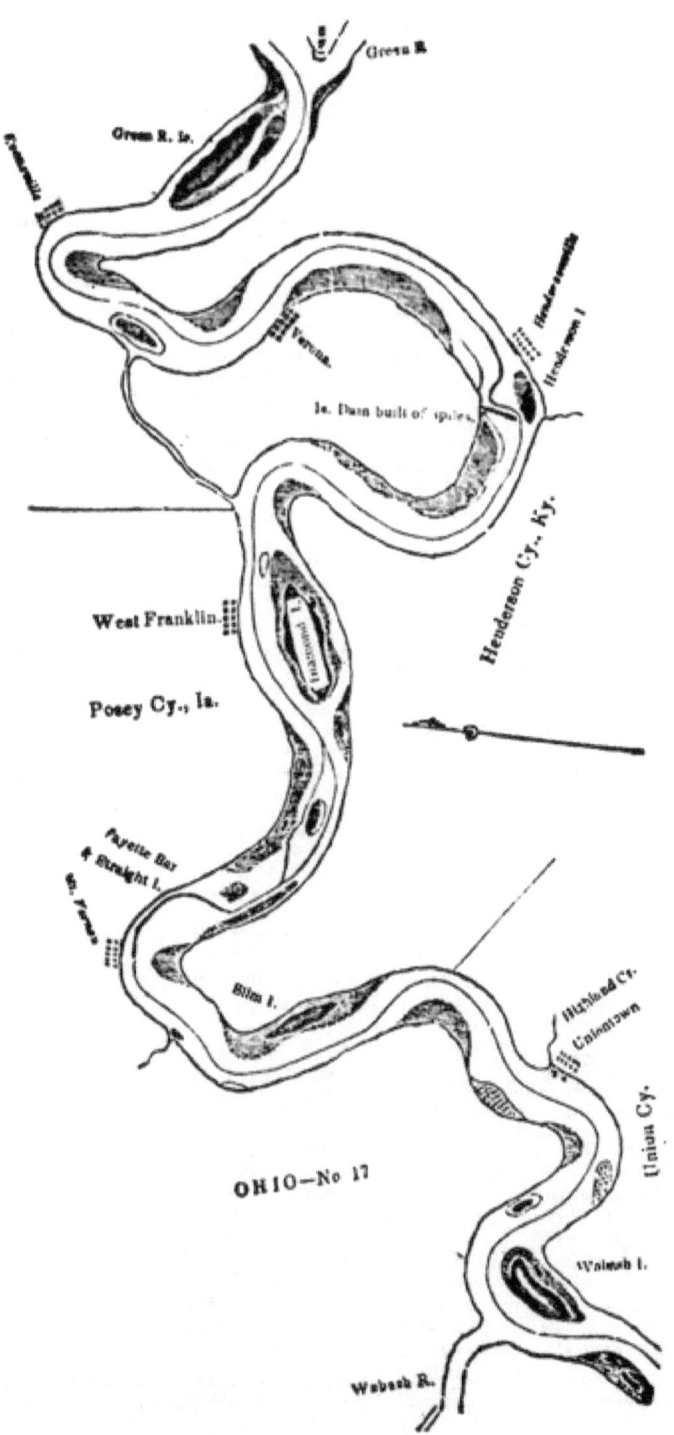

OHIO—No 17

fertile lands in the State. It is navigable for flat-bottom boats, for a distance of 150 miles during high water.

West Point, just below the mouth of Salt river, in Hardin county, is a thriving village. Population about 250. It has an extensive boat-yard.

Brandenburg, 18 miles below, is the county seat of Meade co., Ky. It is built on a high bluff, and contains a court-house, 2 churches, and 2 flouring mills. Considerable quantities of corn and tobacco are shipped from this place. Population 700.

Mauckport, 3 miles below, a small village in Harrison co., Ia.

Northampton, 7 miles below, a small village in the same county.

Amsterdam, 3 miles below, a small village in the same county.

Blue River, a small stream rises in Washington co., Ia., and flows in a southerly direction for about 75 miles, and empties into the Ohio 6 miles below Amsterdam.

Leavenworth, 2 miles below, county seat of Crawford co., Ia., at the Horseshoe bend. It is a thriving town, and well located for business; being at the commencement of the coal region in Indiana. Leavenworth has 2 churches, 1 printing office, and a population of about 800.

Fredonia, 5 miles below, in same co., is situated on high a bluff. Pop. 300.

Little Blue River, rises in Crawford co., and empties into the Ohio at the line between Crawford and Perry counties, Ia. Its length is about 45 miles.

Alton, 13 miles below Fredonia, at the mouth of Little Blue river, in Perry co., Ia., is a small village. Population, 100.

Concordia, 10 miles below, in Meade co., Ky., is pleasantly situated. Population about 100. The hills in this neighborhood abound in beds of limestone rock, from which immense quantities of lime are made.

Rome, county seat of Perry co., Ia., 12 miles below, opposite the mouth of Sinking creek. It was settled in 1811, and now contains a court-house, jail, county seminary, 3 churches, and about 650 inhabitants.

Stephensport, opposite Rome, in Breckenridge co., Ky., at the mouth of Sinking creek, is a pleasant little village, containing 2 churches, several stores, and a population of about 250. It was established in 1825.

Sinking Creek rises in the upper part of Breckenridge co., Ky., and is a considerable stream, supplying abundance of water-power for mills during the whole year. 6 or 7 miles from its source, the creek suddenly sinks beneath the earth, showing no trace of its existence, for 5 or 6 miles, when it re-appears above ground and flows into the Ohio. On this creek is to be seen a natural rock mill-dam, 8 feet high and 40 feet wide, which answers all the purposes of a dam to a mill which has been erected at the place. Near the creek is a large cave, called Penitentiary cave, which has never been fully explored.

Cloverport, 10 miles below, in the same county, is an important point for shipping tobacco and other produce, of which fine crops are grown in the county. Population about 800. There are extensive beds of fine coal in its vicinity. 4 miles in the interior are the White Sulphur, Breckenridge, and Tar Springs.

Tobinsport, Perry co., Ia., is a small village opposite Cloverport.

Hawesville, 14 miles below, the county seat of Hancock co., Ky. Population about 600. It derives considerable trade from its extensive mines of coal.

Cannalton, opposite Hawesville, in Perry co., Ia., is a flourishing town, the largest in the county. It contains several churches and elegant residences, and a large cotton factory, which employs several hundred hands. Population about 2500. This building presents a splendid appearance from the river, it is 300 feet long and 4 stories high, built of variegated sandstone. Extensive beds of coal are found in the adjoining hills, giving the place great advantages for a manufacturing town. Fire-clay and a fine sand-stone for building purposes are found here in abundance.

Troy, 6 miles below, near the mouth of Anderson river, in the same county, is a thriving village, and has the trade of the rich mineral district in the rear and along the margin of this section of the great coal field. Population about 600.

Anderson River, rises in Crawford co., Ia., and flows in a southerly direction and empties into the Ohio near Troy. It is navigable for flat-boats about 30 miles in high water.

Maxville, 1 mile below, at the lower side of the mouth of Anderson river, in Spencer co., Ia., is a small village. Population about 200.

Batesville, 2 miles below, in the same county, is a small village. Pop. 200.

Lewisport, 3 miles below, in Hancock co., Ky., is a small village, extending for some distance along the banks of the river. Population 300.

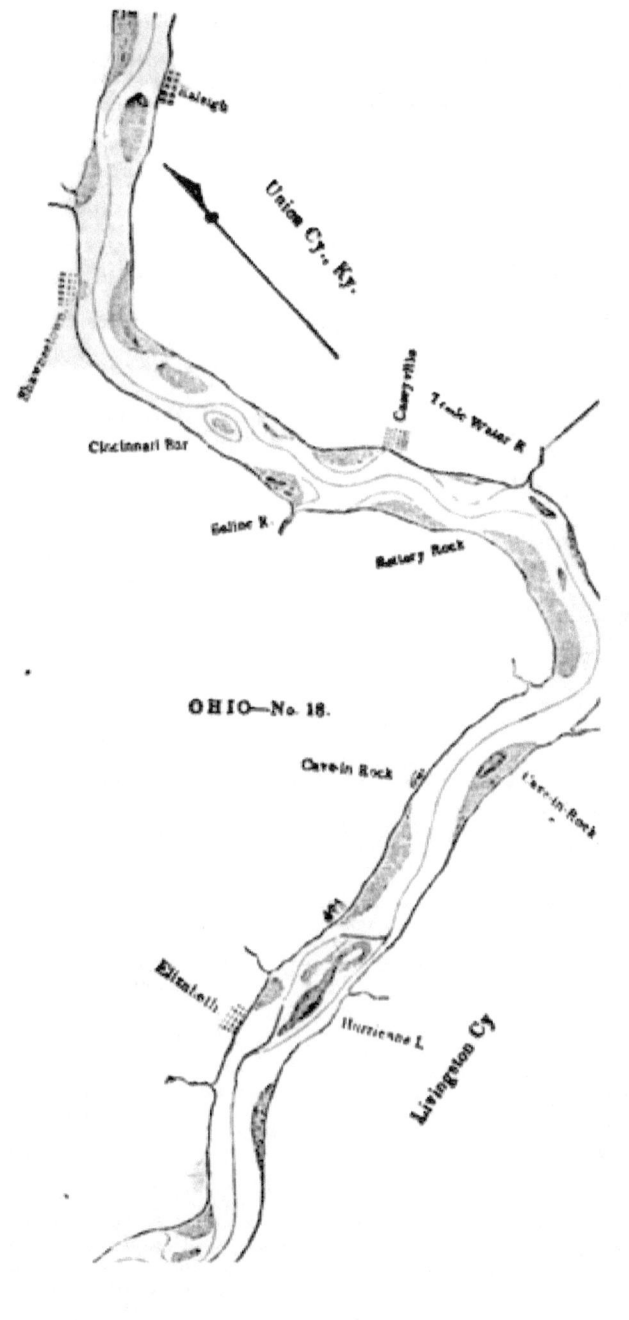

Rockport, seat of justice for Spencer co., Ia., 13 miles below, situated on a high bluff. Population about 1,800. Its name is derived from a hanging rock, known by the name of "*Lady Washington's Rock*;" it is a sandstone formation, and rises to the height of about 30 feet above the general level of the river.

Owensburgh, 9 miles below, is the county seat of Daviess co., Ky. It is a very handsome place, situated in a fertile region, abounding in minerals. It contains a court-house, 4 churches, an academy, a bank, and a population of about 1700.

Bon Harbor, 3 miles below, in the same county, is a thriving village. Population about 300. There is an eddy formed by a bar in the river at this place, which causes an excellent harbor for boats. It is from this circumstance that the name of the place is derived. In the vicinity are fine beds of coal, which render facilities for manufacturing to a large and extensive cotton and woolen establishment.

Enterprise, 3 miles below, a small village in Spencer co., Ia. Population 200. The country adjacent is a rich bottom heavily timbered.

Point Isabel, 1 mile below, a small village, in the same county, at the head of French island.

Newburg, 13 miles below, in Warwick co., Ia., is a finely located and thriving town. It was laid out in 1817, by Michael Sprinkle, and was at first called Sprinklesburg. Population 500.

Green River, 6 miles below, rises in Lincoln co., Ky., and takes a westerly course, until having received the Big Barren river on the south, it turns to the north-west. The current is gentle, and the water generally deep. It is made navigable by means of locks and dams. Steamboats ascend to Bowling Green, on the Big Barren river, 20 miles below the Mammoth Cave, and, during a great part of the year, to the cave, on Green river a distance of 165 miles, bringing down large quantities of corn, tobacco, and other produce. *Brownsville*, capital of Edmondson co., Ky., is situated on Green river about 10 miles below the Mammoth Cave. *Morgantown*, capital of Butler co., Ky., on Green river, below the junction of Big Barren. *Lewisburg*, below, in Muhlenberg co., Ky.

The Mammoth Cave, is situated in Edmonson co., Ky., equi-distant from the cities of Louisville and Nashville (about 90 miles from each,) and immediately on the nearest road between those two places. It is within half a mile of Green river. The cave has already been explored for more than 18 miles. It contains 226 avenues, 47 domes, 8 cataracts, several rivers, and 23 pits, most of them of surprising beauty and startling grandeur. The cave is dry, and exceedingly conducive to health. It is visited by many invalids, for the purpose of inhaling its air; and, in many instances, proves highly beneficial.

Evansville, 9 miles below the mouth of Green river, is the county seat of Vanderburg co., Ia. It was laid out in 1816, and received its name in honor of Gen. R. M Evans, who was one of the early settlers of the place. It is situated on an elevated bank. The trade of Evansville is considerable, and rapidly increasing. The Wabash & Erie Canal, terminates at this place. The Evansville & Terre Haute Railroad, via Vincennes, has its terminus here—bringing Evansville in connection with many points by the intersection of other roads. A *very* large amount of produce is annually shipped from this point—corn, oats, hay, pork, &c., &c. Evansville contains a court-house, jail, 9 or 10 churches, 6 printing offices, and a large number of business houses, &c. Population 21,830.

Verona, 7 miles below, in the same county, is a small village.

Henderson, 5 miles below, is the county seat of Henderson co., Ky. It is a flourishing place, and the principle shipping port for the produce of the country bordering on Green river, exporting large quantities of tobacco, corn, &c. It contains a court-house, 6 churches, 4 schools, 5 large tobacco factories, and a population of about 2000. The country adjacent is well adapted to the cultivation of tobacco and corn. Iron ore is also found in it, and large beds of stone coal, of an excellent quality. About 75,000 bushels of corn, and 7,000,000 lbs. of tobacco are annually exported from it.

West Franklin, 14 miles below, in Posey co., Ia., is a small village.

Mount Vernon, county seat of Posey co., Ia., 12 miles below, on a fine bluff. t was settled in 1803, and contains a court-house, jail, and county offices, 3 churches, and about 2300 inhabitants. A plank road extends to New Harmony on the Wabash river.

Uniontown, 10 miles below, at the mouth of Highland creek, in Union co., Ky., is a thriving town, shipping large quantities of corn to the southern markets. Population about 500. The country is very fertile. A few miles from Uniontown, on Highland creek is a fine Tar spring. There are a number of curiosities in this county, worthy of observation. One is a large flat rock, with perfect resemblance of the naked feet of men, and animals deeply imprinted in it. There is also a cavern, which is thought to be of great extent, but has not yet been fully explored.

Wabash River enters the Ohio 5 miles below Uniontown. (*See page 125.*)

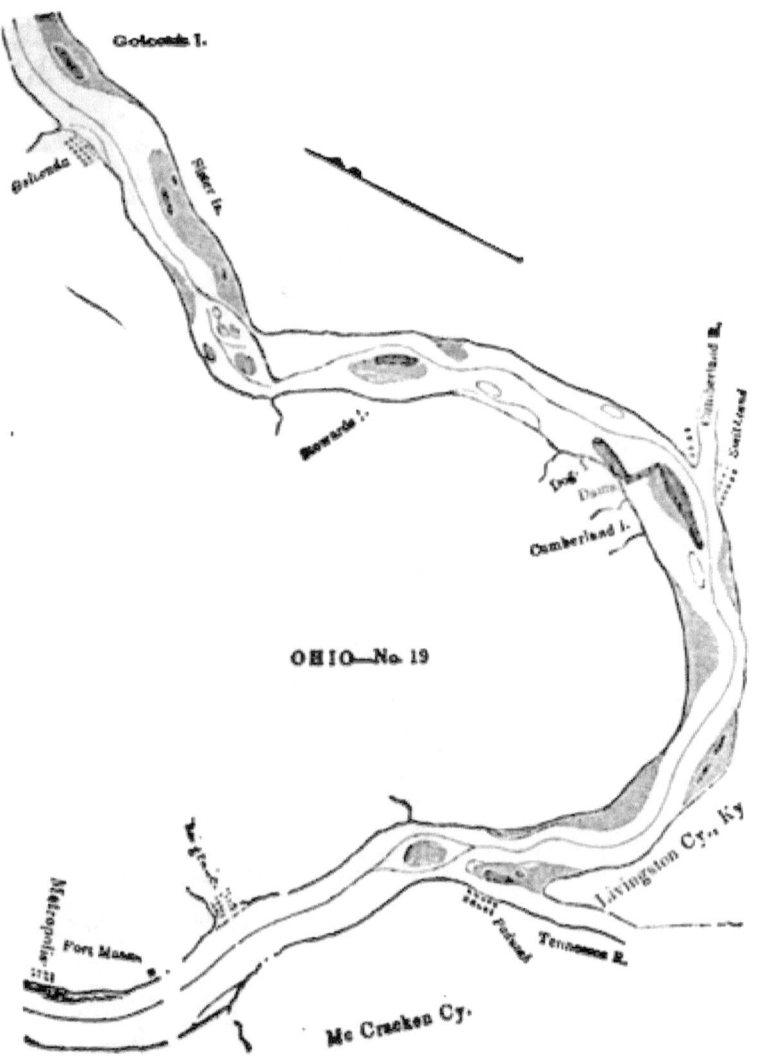

Raleigh, 6 miles below the mouth of the Wabash, in Union co., Ky.

Shawneetown, 5 miles below, in Gallatin co., Ill., on a low bank of the Ohio. It is liable to inundations from the river. It is, however, a place of considerable business, and the largest town in southern Illinois. It was laid out in 1814, and now contains 3 churches, a land office, and a population of 2000.

Caseyville, 10 miles below, in Union co., Ky., is a small village containing a population of 250. About 3 miles from Caseyville, may be seen a natural curiosity, termed the ANVIL ROCK. It is a large rock, some 50 feet high, 20 feet wide, and 2 feet thick, and bears a striking resemblance to a blacksmith's anvil. This rock stands upon level bottom land, and is entirely isolated.

Battery Rock, 2 miles below, in Gallatin co., Ill., is a high, rocky bluff, extending some miles along the river, giving a picturesque appearance to the scenery.

Cave-in-rock, 12 miles below, in Hardin co., Ill., is a noted place, and viewed with interest by all travelers on this river. It was the rendezvous, about 1801, of a celebrated outlaw, by the name of Mason; and his comrades, who subsisted by plundering the flat-boats and arks, descending the river with produce, or waylaying the traders on their return with the products of their sales—robbing and murdering them. They continued this nefarious business for several years, until their depredations became so alarming, that the Governor of Mississippi offered a reward of $500 for Mason's head. Mason was shot, and his head carried to Washington, then the capital of Mississippi, by one of his own band named Harpe, a notorious outlaw, who had escaped from Kentucky.

Elizabethtown, county seat of Hardin co., Ill., 6 miles below, at the foot of Hurricane Island. Population about 200.

Golconda, 23 miles below, is the county seat of Pope co., Ill. It is beautifully situated on an elevated plain, and contains a court-house, and population of about 250.

Cumberland River, enters the Ohio, 15 miles below. (*See page* 127.)

Smithland, county seat of Livingston co., Ky., just below the mouth of Cumberland river. It is a place of considerable commercial importance, being favorably situated for reshipping goods to and from the interior of Kentucky and Tennessee. Smithland contains a court-house, jail, and county offices, 2 churches, 1 foundry and machine shop, a boatyard, an extensive tannery, and a population of 1500.

Tennessee River, enters the Ohio, 12 miles below Smithland. (*See page* 128.)

Paducah, county seat of McCracken co., Ky., just below the mouth of the Tennessee, was laid out in 1827, and received its name in honor of the celebrated Indian chief, Paducah. It is the depot for the vast and growing trade of the Tennessee river. It contains 4 churches, a court-house, a fine hotel, and a population of 3000.

Belgrade, 8 miles below, in Massac co., Ill., is a small village.

Fort Massac, 2 miles below, in the same county, is the spot the troops occupied, who were sent to intercept the plans of AARON BURR. The fort was burned many years ago, and nothing is to be seen now to mark the spot.

Metropolis, county seat of Massac co., Ill., 1 mile below. Pop. about 700.

Hillaman, 8 miles below, in the same county.

Wilkinsonville, 7 miles below, in Alexander co., Ill., is a small village, named in honor of General WILKINSON.

Caledonia, 10 miles below, county seat of Pulaski co., is a small village.

America, 3 miles below, in the same county.

Emporium, formerly Mound City, 3 miles below, in same county, above the mouth of Cache river, is an enterprising town, and landing point for steamers, connected with the Ill. Central R. Road by a road 3 miles in length.

Cairo, 6 miles below, in Alexander co., Ill., at the junction of the Ohio and Mississippi rivers, has acquired considerable celebrity by the repeated attempts which have been made, to build up a large city on its site. Situated, as it is, at the junction of these two mighty rivers, it, undoubtedly, presents one of the finest points for a city which can be found in the West; being placed so as to command the immense and incalculable trade of the whole west, north-west and south. But there are difficulties to be surmounted, in the location of the ground, and the surrounding country, which will take an immense amount of capital and labor. The banks of the river are here very low, and the surrounding country is still lower. Both are subject to overflow, and from the marshy nature of the soil are generated miasms, which render it very unhealthy. But, by a scientific system of embankment, filling up, and draining, all this may be overcome. A levee has been thrown up, at a cost of about $1,000,000, which protects it to a great degree.

The Great Illinois Central Railroad has a terminus here, and extensive depot buildings

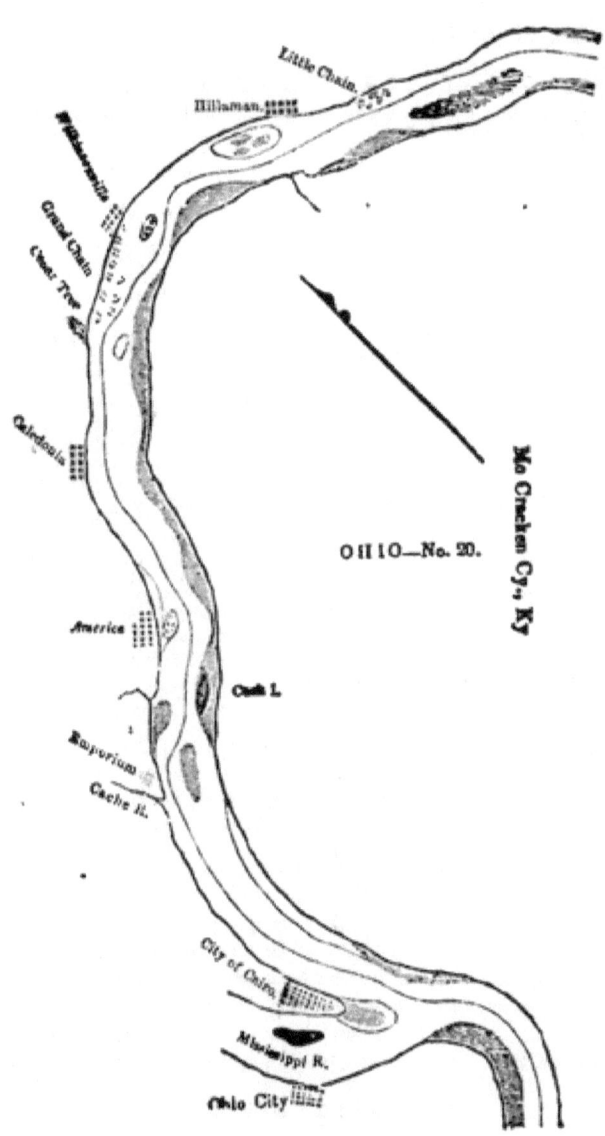

THE MUSKINGUM RIVER

Is formed by the junction of the Tuscarawas and Walhounding rivers at Coshocton, O. It is the largest river, lying wholly in the State, and has been made navigable by means of dams and locks, and short canals, to Dresden, about 96 miles from Marietta. The numerous falls of the Muskingum afford water-power to almost any extent, and most excellent advantages for manufacturing.

Coshocton is beautifully situated at the head of the Muskingum river, 113 miles from Marietta, and is the county seat of Coshocton co., O. It was laid out in 1802, and called Tuscawara, which name it retained until 1811, when it received its present appellation. It contains 4 churches, 2 newspaper offices, a flour mill, and woolen factory, and a population of 1800. When the river is very high, steamboats occasionally ascend as high as this point. The Ohio Canal passes through Coshocton, also the Steubenville & Indiana R. R.

Dresden, 17 miles below, in Muskingum co., is a flourishing and active business place, well supplied with water-power. Coal and iron ore abound in the vicinity. Population about 1500.

Zanesville, 16 miles below, and 80 miles from Marietta, is the county seat of Muskingum co., and one of the principal towns in Ohio. It is connected with Putnam, West Zanesville and South Zanesville by bridges. The town was laid out in 1799, by Ebenezer Zane, and John McIntire, and was first called Westburn, which name it bore until the establishment of a post-office, when it received its present name. Population about 10,000. Zanesville affords superior advantages for manufactories of all kinds. The fine water-power, abundance of bituminous coal in its vicinity, and its great facilities for transportation and exportation—being the terminus of the Wilmington & Zanesville Railroad, extending to Cincinnati; the Central Ohio Railroad passing through it, also the National Road; the Muskingum, opening immediate intercourse with the Ohio and all the southern countries; the Ohio Canal, reaching to the Lakes on the north, and south through the finest portions of the State, all seem to mark it out as one of the finest positions in the west for manufacturing purposes. The water of the river is distributed through the city from a large reservoir, on a hill 160 feet high. The water is forced up by means of a powerful force pump.

Duncan's Falls, 9 miles below, in Muskingum co. Population about 300.

Taylorsville, just below, on the opposite (west) side of the river, in same co. A dam across the river here gives the place advantages of large water-power, and a number of mills are in successful operation. Population about 1000.

Eagleport, 11 miles below, in Morgan county.

McConnellsville, 10 miles below, a thriving town on the east bank of the river, is the county seat of Morgan co. There are large salt manufactories in the vicinity. Population near 1700.

Malta, on the opposite bank of the river. Population about 750.

Newcastle, 3 miles below, east bank of the river, in Morgan co.

Windsor, 7 miles below, west bank of the river, in Morgan co.

Big Rock, 8 miles below, east bank of the river, in Morgan co.

Beverly, 10 miles below, on the east bank, in Washington co.

Waterford, nearly opposite, in the same county.

Lowell, 10 miles below, in same co., on the east bank of the river.

Marietta and Harmer, 12 miles below, at the mouth of the river. (*See Ohio River.*)

THE SCIOTO RIVER

Rises in Hardin co., O., and flows in a south-easterly direction, and empties into the Ohio river at Portsmouth. It is navigable for steamboats but a short distance from its mouth. Flat-boats, in high stages of water, are brought down from a distance of 130 miles. Its length is 160 miles, and it is 150 yards wide at the mouth. The counties through which the river flows, are among the most fertile and highly cultivated in the State of Ohio. It is the second river in size which lies wholly in the State.

Columbus, capital of the State of Ohio, and county seat of Franklin co., is beautifully situated on the east bank of the Scioto river, 90 miles from its mouth. The National Road passes through it from east to west. The Ohio Canal, also has a branch extending to this place; and it is the center of Railroads diverging in nearly all directions. (See James' Railroad and Route Book.) The present site of the city was, in 1812, an unbroken forest. It now contains a population of about 32,000. It is laid out regularly, with wide streets, and adorned with many beautiful buildings. The public buildings are constructed on a magnificent scale, and do honor to the State. They are, a magnificent

State-house, a Lunatic Asylum, an Asylum for the Blind, one for the Deaf and Dumb, and the Ohio Penitentiary.

Circleville, county seat of Pickaway co., O., is a flourishing town, situated on the Ohio Canal and Scioto river, 26 miles south of Columbus. The Cincinnati, Wilmington & Zanesville Railroad passes through the place. The town is built on the site of an ancient fortification, and was laid out in the year 1810, by Daniel Dresbach. It derived its name from the circular form of one of the ancient ruins which were found here. These ruins have long since disappeared before the steady march of improvement, which has marked the settlement of our western country. Population 5,400.

Chillicothe, county seat of Ross co., on the west bank of the Scioto river, 19 miles south of Circleville, is a place of considerable importance in the State. It was first laid out in 1796. In 1800, the seat of Government was removed from Cincinnati to it, where it remained till 1816, when Columbus was made the permanent capital. Chillicothe is the principal point of trade for the great Scioto valley. Population 9000. The Cincinnati & Marietta Railroad passes through it; also the Ohio Canal.

Piketon, capital of Pike co., O., 20 miles below. Population about 750.

Jasper, 2 miles below, in the same county, is a small village.

Lucasville, Scioto co., 10 miles below, and 13 miles above the mouth of the Scioto river.

THE KENTUCKY RIVER

Rises in the Cumberland mountains, and interlocks with the head waters of the Licking and Cumberland rivers—length about 200 miles. It is navigable for flat-boats over 150 miles. To Frankfort, 60 miles from its mouth, it has been made navigable by means of locks and dams, of which there are 17, built at a cost of $2,300,000. The perpendicular height overcome by these locks, is 210 feet.

The scenery along the banks of the Kentucky river is not surpassed by any other in the Union, unless it be the Hudson. The channel, for the greater part of its course, runs through beds of solid limestone rock. In the neighborhood of the mouth of the river, there are many remains of ancient works, relics of a race whose history is beyond the present limits of human knowledge, and whose deeds are buried in the impenetrable mysteries of the past.

Boonesboro, in Madison co., Ky., on the Kentucky river, is celebrated in the history of the west for its memorable sieges by the Indians. A fort was built here by Daniel Boone, in 1775.

Cogar's Landing, below Boonesboro, and 104 miles from the mouth of the river.—*Monday's Landing*, 4 miles below Boonesboro.—*Cumming's Landing*, 4 miles below Monday's Landing.

Oregon, 10 miles below, in Mercer co., is a flourishing village. This is the landing place for *Harrodsburg Springs*, situated about 8 miles from the river. *Harrodsburg* is the capital of Mercer co. Population about 3000.—*McCowan's Landing*, 3 miles below Oregon.—*Wilson's Landing*, 4 miles below.—*Sherlock's Landing*, 4 miles below.—*Woodford Landing*, 4 miles below.

Frankfort, 12 miles below, is the capital of the State of Ky., and county seat of Franklin co. It is situated in a beautiful plain, surrounded by precipitous hills. It was laid out in 1773, and made the seat of government in 1792. The State-house is a handsome edifice, built of Kentucky marble, quarried in the vicinity. Frankfort contains the State Penitentiary, a fine court house, 2 banks, 7 printing offices, 4 or 5 churches, 3 bagging factories, and a population of about 5000. The Lexington & Louisville Railroad passes through Frankfort, and a bridge connects it with South Frankfort.—*Flat Creek Landing* is 15 miles below.

Monterey, Owen co., 3 miles below Flat Creek Landing, is a flourishing village. *Owenton's Landing*, 5 miles below.

Lockport, Henry co., 6 miles below Owenton. *Gratz*, 3 miles below Lockport.

Drennon's Springs, Henry co., 8 miles below, and 1 mile from the river, is a fashionable watering place.—*Springport*, 1 mile below.

Marion, 4 miles below Springport, in Owen co. *Law's Landing*, 3 miles below.—*Worthville*, 4 miles below.

Carrollton, 8 miles below, at the mouth of the Ky. river, (*See Ohio river*.)

THE WABASH RIVER

Rises in Mercer co., O., near the western boundary of the State, and flows first north-west and then in a general southerly direction through a portion of the State of Indiana and forms, for a distance of nearly 200 miles, the boundary between Indiana and Illinois, and empties into the Ohio 142 miles above the mouth of the latter. It is navigable for flat-

126   THE WABASH RIVER.

boats about 400 miles, and in time of high water steamboats ascend as far as Lafayette. The total length of the Wabash is estimated at 550 miles. Bituminous coal is found along its course, almost everywhere below Lafayette. It receives, in its course, the waters of many respectable tributaries, among the most important is WHITE RIVER, which passes through the State from east to west, and waters a great extent of fertile and well settled country. Perhaps no river in the world, of its magnitude, drains a more extensive and fertile country than the Wabash and its tributaries. It forms the heart of the State of Indiana. The following places are located on or near the banks of the Wabash, commencing near its source : *Alexander*, Adams co., Ia.; *Newville*, *Bluffton*, and *Lancaster*, Wells co., Ia.; *Tracy*, *Mt. Etna*, and *Huntington*, Huntington co., Ia.; *Utica*, *La Cros* and *Wabash*, Wabash co., Ia. *Peru*, Miami co., Ia.; *Lewisburg*, *Circleville*, *Logansport*, and *Amsterdam*, Cass co., Ia.; *Lockport*, *Burnettsville*, *Tiptonsport*, *Carrollton*, *Paragon*, *Delphi*, *West Delphi*, and *Pittsburg*, Carroll co., Ia. *Americus*, Tippecanoe co.

Lafayette, county seat of Tippecanoe co., Ia., is beautifully situated on the Wabash river, 378 miles from its mouth. It was laid out in 1825, on land bought at government prices. Its progress has been steady and rapid, and it is now among the first towns in the State in population and commercial importance. The Wabash & Erie Canal passes through this place, bringing it in connection with Lake Erie. Lafayette contains a fine court-house, jail, and public offices, 8 or 10 churches, 4 printing offices, a county seminary, 2 paper mills, and several pork-packing establishments. Population about 15,000. It is in direct communication by Railroads with Indianapolis, Chicago, and New Albany. An immense amount of produce is forwarded from this place, via canal and railroads.

Wheaton, 9 miles below, in same county, is a small village.

La Grange, 3 miles below, in same co.—*Maysville* 5 miles below, in Fountain co., Ia.—*Independence*, Warren co., 1 mile below.

Attica, Fountain co., Ia., 8 miles below Independence, is a flourishing place, surrounded by splendid forests and beautiful prairies, with a soil of great fertility. A large and increasing trade is centered here. Population about 2100.

Williamsport, 2 miles below, county seat of Warren co., Ia., is a thriving town, with an active trade. *Portland*, Fountain co., Ia., 8 miles below; *Baltimore*, 6 miles below, in Warren co., Ia.

Covington, 4 miles below is the capital of Fountain co., Ia. It is a shipping point for large quantities of grain. Stone coal and iron are found in abundance in the vicinity. Population about 1800.

Perryville, Vermilion co., Ia., 9 miles below, is finely located, and has a large and active trade. Population 1100.

Vermilion River, empties into the Wabash 10 miles below Perryville. It takes its rise in Illinois, and is navigable for about 90 miles, to Danville, Ill., during high water.—*Lodiville*, 2 miles below the mouth of Vermilion river, in Parke co., Ia.

Newport, 7 miles below Lodiville, and 1 mile from the Wabash, on Little Vermilion river, is the capital of Vermilion co., Ia. Population 600.

Montezuma, 6 miles below, in Parke co., Ia., is an active village. Population about 500.—*Armiesburg*, 2 miles below, in the same county.

Clinton, 10 miles below, in Vermilion co. Population about 550. Large quantities of produce are shipped from Clinton.—*Numa*, 2 miles below, in Parke co.—*Harrison*, 14 miles below, in Vigo co.

Terre Haute, 4 miles below Harrison, is the capital of Vigo co., Ia. It is situated on the east bank of the Wabash, also on the National Road, and the Wabash & Erie Canal. It was laid out in 1816. It is a center of railway communication; one to Indianapolis, one to Springfield and Alton Ill., and one to Evansville, Ia., connecting with the Ohio and Mississippi R. R., to Cincinnati and St. Louis, at Vincennes. Also, one to Crawfordsville, intersecting the New Albany & Salem R. R. to Michigan City. Terre Haute is beautifully situated on a high bank of the Wabash, and is the center of a large and increasing trade. Large quantities of flour, pork, and grain, are shipped by the canal and river, also by the railroads. The town contains 6 printing offices, 10 or 12 churches, 3 banks, a court-house, a town hall, and a large academy. Population 17,100.

Darwin, 25 miles below, is the capital of Clarke co., Ill. It is a thriving village — *Yorke*, 16 miles below, in Crawford co., Ill.—*Hudsonville*, 9 miles below, in Crawford co.—*Merom*, Sullivan co., 8 miles below.—*Russellville*, 25 miles below, in Lawrence co. Ill.

Vincennes, county seat of Knox co., Ia., 18 miles below Russellville. This place derives a great interest in the history of the West, from the fact of its being one of the first settlements formed in the valley of the Mississippi. It was first occupied by the French settlers, as a military post, in 1735, and called Post St. Vincent. In the year 1749. the name of Vincennes was given to it, in honor of F. M. De Vincenne, a gallant and much respected French officer, who fell in battle with the Chickasaws, in 1736. A large and beautiful prairie is in the vicinity, the soil of which is very productive. The seat of the territorial government was here until 1813.

Vincennes contains a large, commodious city-hall, court-house, jail, and county offices, 6 or 8 churches, among them a fine cathedral, St. Gabriel College, a theological seminary, several manufactories, and a population of 4,000.

The Ohio & Mississippi R. R., connecting Cincinnati with St. Louis, and Evansville & Vincennes, connecting with the Terre Haute & Vincennes road to Chicago, cross each other here, thus opening through this city an outlet north, south, east, and west.

Mount Carmel, 36 miles below, capital of Wabash co., Ill., is beautifully situated, and a very thriving business place. Population about 1600.

Graysville, 45 miles below, in White co., Ill., is a flourishing village, with an active trade. Population about 650.—*New Baltimore*, 9 miles below, in Posey co., Ia.

New Harmony, Ia., 6 miles below, New Baltimore, and 16 miles from the nearest point of the Ohio, though about 60 miles from the mouth of the Wabash, following the meanders of the river. It is surrounded by a fine, rich, and heavily timbered country, interspersed with small, rich prairies. It was first settled in 1814, by a religious sect of Germans, called Harmonites, under the guidance and control of George Rapp, in whose name all the lands and property were held. They erected about 200 substantial buildings, planted vineyards and orchards, built mills and manufactories, and were wonderfully successful in converting a wilderness into a finely cultivated plantation in a short time. They had even the luxury of a botanic garden, and a green-house. Their great house of assemblage, with its wings and appendages, was nearly 100 feet square. In 1824, the celebrated Robert Owen, of New Lanark, Scotland, purchased the entire possession of the Harmonites, at $190,000, for the purpose of establishing a community upon the plan of his "social system." The plan proved a failure, and was finally abandoned. A plank road extends from New Harmony to Mt. Vernon. The Population of New Harmony is now about 500.

Chainville, 20 miles below. in same co., and 40 miles above the mouth of the Wabash.

THE CUMBERLAND RIVER

Rises in the Cumberland mountains, and interlocks with the head waters of Clinch and Kentucky rivers; flows southwesterly through Ky., more than 250 miles; enters the State of Tenn., and after a further meandering course of about 130 miles it reaches Nashville in Lat. nearly 35 N. Thence flowing north-westerly 203 miles, it empties into the Ohio at Smithland. The Cumberland, the second largest tributary of the Ohio, is about 600 miles in length, and drains a territory estimated at 18,000 square miles. It is navigable about 6 months in the year for steamboats as far as Nashville, and for flat and keel-boats some 300 miles further. This river passes through a country of remarkable fertility, some portions of it rich in iron ore, and, no doubt, other valuable minerals.

The following towns are located on and near the banks of the Cumberland.

Mt. Pleasant, Harlan co., Ky.—*Barboursville*, Knox co., Ky.—*Williamsburg*, Whitley co., Ky. (About 12 miles below this point the river has a perpendicular fall of 60 feet, which presents one of the most remarkable scenes in the State.)—*Creelsburg*, Russel co., Ky.—*Burksville*, Cumberland co., Ky.—*Celina, Meigsville, Gainesboro*, and *Granville*, Jackson co., Tenn.—*Carthage*, Smith co., Tenn.—*Cairo*, Sumner co., Tenn.—*Lockport* and *Rives*, Wilson co., Tenn.

Nashville, capital of the State of Tennessee, and seat of justice for Davidson co., is pleasantly situated on the Cumberland river, 203 miles from its mouth. The city stands on a solid rock, elevated to the height of from 50 to 175 feet above the level of the river. The commerce of Nashville is very extensive, and is rapidly increasing. The principal article of export is cotton, of which large quantities are shipped to the southern markets. There are some fine public buildings and institutions of note in Nashville, among which, are the State-house, Penitentiary, Hospital for Lunatics, the Nashville University, a female seminary, several schools, and a large number of churches for the various denominations. The University was founded in 1806. The library contains 12,000 volumes.

Besides the buildings mentioned, Nashville contains several manufacturing establishments, a large number of wholesale and retail stores of all kinds, and a population of about 21,000. The terminus of the Nashville & Chattanooga Railroad is here; and railroads to other important points are constructing.

Clarksville, Montgomery co., Tenn., 55 miles below Nashville, is a thriving place, and has considerable trade. Population about 3000.

Palmyra, 15 miles below, in same co., is a small village.

Dover, 30 miles below, capital of Stewart co., Tenn.

Fort Donelson, about 1 mile below Dover, in Stewart co.

Tobaccoport, a small village, 14 miles below, in same county.

Canton, 16 miles below, in Trigg co., Ky. Population about 300.

Rockcastle, a small village, 5 miles below, in same county.

Eddyville, 17 miles below, (and 50 miles above Smithland, at the mouth of the Cumberland,) in Caldwell co., Ky., is a thriving village. Population about 700.

THE TENNESSEE RIVER,

The largest tributary of the Ohio, and one of the largest rivers east of the Mississippi, is formed by the union of the Clinch and Holston rivers, which rise in the Alleghany mountains of Virginia, and unite at Kingston, Tenn. It then takes a south-west course, traversing the northern part of Alabama, and then changing, flows in a northerly direction through Tennessee and Kentucky, and enters the Ohio at Paducah, in Latitude 37 north. The total length of this river from the head waters of the Clinch and Holston, is about 1200 miles; being longer than the Ohio from Pittsburg to the mouth. The obstructions to navigation are few, and could easily be remedied. The first obstruction is the muscle shoals at Florence, Ala., about 250 miles from the mouth. Up to this point, steamboats can ascend at almost any season of the year. Above these shoals the navigation is entirely unobstructed for the distance of nearly 500 miles.

The country through which the Tennessee flows, is mostly fertile, but is thinly inhabited. On the upper part of its course, it has much beautiful mountain and valley scenery. The area drained by this river and tributaries is estimated at upward of 40,000 square miles. The following towns are situated on or near its banks.

Knoxville, on the Holston river, county seat of Knox co., east Tenn., is a flourishing city. The situation is beautiful, elevated, and healthy, with a fine view of the surrounding country, and the mountains in the distance. Knoxville has manufacturing establishments of various kinds, among the most important is that of Window Glass, which is carried on extensively. It is, also, an important railroad center. It was laid out in 1794, and was the State capital till 1817. Population about 5000.

Louisville, is a flourishing place, in Blount co., Tenn., about 20 miles by land, below Knoxville.

Kingston, county seat of Roane co., Tenn., at the junction of the Holston and Clinch rivers, is a town of considerable business.

Washington, county seat of Rhea co., Tenn.

Harrison, county seat of Hamilton co., Tenn. Iron and stone coal are abundant near this place. Population about 500.

Chattanooga, about 250 miles below Knoxville, in Hamilton co., Tenn., is a flourishing town. The terminus of the Chattanooga Railroad is here. Stone coal and iron ore abound in the vicinity. Manufacturing is carried on to a considerable extent, and it is an important shipping point. Population about 4000.

Whitesburg, is a small village of Madison co., Ala.

Triana, a small place, in same county.

Decatur, Morgan co., Ala., is a thriving town, and is the eastern terminus of the Tuscumbia & Decatur Railroad.

Muscle Shoals, a name given to the rapids in the Tenn. river, dividing the counties of Lauderdale and Lawrence, Ala. These rapids extend 20 miles, the fall being, in that distance, about 100 feet, and an impassable obstruction to navigation, except during the highest stages of water.

Florence, county seat of Lauderdale co., Ala., is at the head of navigation below the rapids, and 280 miles from the mouth of the Tennessee. This is the principal shipping point for the produce of the surrounding country, with which it has a large and increasing trade. A fine bridge crosses the river here. There are several large cotton factories at and near Florence. Population about 2500.

Tuscumbia, Franklin co., Ala., is 1 mile south of the river, and is the western terminus of the Tuscumbia & Decatur Railroad. Population about 2000. At Tuscumbia there is a very remarkable spring, which flows from a fissure in a limestone rock, and which is said to discharge 20,000 cubic feet of water per minute.

Newport, a small place, in same county.

Chickasaw, a thriving village, in same county.

Waterloo, Lauderdale co., Ala., is a small village, about 30 miles below Florence.

Pittsburgh Landing and Shiloh Battle Ground, 28 miles below.

Savannah, capital of Hardin co., Tenn., is a place of considerable business, 7 miles below. Population about 1000.

Carrollville, 35 miles below, is a small village in Wayne co., Tenn.

Sharonsville, a village in Perry co., Tenn.

Perryville, in same co., 20 miles below Carrollville. A large quantity of cotton is annually shipped from this point. Population about 300.

Reynoldsburg, 50 miles below, in Humphrey's co., Tenn.

Fort Henry, 45 miles below, in Tenn., and about 65 miles above the mouth of the Tenn. river.

www.ingramcontent.com/pod-product-compliance
Lightning Source LLC
Chambersburg PA
CBHW020112170426
43199CB00009B/506